GOOD AS GOLD

GOOD AS GOLD

An autobiography in three parts

by

Ralph Gold

Ralph Gold
July 2003

 Robson Books

This paperback edition published in 1998 by Robson Books Ltd.

First published in Great Britain in 1997 by Robson Books Ltd,
Bolsover House, 5–6 Clipstone Street, London WlP 8LE

British Library Cataloguing in Publication Data
A catalogue record for this title is available from the British Library

ISBN 1 86105 234 0

Typeset in Century Schoolbook by FSH Ltd. London
Printed in Great Britain by St Edmundsbury Press,
Bury St Edmunds, Suffolk

To Annie, In Loving Memory

Acknowledgements

Sandra and Michael Vaughan

When they agreed to take on the task of correcting my work they did not know what they were letting themselves in for. Without their dedication and motivation I would have given up long ago.

My brother David

who encouraged me every step of the way and, 'Good as Gold', unhesitatingly agreed to take on the extra burden of running the business while I wrote this, my autobiography.

Foreword

I asked Ralph Gold to allow me the honour of writing a foreword for his autobiography *Good as Gold* having seen, over four years, the effort and resolve which he has applied in writing it.

It is a unique 'rags to riches' story which tells of a lifetime struggle, along with his brother, David, to overcome the narrow-minded attitude of 'the establishment' and the media towards them.

As private individuals they were described as reclusive and suffered prejudice with a dignified silence which added intrigue and mystery leading to 'Porn Barons' headlines and contrived media stories.

The truth is very different – Ralph tells of their involvement in the building of a successful publishing empire, as well as their takeover of 'Ann Summers', which went on to become one of the largest party plan organizations in the world.

From a life of virtual poverty they became international sports-men and later took to the air, participating in the world famous Malta Air Rally, which David won on two occasions before experiencing the despair of tragedy as his friends died in the blazing inferno of a plane crash. Ralph, too, experienced a great personal loss and, to overcome his sadness, took to playing the piano.

Their energy and application has taken them through highs and lows to achievements beyond most people's dreams. As they approach the age when success usually means comfort and slowing down they are both increasingly busy with yet another goal... to take their own club, Birmingham City, to the top of the football Premiership.

The poverty, the hard work and the determination, the joy and the pathos will grip you as it did me as the fullness of their lives unfolds. For me it was summed up at Wembley in 1995 when Birmingham City won the Auto Windscreen Trophy in front of 76,000 fans chanting...

'One Gold Brothers, there's only one Gold Brothers'

MICHAEL VAUGHAN
CHIEF EXECUTIVE
GOLD GROUP (INTERNATIONAL)

A man who moralizes is usually a hypocrite, and a woman who moralizes is invariably plain.

Oscar Wilde 1896

* * *

'In 1996 what outrages the sense of morality is the mass genocide in Bosnia, not the behaviour of consenting adults in relative privacy.'

Paul Higham, Defence Barrister, Southwark Crown Court – securing the acquittal of the manager of 'Club Whiplash' charged with running a disorderly house.

* * *

Prologue

'How's business?' a friend asked of me at my son Bradley's wedding to Liane. He had the trace of a smile, as though there were no reason to ask. He already knew the answer.

'Fine,' I said. 'Ann Summers' is doing better than ever, and almost everything else is holding its own, so I can't complain.'

It had been in *The Times* only six weeks earlier that David and I were considered to be the 188th richest people in Great Britain, so I suppose 'fine' was an understatement.

But it wasn't always 'fine'. There were times in my life when there was positively nowhere to go but up. The downs were not a requisite of being poor and the ups not necessarily a result of being rich. It just seemed better to have more than less ... So I strove for more.

I would like you to read my story from the very beginning. The wedding will take place in fifty-four years time.

Part One

THE ONLY WAY IS UP

In The Beginning

I was born in July of 1938, fourteen months before the beginning of the Second World War, in a first floor, two bedroom flat opposite the railway track in Hampton Road, Forest Gate, in the East End of London. I am told that the temperature that night was a near record high and my poor mother was suffering because I was taking such a long time to arrive.

My mother, Rose, so much wanted me to be born on her birthday, the 9th of July, but it was not to be. Her nine pounds twelve ounce boy was delivered by the midwife at 2 a.m. the following day.

David, my brother, was brought in to see me very early the next morning. His birth had been far more dramatic than mine. He weighed just four pounds and was immediately placed in one of the newly invented incubators. His survival was nothing short of a miracle. Godfrey, our father, was not around for either of his new arrivals. But then he was often 'not around'.

My mother and father had first met in Doncaster. He was an eighteen year old corner spiv selling bath salts and my mother was a twenty year old bus conductress and Sunday school teacher. She was a virgin, he was a womanizer, but the chemistry was right. Just one chat up line and my mother was hooked. She fell hook, line, and sinker for this cocky Cockney. Within three days she lost her virginity. Within three days and three minutes she was pregnant.

The family – no Godfrey

The abortion was to be performed in London, but first they had to inform my mother's mother that they were going to London to get married. My father was Jewish and my grandmother was not at all happy about that. She forbade her daughter to go. Rosie, however, would listen to no one on the subject. Her mind was made up; she had found her dream man and was determined to make the trip to London for the abortion and for the marriage. I don't know which one came first but I do know that each of these matters was taken care of.

Rosie met her future in-laws and despite the fact that she was not Jewish she ultimately developed a good and lasting relationship with them. They were never very happy about their son Godfrey. He was undoubtedly the black sheep of the family. Even at thirteen years of age when all good Jewish boys make their Barmitzvah, he had refused to go through with the necessary studies and remained the only one of the four sons to dissent.

Shortly before my birth, Dad had been released from Exeter jail after serving 80 days of a four month prison sentence for stealing a fountain pen. After his release he returned to his old profession – selling bath salts and starch substitute on street corners, and in markets. He would trade in the markets without an official hawker's licence, which was risky, as he hardly ever had the money to pay the fines. On occasions he was arrested and the rent book, always in Mum's name, would be put up to the court as collateral until the debt was cleared.

He was far more successful when trading 'up north', so Mum saw little of him and her being nine months pregnant did not cause him to change his way of life. However, he did come home soon after I was born. He arranged for his mother, Miriam, to go with my mother and me to the East Ham Memorial Hospital for my circumcision – my brother had been circumcised by the Beth Din only days after his birth but my 'chop' was less formal.

We lived at Hampton Road for a further four years, but it was not until the last few months at the Hampton Road flat that my sister, Marie, was born. I can remember very little about those early years. War had been declared and 'Anderson' air raid shelters were installed. At Hampton Road we had one garden but two shelters. The shelter to be occupied by the ground floor family was the one closer to the house. Ours was a little further away. This was no problem ... except in an emergency. One such emergency occurred very early on. The air raid siren had sounded and within only a few minutes searchlights flooded the sky and bombs were falling all around us. The anti-aircraft guns were being fired from the local Wanstead Flats. Above the din I could hear the bells of both the fire engines and ambulances as they sped along the main Romford Road.

The three children of the household were taken from their beds to the back door. We were to be carried, still in our pyjamas, to the first shelter. It was considered too dangerous for us to go one step further than was absolutely necessary. The father of the boy downstairs had me in his arms when a bomb landed nearby, and a large piece of shrapnel landed within twelve inches of us.

The next day we came from the shelter to gaze at the devastation of war. I can remember the smoke filled fog, the dust, but most of all, the shrapnel. These were fragments of bombs that most boys collected with relish.

Before my fifth birthday we moved to our new home at the Boleyn end of Green Street, one of the more famous roads in the East End of London. One of its earlier residents, as legend would have us believe, was Ann Boleyn. The Boleyn Castle was almost opposite our house and during my early days we would have great fun exploring and playing around this old ruin.

Green Street's other claim to fame was (or should I say is) the West Ham Football Club. Some years earlier, the team had played in the first ever F.A. Cup final at Wembley, only to lose to Bolton Wanderers by two goals to one. David and I used to support the side from the 'chicken run', which was the cheapest part of the ground to get into. We could get in for nothing when the gates were opened, twenty minutes or so before the end of the game, and for years that was what we did.

Three days before we moved house, Mum took my brother David, my sister Marie, and me to see our new, albeit humble, abode. It was early in the afternoon on a Friday and the Queens Road Market was in full swing. The stall holders were loudly broadcasting their wares. On the corner of the market stood the Queens Road pub. The piano player had played his last tune for the afternoon and 'last drinks' had been called. Most of the customers were drifting away to go about their business. A few children stood patiently at the doorway waiting for their parents to drain the last drop from their glasses. One of the heavier consumers swayed through the door, looked around and whistled at my mother. He inoffensively said, ''Ello luv,' and Mum just smiled back at him displaying an almost perfect set of teeth. As she walked on she also displayed to her admirer a fine pair of legs ... Mum was a very attractive lady.

Our arrival at 442 Green Street was depressing. The house, that we had been so excited about seeing for the first time, was a wreck. Our flat at Hampton Road was a dump but at least it had a roof! There were still tram lines on the road, even though the trams had ceased to run. Now there were trolley buses with their arms reaching up to touch the electric cables suspended across the street at regular intervals. On that day, a number of people carrying jugs, kettles and buckets were queuing at the corner of Selsdon Road, which was only twenty-five yards away from our new home. They were waiting for the arrival of the water cart bringing supplies for those whose mains had been cut off following an air raid. I was soon to find myself in that queue. It was not surprising to see the entire line stand to attention and for the men to remove their hats as a funeral car went slowly along the main road.

Ladies scrubbed their doorsteps despite the dust and smoke created by the constant bombing that had taken place over recent months. The smell of poverty was all around me.

The smell of it was in the house. The small kitchen had a gas oven that was black with grease and grime. It looked as though it could never be brought back into use. My mother knew otherwise and it was only a matter of weeks before she had it gleaming. It was still unusable most of the time as the gas mains were forever being turned off.

As an alternative we had a black-leaded kitchen range which was situated in the tiny living room. It comprised a large oven next to the fire and above both were four hobs on which we were to place our saucepans and the kettle.

David and I went into the garden. There was a great deal to explore – a rickety fence surrounded no less than 800 square feet of weeds and rubble. Attached to the house was a scruffy toilet with a door that did not fill its frame, and had a gap of at least twelve inches at both the top and the bottom.

In the centre of the garden was an eight feet by five feet Anderson air raid shelter. I could just see the round corrugated roof protruding above the ground by a couple of inches. I could not wait to go down the three or four wooden steps to see the inside. Little did I know that I would be spending a large proportion of the next three years of my life practically living in this hovel, sleeping there most nights during the big bombing raids.

Countless times we could hear the dreaded sound of the air raid siren and run down the steps into the dank-smelling sanctuary and wait patiently, sometimes hours, for the 'all clear' siren. I remember the mattress that practically provided wall to wall carpeting, the paraffin heater that kept the kettle permanently on the go, and the large brown tea pot that was chipped around both the lid and the spout. We drank tea like there was no tomorrow, and when I think of the bombings ... to the grown ups, tomorrow was an unlikely event.

In the next terraced house to us lived the McCloud family. Their bomb shelter was much bigger than ours – but then their family was much bigger too. There were six kids; four girls and two boys. Mr McCloud, a Scot, was a big man. He worked in the docks, and like most dockers he enjoyed his pint or two of beer. He would come home from the pub each night, very much the worse for wear. Through our paper thin walls we could hear the most almighty rows, and although we obviously could not see what was

Gold Brothers early days

going on, the next day, Mrs Mac's face would say it all.

On rare occasions I went into the McCloud house. It was not very nice in there. After I had been told that Mr Mac had drowned six baby kittens, soon after their birth, by sticking their heads into the bowl of the toilet, I vowed to keep away from the place forever.

We had not lived at Green Street for very long before Mum bought a four foot six inch tin bath. It was too big for the house and had to be hung on the garden wall next to the toilet. We carried it in every Friday night to be used by the whole family. Two full kettles and two large saucepans were kept permanently on the boil over the coal-fired hob. Cold water was brought in from the kitchen. The first bath, normally for my sister Marie, was only about eight inches deep and by the time Mum took her bath the water was not so clean, and not so hot, but at least the tub was nearly full. After each bath we were fully dried off and Mum saw to it that a piping hot tin mug of cocoa was ready and waiting. In the evenings, whenever there were no air raids, standing in front of the fire was a favourite pastime.

We had two large armchairs parked each side of the fireplace and a few wooden dining chairs. They had all been bought from the local rag and bone man. We would warm our bottoms in front of the hob then sit into one of the chairs. Over the years this became a family habit and there developed an unwritten agreement, whereby one person would get up and nudge the individual at the fire to move away, and he or she would sit down. This would go on all evening and not a word needed to be said about it. We could easily tell that we had been too close for too long because little patches of blue veins would form on our legs.

The radio was our main source of entertainment. During the day we loved to listen to 'Music While You Work', later perhaps some Vera Lynn songs or the 'Billy Cotton Band Show'. One programme that was a must was the news broadcast on the 'Home Service' at six o'clock. We waited in anticipation for the latest bulletins from the war zones. On occasions, we actually heard the voice of Winston Churchill. It was a great morale booster.

One cold and miserable November morning we awoke, having spent the night in the shelter. My mother was eight months pregnant. She had gone into the house to light the fire and to make breakfast. Once again my father was 'taking care' of other things. Suddenly we heard a scream. It was a scream of horror and pain. It stunned David and me into a state of panic. My brother ran into the house to find Mum sitting at the tiny living room table with her head in her hands, sobbing. She was clutching a telegram. David tried unsuccessfully to comfort her. I just cried and cried not knowing what was wrong but it was obviously something very serious.

We were soon to learn that Uncle Jim, my mum's favourite brother, her favourite person in the whole world, was lost at sea presumed dead. We could not conceive of the deep love that existed between them, but through our lives we have heard so many splendid things about him from my mother and her family that I can truly understand the pain that she went through on that terrible day.

Uncle Jim

For the next few months she slept with this poem beneath her pillow:

Deep in my heart is a picture
More precious than silver and gold
'Tis the picture of a dear brother
Whose memory will never grow old
No one knows my longing
For few have seen me weep
I shed my tears from a broken heart
When others are asleep.

It was months later that she was to learn that he had died such a horrifying death. He had been one of eighteen hundred prisoners being held aboard the *Lisbon Maroo* – a Japanese ship en route from Hong Kong to Lisbon. The conditions on board were almost indescribable. The prisoners were overcrowded and under-nourished, many had contracted diphtheria, dysentery and other diseases, they had no medical provisions and no sanitation. No attempt had been made to remove the bodies of prisoners who had died.

The vessel, which was not displaying a Red Cross flag, was torpedoed by a 'United Nations' submarine. The Japanese officers, soldiers and crew left the prisoners under the hatchways and abandoned ship. For twenty four hours the ship remained afloat but rescuers never came. Death was a blessing.

Only One God

My father didn't make it into the army ... hay fever I think, although I don't remember ever hearing him sneeze! His contribution to King and Country was to look after the bookmakers, club owners and many of the unfortunate women that were temporarily (or in some cases permanently) without their man to take care of them.

He 'took care' of my mother too, but at six years of age I was unable to distinguish the difference between screams of joy and the screams of pain. Later my brother David was able to tell me what was happening after we removed the glass tumblers from our parents' bedroom wall.

'Those sounds are made by mums and dads at the end of a good bunk up,' he told me.

'What's a bunk up?' I asked.

'Well, its like a piggy back ride, only it's even better.' ... He was quite clever for an eight year old.

I remember lying in bed one night while my mother was in bed in the front room and my father was supposedly at the gambling club which was next door to the Carlton Cinema in Green Street. It had been a dreadful day, hot and humid and sure enough violent storms had followed. My sister Marie was asleep but David and I lay awake waiting, listening for each crack of thunder. The storm abated but at around midnight we heard an almighty explosion ... without warning a bomb had landed on the Carlton

Cinema killing more than fifty people.

My father was not among them. He was 'somewhere else' that night. Our house was less than five hundred yards from the blast and was badly shaken. The whole window frame fell into my parents' bedroom. Thankfully my mother was physically unhurt, but she was obviously in a state of shock as my sister began to cry and my brother tried in vain to stop me from panicking. I believed that the house was about to fall in.

I remember so well the next morning when my dad arrived home. It was such a beautiful day. Everything was so calm. He had come home very early with his prepared statement ... he was so confident when he lied, that whatever the story, it had to be believed. He was so arrogant, so cock-sure (to a degree I inherited his arrogance, but cock-sure? I'm not so sure). My father should have been dead! so what did he mean by waltzing in at 8.30 in the morning? An argument developed that, as far as I was concerned, lasted for twenty five more years. But despite these arguments the screams of pleasure from the front bedroom continued.

The relationship between my parents always seemed to be in chaos. My father was always away. The only knowledge that we had of his whereabouts was from his sister, Bella. She was also in the business of buying and selling bath salts and would regularly see Dad at the wholesalers in Whitechapel. She would learn of his movements and sometimes report back to my mother. Regardless of the fact that we saw little of Dad, he did provide his wife with a fairly regular income, which resulted in the family eating regular meals.

There was talk that Dad intended to go into business with a man called Billy Ross. He used to work for the wholesalers where Dad had bought his stock. It was suggested by one of them that they could by-pass the middle man and produce starch themselves, and a partnership was formed. They soon opened a little workshop in Leytonstone and for a time their product, which they called 'Golden Brand', was a success.

There were controls regarding the manufacture of starch and, as I understood it, contact with the black marketeers was an essential ingredient ... it was an ingredient that my father just happened to have.

I liked Billy. He was a kind man, happily married and, compared to the normal associates of my father, a decent man. Dad worked very hard and for long hours. The company made good progress and soon they needed to take on staff. To start with, Gerald, Dad's brother, was employed and later my mother's half brother John came on the scene. He too went to work in the Leytonstone factory.

But they were young men and it was not long before they would be needed to fight for King and Country. Gerald volunteered to go into the Royal Air Force. Although he was under-age, he managed to forge his papers, and at sixteen and a half he began training to become an airman. During his days on leave he continued to help at the factory. John waited for his call up papers before he joined the Royal Fusiliers but that was towards the end of the war and he did not fire a shot in anger.

My mother's best friend, Ethel Jude, lived in the house that backed on to ours. She was always so friendly and supportive, and it was reassuring to know that she was there in times of need. And there were plenty of those. We liked her immensely.

Ethel had two children at that time, a son Ken, who was my age, and a daughter named Joan who was two years younger. There was no fence between the two houses and we would treat each other's home as our own. Tea was the order of the day, every day, all day, and Ethel's large kettle with the thin spout was continually on the boil. Ethel's husband, Stan, was taken prisoner early on in the war and, with Godfrey never home, a great relationship grew between the two families.

Trixie, our dog, was free to use the Jude house as a walk through to Selsdon Road. Trixie was a dog, not a bitch. We spent hours searching for an indication when he was given to us as a puppy. Even Ethel was called over for consultation. We were still unable to find a thing between his legs and were convinced that he was a girl, so we called him Trixie, and Trixie he was to stay. Despite the appearance of a distinctive willy.

Back yard, Mum, Marie, Trixie and Ethel at window

Each time I came home, Trixie greeted me with great enthusiasm. One day I was told that there had been an awful commotion in the garden. Ethel's youngest daughter had run into our house in panic.

'Something terrible's happened to Trixie!' she screamed.

David went into the garden to find Trixie and Manda, a bitch that belonged to the new people along the road, stuck together, bottom to bottom. David didn't know what to do. Neither did Ethel. David told me later that he was scared, and had never seen anything like it before. He had no idea that this was puppies in the making.

Ethel's first priority was to see that her daughters were sent into the house. Then it was time to panic.

'Dirty buggers!' she said to David. 'I'll get a bucket of water.' She gave it to David, and he threw it at the dogs. He missed. Another bucket, another miss. This went on until they gave up twenty minutes later ... Nature was then allowed to take its

Mum with Trixie

course. Eventually Trixie came home, bedraggled but with a look of satisfaction on his face ... Trixie had proven beyond doubt that he was a he.

Trixie survived the war. He continued to survive at least a dozen cars a day at our end of Green Street. He had been with us for twelve years but one day he just disappeared. We searched the streets for days but found nothing. Despite his name and address tag, we heard no more of him.

The visit of the King and Queen to nearby Canning Town caused a great deal of excitement. David and I walked for miles in the hope of catching a glimpse of them. He was successful, but then David was much taller than I in those days. I remain unsure as to whether or not I had seen them. I saw a man and a woman and the man wore a uniform ... and that was good enough for me.

Credon Road school was in a sorry state since it had been hit by a V1 flying bomb in the summer of '43. Five minutes before the missile landed, David and I had been playing cricket only fifty yards away, using a wicket chalked up on the wall of the local shirt factory. The 'doodlebug' had stopped humming which, although I didn't know it at the time, meant it was about to come down. The street was suddenly empty, and I knew that something was wrong. On arriving home my mother was in a state of panic, and we were quickly ushered into the shelter.

Within seconds the whole garden shook, and half my school was gone. Half of the playground was a crater, most of the spiked railings were lying flat, and half of the bicycle hut had disappeared, taking with it half of the drill shed. But half was better than nothing, and within three weeks lessons were resumed.

My brother had been sent to Harold Road school and this too was partially destroyed by a direct hit so David was moved on yet again. He was involved in many little incidents at his various schools. He was told on more than one occasion to put on his gas mask and instructed to stay in the air raid shelter until they were given the 'gas, all clear'.

Many of his friends were 'bombed out,' this was an expression used when families were forced to pack up and go after their homes were either hit or became unsafe due to a 'near miss'.

My brother is much older than me ... well 22 months actually and he can understandably remember so much more about the war. In recent times we hear his war stories over and over and I must say I still enjoy every word although his story about being treated badly at Plashet Road school was particularly disturbing. He was in a class of more than forty pupils and was already behind in his studies because of the bombings and evacuations.

David came home one day and Mum saw he was very upset.

'What on earth is wrong David,' she asked. At first David would not answer but Mum persisted. Eventually David broke down and explained the problem to her through his sobs. His teacher was producing the school play and every one of his class-mates was taking part except him, he was excluded but did not know why.

*

The following day after lunch his teacher came into the classroom and beckoned David to follow her to the headmaster's office where to David's amazement stood Mum in her Sunday best clothes.

'Why isn't my son in the play?' she blurted out as David and Mrs Green entered the room.

'Mrs Gold,' Mrs Green said indignantly, 'The play is a nativity and as your son is Jewish, I thought it inappropriate that he should be included.

'Mrs Green,' Mum exclaimed, now clearly becoming angry, 'he is a ten year old boy,' she said, pointing to David, 'and he doesn't understand "Jewish". If it helps, make him a "Jewish" shepherd but for goodness sake put him in that play.' Mrs Green looked away as if to say, 'It's not possible'.

'And,' my mother went on, 'if you don't it might be inappropriate, but I will not leave this office until I have your assurance that you intend to change your mind.'

He took part in the nativity play but generally things did not improve, and eventually Mum arranged for him to return to the already overcrowded Credon Road School.

The Blitz was reaching its peak when my mother decided to take us to stay with people in her home town. Evacuation to Doncaster meant a long train ride. For the first time, in real life, we would see cows and sheep and lots and lots of grass. Apart from Wanstead Flats there was not a lot of grass to be seen in our manor, so it was a very exciting adventure.

We left for Doncaster from Kings Cross station. David and I carried our own gas masks and my mother carried protective equipment for Marie that fitted over the front of her push chair. The train journey was every bit as exciting as we had previously pictured, the grass seemed greener, the cows bigger and the sheep carried more wool than I had ever imagined ... it was wonderful.

I can remember putting my head out of the window and taking in the smell of the steam and then going through tunnels that seemed to go on forever.

On arrival in Doncaster we were met by my Auntie Gladys. She was Mum's sister and affectionately known as Aunt Gag. Her husband, Ted was as deaf as a post, but I liked him. They were a nice couple. They had a smallholding, where they grew vegetables. Their home was a bungalow in a little village on the outskirts of Doncaster. At night the area was lit by gas lamps and I can recall the gas man coming round each morning to put them out. We stayed with them for a few weeks and it was wonderful ... there was food in abundance.

One morning my mother received a telegram. She seemed very distressed, as if someone had died. I learned later that my father had fallen in with a bad crowd, and been arrested for being the receiver of stolen goods. He was given a prison sentence of four years and had to serve his time in the dreaded Dartmoor jail. David and I were oblivious of this, and were able to go about our lives in Doncaster as though nothing had happened.

We were unable to stay for long with Auntie Gladys and Uncle Ted and Mum had to find someone else to take us on. Marie was looked after by my other auntie, Aunt Joan, who was married to a bookmaker with a 'pitch' on the Doncaster race track. Relatively speaking, they were rich, and David and I would have liked to have gone to them, to be with our baby sister. But Aunt Joan could not possibly have coped with all three of us, and so, for the first time, government assistance was called upon.

The government paid 8/6d per week for the keep of evacuees, and friends of the family offered to take us on. We went first to the Blackburns, a family that lived only a stone's throw from our grandmother. Mr and Mrs Blackburn had seven children, and their home was even more of a hovel than ours in Green Street. There were no carpets and most rooms were even without lino. The strangest thing about their standard of living was that there were only four or five chairs in the whole house, and the kids, us included, would eat meals standing up.

Fortunately we only stayed there for a few weeks, after which we moved on to the Tart family. My father had boarded there many times when he was selling his wares up north. They were very fond of my dad and he too thought the world of them ... This home was highly recommended.

Mr and Mrs Tart had three strapping lads, all more than six feet tall, who were coal miners. They were really nice people, and it was our first involvement in what was clearly a loving and caring family scene.

David and I were taken to the swimming baths nearly every day. We became very good swimmers and with the encouragement of the Tarts I started to dive from the higher boards. Before we went back to London I could dive from the six foot high shoulders of Peter Tart standing on the very top board at the local baths. This would create a great deal of interest and I began to realize that I was becoming a bit of a show off. In those early years I didn't have much to show off about.

However ... things did improve

Painful Times

We went back to London and started school again at the beginning of the spring. The war was coming to an end and there was no further need for blackouts. Air raid wardens were practically redundant and the women folk were ending the relationships with their American boy friends. They were going to miss their regular supplies of nylon stockings, chocolate and chewing gum, but preparations were to be made ... Our boys were coming home.

I had missed the old school. I could understand the kids better. The Cockney accent that we all used was like a foreign language but it was our language and if you didn't speak in that way, you might as well be a foreigner. I became quite a mimic, this was part of the 'show off' in me, and speaking with a northern accent or 'posh' or very heavy Cockney presented no problem to me.

The school was in a sorry state. Since the 'bomb' most of the older boys were sent off to other schools but I was one of the lucky ones as my class room was still intact.

Everything seemed the same in our home, except for the fact that my father wasn't there. He was never really there, but somehow it was different this time. I knew that something was wrong and it worried me. At six years of age I was starting to feel concerned about being loved. My mother was wonderful and loved us all dearly. I don't know why, but that in itself wasn't enough. I wanted both of my parents, and my father's absence was disconcerting. I was not to find out for a long time as to why he just 'wasn't around' this time.

We had only been back at school for about a month when one morning David and I experienced terrible stomach pains. We were sent home and Doctor Davis from Plashet Road was called in. Within twenty minutes we were both on our way to Samson Street hospital and immediately placed in the same special quarantine room. Our illness was at once diagnosed as dysentery, a disease that was associated with filth and poverty. I would accept the fact that we lived in poverty, but cleanliness had always been important to our family.

We were in hospital for over two weeks and my mother still hadn't been in to see us. This was very worrying as I had begun to realize that parents did 'disappear'... After all my dad had. David had said that he was at sea and I suppose that I was too young to really care, but I cared a lot about my mum. We were to learn later that she too was unwell, but could not have any treatment as she could not afford to lose her job cleaning at the local café. When she did eventually visit us it was wonderful to see her, but she looked very ill. She had lost a lot of weight, and I now believe that she was close to death at that time.

One day as we lay in hospital, fretting about Mum, a third patient was introduced to our little quarantine ward. We were shocked to discover that it was our baby sister, Marie. In the third week of our stay at Samson Street hospital, Marie escaped from our room and toddled into the scarlet fever ward. She was caught but it was too late. On the day that we were all declared cured of dysentery, Marie was found to have ... yes, scarlet fever. Nevertheless, she was home within a fortnight and life was able to resume some semblance of normality.

My mother held on to her job at the café across the street from us. She did not wait at tables. Her job was primarily to clear and clean them and, in addition, to scrub the floors. The wages were understandably not high. Our family funds had deteriorated to a state of absolute poverty. Mum often brought home bones that were supposedly for Trixie. He did get them eventually, but not until Mum had cooked them for hours in order to make stock for our vegetable soups.

Friday night, pay night, was a time that we could guarantee a good meal, although sometimes the shops would be closed before the wage earner arrived home. During the week we would often borrow money from Ethel to buy bread and jam. 'Dripping' always seemed to be in the cupboard, but often the bread had long been consumed. We always bought bread in half loaves which was necessary but bad economics because two half loaves were a half penny more than one whole loaf ... times were hard.

The café where my mother worked was owned by the Barnes's. They had a beautiful eighteen year old daughter named Doreen who was madly in love with my mother's half-brother, John. He was 21 years old and married to Silvia. They had a son named Jan, but their marriage was on the rocks and John moved in with us on a so-called 'temporary' basis which lasted, on and off, for nearly ten years.

My mother had to tolerate him because the one pound twelve and sixpence a week for his keep was vital to our existence. He quite liked Marie, but David and I did not get on too well with our uncle. A roofer by trade, John was quite handsome despite the big ugly tattoos on his arms, and was a drinker and womanizer. Notwithstanding this – or possibly because of it – Doreen found him irresistible.

One day I caught them doing things on our arm chair. Doreen's tongue appeared to be stuck in John's ear and his hand was up her skirt. I was becoming aware that men liked to touch 'there'. However, it was many years before I found out that women liked that too. Her knickers were on the floor and she was holding John's erect penis in her hand. It was exceptionally large and I remember thinking that the skin on the end was stretched to bursting point.

My intrusion brought him out in a rage.

'Fuck off you little bastard!' he yelled.

Why he was so cross I couldn't understand. Now I realize that he was about to get his 'leg over', and in those days it took a lot of working on.

John was a pig to my brother. David, only ten years his junior, seemed to annoy him in some strange way. John would hit us both but David took the main brunt. I can remember a time when we were playing in the back yard and John was indoors, drinking tea and listening to the racing on the wireless. We were in high spirits and I made a 'dare' to David ... we were big into 'dares'.

'I dare you to tell Johnny that he has got a face like a penguin's penis,' I said. David did just that. He squeezed his little fingers into the tiny gap beneath the living room window, opened it just a couple of inches and said the words verbatim. John went mad. He came out of the house and literally beat David up ... This was child abuse, 1946 style. David's face was bruised for weeks but we were too scared of John to report the incident to anyone.

I am very proud of the fact that throughout my life I have always managed to repay my debts. I have never stooped to begging or stealing, although I must confess to some activities that were 'marginal'. One such activity was 'bunking-in' the pictures. David and I went regularly to Saturday morning pictures at the Boleyn Odeon, but we could not always afford the sixpence entrance. Roy Rogers and his horse Trigger was a weekly serial that just could not be missed. We had to get in somehow. The emergency exit was the answer. A pal inside would go to the toilet, the emergency door was nearby and a push on the bar would let us in.

One late afternoon I went alone to Green Gate, which was about a mile and a half from home. A 'flea pit' cinema stood on the corner, showing an 'A' film, which meant, of course, that it was for adults only. I went to the fire exit door and probably had in mind the Saturday morning 'trick'. When a lady came out, I actually held the door open for her and when she left, I walked inside. The cinema was quite full and I sat down on the first seat that I could find.

Familiar music immediately filled my ears as the 'Pathe' newsreel cockerel filled the screen. Even today my skin creeps as

I think of the horror that I was about to experience.

On the screen were pictures of thousands and thousands of bodies piled mountain high. Some that were not yet dead were still moving. I was horrified. I did not understand what the Holocaust was, nor did I know that the victims were Jews. I started to cry and ran out of the same door that I had used to get in. It was a dreadful experience and I suffered for many years with the memory of it.

My Nan knew that I was upset about something and we sat and talked. It was then that I found out that those men, those bodies, were the bodies of dead or dying Jews. While I'd been at Doncaster I had experienced for the first time the significance of being called Gold. Gold, according to a school friend, was short for Goldburg, and Goldburg was a name for Jews. And Jews, according to him, were misers. He knew because his dad told him, and I felt that his dad wasn't keen for him to play with me. Afterwards, I had asked my mother what a Jew was. She told me then that Dad was a Jew and I bore his name. As to why Phil's father didn't like Jews, she didn't give me a satisfactory answer.

But I was too young to really accept that there could be so much hate for these people. 'Why, Nan?' I asked. Tears welled up in her eyes, she turned away and I knew that she was crying. Her own experience as a young girl in Poland had been quite terrifying, but she rarely spoke of the way in which she and her family had been treated. She said that the reasons for the persecution of the Jews went back for thousands of years. However, in modern times the Gentiles could not forgive the Jews for what they did, or for what they did not do, to save Jesus.

'But wasn't Jesus a Jew?' I asked.

'Yes,' she said, 'and so am I, and so could you be, one day.'

'But then if I were a Jew would people hate me?' I asked.

'No, not all people. Some people today are unhappy that Jews have a fellowship that excludes others, and that Jews seem to succeed where others fail.'

These words left me with a complex, and I was to find out that it was not without foundation. Granddad was less tolerant of the behaviour of some Gentiles. He was of the opinion that there was a certain amount of jealousy of Jews. They were, in the main, achievers and many people including Hitler, resented them for that alone.

In Peace

The biggest anti-climax of my life was the end of the Second World War. I don't know what I had expected but to me it was a damp squib. There was a street party in Selsdon Road which I found disappointing. The dancing and the cuddling seemed to be a silly way to carry on, but then I was only seven years old. Apart from the time that I played doctors and nurses in a wardrobe cupboard with a pretty little girl in the neighbourhood, I knew nothing of the extent of the excitement created by these encounters.

Nor could I understand the difference between VE Day and VJ Day. It was not made clear to me. Whilst celebrating the end of the war at the street party, I was told that the war was not actually over and I had visions of the doodlebugs spoiling the whole affair. It was very confusing.

It was very confusing and indeed shocking when Uncle David returned from the war. He had been released from a prison-of-war camp in Italy. My grand-parents, Charlie and Miriam, had arranged a big homecoming for their son David and all of the family were invited. We arrived at Rixen Road in Manor Park to discover banners all over the place.

'David Gold – welcome home' .... 'Good luck David' .... 'We welcome our hero'. I had been told all about Uncle Dave. How he had been captured by German soldiers and had been sent on to

Italy as a prisoner-of-war. According to Nan he was going to be bringing home a German helmet, a bayonet and a sword once worn by an Italian officer. I was so excited and as the warm August morning passed on, the excitement of seeing my 'hero' Uncle Dave for the first time in memory was so enormously intense. Soon after lunch we were advised by a neighbour who had a phone (a rare luxury in our part of the world) that he had left his base and would arrive soon by taxi. The tension mounted.

I had never thought to ask just how big my uncle was or to even consider that he was other than a 'giant' of a man who had practically won the war single-handed. I was astounded when he alighted from the taxi. He was carrying the sword and it was nearly as big as he was. Five feet four inches tall, he must have weighed no more than five stone and looked even older than my grandfather. Fifty years later, he is fit and well and continues to be a powerful force in the publishing industry.

A month or so later I fell in love. Not yet eight years old, I met Marian Ray. My first sweetheart was a beautiful little girl with long golden ringlets. Our romance lasted for over four years although we never ever kissed or even held hands. She went to tap dancing school and appeared on the stage. In her teens she was invited to Hollywood to appear in a musical film which, I was informed, was produced in 'Technicolor'. I never saw it but I was so proud that she had been my girlfriend – we had even played 'gobs' (fivestones) together.

Because of Marian I started to be more conscious about my appearance. A bath once a week was not really enough. We had a bathroom, with a just a single cold tap which occasionally produced water that was a dirty brown colour, so it was better to take the tin bath from the garden wall into the living room and fill it with water boiled on the iron stove in kettles and saucepans.

The clothes that we wore were literally rags. The rag man would pass our door once a week calling out, 'Any old iron, old rags, bring au't your lumber.' We never had anything to sell, but every now and then, when Mum had some spare cash, she would send me along to buy some clothes.

I can remember going to the rag man's yard in Southern Road, which was not far from Samson Street hospital. The whole scene was not unlike the one in 'Steptoe and Son'. There was wooden spiked fencing that surrounded a cobbled yard where a horse stood chewing his hay from a sack-like bag strapped under his chin. The horse was still attached to his empty cart.

I arrived soon after he had returned from his rounds. The rags had been sorted into huge piles. There were wools, cottons, jumble and old iron. I had 1/3d to spend and, with permission, I scrambled over his stock to pick out some items. There was a variety of smells, some quite revolting but others were surprisingly pleasant, and I quite enjoyed rummaging through his stock. When I had found a few items it was time to discuss the price. It was my first experience of negotiation. He wanted 1/6d and I managed to buy them for a shilling. Through life, I have always been a tough negotiator and through life I have always been honest ... I gave my mother the thru'pence change.

Mum went immediately to the first aid cabinet in the cupboard under the stairs and brought out the 'flea comb'. This was used at least twice a week, but after visiting the rag shop it was crucial that immediate action was taken. We had a saying in those days; 'If your hand itches, you are about to get something. If your head itches, you have already got it.'

It was a common sight to see young children with their hair shorn and with 'Gentian Violet' lotion applied to their bald head. To the kids it was somewhat shameful, so I willingly allowed my mother to untangle my mop of unruly hair by pulling this extremely fine comb through it.

I also knew that I could not go up to Doncaster if I had fleas, and I was looking forward to seeing my gran and my aunts and uncles again. After doing the rounds, David and I were delighted when Mum suggested that we spend some time with the Tart family. They had once lived in Birmingham and on the Saturday we were invited to go to a match at St Andrews with Mr Tart and a friend. It was the first time that we had actually seen a full game of professional football with 'paid for' tickets. We stood in the Kop watching Birmingham City take on Manchester City. With more than 50,000 other supporters, I was glad of a pair of shoulders to sit on. Whilst up there, I was able to tell David, who was too big to be carried, exactly what was going on. When the 'Blues' (Birmingham City) scored I thought I would lose him in the crush. He survived and we won 5–0.

After the game my uncles (which was what we called them) went for a drink in the local pub. As we stood outside waiting for our bag of 'Smiths Crisps' and glass of lemonade, I remember seeing crowds of people, far more than we had ever seen leaving the 'Boleyn' ground at West Ham. Most of them were wearing a cloth cap and scarf and as they walked past us, many of them smiled or passed a kind remark.

We got home very late and I was worried that my uncles would be in a lot of trouble from Mrs Tart but on the contrary she was really interested in hearing about our exciting day. We stayed up for ages telling her about it. Lying in our beds David and I discussed the possibility of going to St Andrews again, but we knew that it was very unlikely.

During the winter of my ninth year the flu bug got to me. This meant that Ethel had to look after me while my mother took my brother and sister to see Dad in Dartmoor Prison. David knew from the start where Dad was, but he kept it from me. He has always been able to keep a secret, and he managed this one very well, although I was starting to have suspicions.

His sentence was coming to an end when David, Marie and Mum went there. The trip was paid for by the National Assistance people and included a stay in a bed and breakfast establishment. Marie was very young, but I know that the sight of that horrid building in the morning mist had a profound effect on David.

My father's imprisonment and the necessity for my mother to claim assistance from the Relief Office caused David and me a great deal of unhappiness. The East End had more than its fair share of prejudice. There was prejudice against Black people, Jews, Asians and many other minorities, one of which was the 'scroungers' and we went under that label. We were on the 'RO'. Claiming free dinners at school was unnecessarily cruel. We were asked to put our hands up each morning to claim our free meal while others had their fivepence collected by the teacher. It was humiliating. Somehow it was a great sin to be poor.

'If you can't eat it, don't take it,' was the school dinner slogan. The unwritten slogan was, 'If you get it for free, eat it or else...' The gristle was not exempt. I stuffed mine into my pocket to take it home to Trixie, but I was afraid of being seen.

By now some of my school friends were finding out that my dad was not at sea, and their parents had expressed concern that they (through the government) were paying taxes for the keep of both convicts and their offspring.

The ultimate humiliation was our visit to 'Granditers' the clothes store in Canning Town. We queued for hours to collect our free garments, paid for by the Relief Office. The free clothes consisted of two vests, two pairs of pants, two pairs of grey army type socks and a pair of heavy army style boots. The boots were already fitted with 'Blakys', flat iron studs that scraped along the ground and told people a mile away that a poverty-stricken scrounger was coming. We removed our shoes in the store and put on the boots. At first it was kind of funny and David and I had a little joke; he called me 'Cliperty' and I called him 'Clop'. The reality of the situation grew on us as my mother told us that we should wear these items as much as possible because, if an inspector caught us without our benefaction, we would be in trouble.

David

I cried, and David was not exactly happy either. We went straight from Canning Town to school. It was late morning and lessons were in progress. I knocked on my classroom door and Mr Nathan called me in. I opened the door and thirty two pairs of eyes were looking at me in my short trousers and my heavy boots. I then walked to my desk. On the wooden floor the studs sounded even louder and I began to cry again. At nine years of age you do not cry, but I did. I experienced real misery and at lunch break I changed into my plimsolls. In the soles of this footwear I used cardboard to protect my feet from the rain. When I put them on that day I felt like Cinderella ... Well, the male equivalent, anyway.

The Fight Game

One day there was a survey at school and the teacher asked the names of our parents. I had not seen my father for nearly two years and could not remember his name. I was getting quite panicky as each child before me was asked, and replies like, 'Ann and George,' were stated confidently.

Miss Stevens eventually reached me and I replied, 'Rose and God.' This caused an uproar of laughter, and Miss Stevens thought that I was having her on, but I insisted. I did remember my mother speaking to him before he was sent away and she did call him 'God'. This was short for Godfrey but I must say, looking back, calling him 'God' was stretching things a bit far. Miss Stevens asked for a note from my mum and this sorted it all out ... My embarrassment lingered on for some time.

Miss Stevens was good to me. I liked her. It was Miss Stevens who talked with me one day about my problems. We spoke about my dad, but of course I would not divulge to her my suspicions. We talked about other things like religion. I was by now starting to be aware that many of my so called 'friends' were treating me differently. This was undoubtedly a combination of my many social discriminations such as being poor, being the son of a convict, but most of all being the son of a Jew.

Miss Stevens said that I was imagining most of the things that I had told her about, and that I should not be so concerned what others thought or said. That was sound advice, but it was a long time before I could put it into effect. 'Jew baiting' was to haunt me.

I recall an incident at 'Ralph's' fish and chip shop on the corner of Selsdon Road and Walton Road. There was a long queue, maybe ten or twelve people, I was one of them. A younger boy with a skull cap came in and walked to the counter. A man went up to the lad, picked him up physically and threw him out. In doing so he said, 'Jews, they're all the bleedin' same.'

One of my friends was called Warzofski. He was the son of a tailor who lived just along the road from us in Green Street.

He was a good, kind and generous person and very often could be seen to hand out a whole packet of sweets to his school-friends. Sweets were on ration but I would think that if you had the money, rationing would not have been a problem, and the Warzofskis had money.

One day I heard that Sammy had been beaten up at school. His nose, which was somewhat larger than average, had been broken and his lip was split open. Sammy Warzofski was the most placid and agreeable person I knew but, as young as I was, I realized that there were a lot of people around who did not like him just because he was a Jew.

I liked Sammy. He was a 'proper' Jew and went regularly to our local synagogue which was situated at the end of the road directly opposite my house. He once asked why I didn't go, and I had no answer. I didn't even know what it meant to be a Jew, and anyway, I'd started attending the Baptist Church in Plashet Road so that I could be a 'Lifeboy', the junior version of the 'Boys Brigade'. Surely I could not do both?

The fact that I had been told that I was a Jew did not concern me. I just wanted to be a Lifeboy and that was that. It did, however, concern Uncle Gerald. He is my father's brother and, with the exception of my grandmother, the only real Jew in the family. Every Sunday we went to my Nan's house in Rixon Road, Manor Park. It was known as Nan's and not Granddad's because she was the driving force. She was a wonderful person, a real down to earth Polish Jewess who loved to love and be loved, but ruled with a rod of iron.

Parents and children congregated every Sunday, and those who failed to turn up needed an exceptionally good excuse. Nan, with the help of her daughters-in-law, would cook while the children played, and the menfolk would usually participate in a traditional Jewish card game called 'Club Yos'.

Nan must have known that she had lost the fight to maintain a real Jewish home and family. Her oldest three sons had married 'Shiksas' and her only daughter, Bella, had married a strict Protestant army captain and had gone off to live in Barry Island near Cardiff.

The Jewish home, however, was to be just that. Nan's rules were to be obeyed. She fasted at 'Yom Kippur' and the family, her sons anyway, were expected to observe. A few years later, when David was thirteen, Gerald persuaded him to participate in this ritual. He fasted only from dusk till bedtime, but then he went to the toilet at one o'clock in the morning and found everyone except Nan standing around the pantry cupboard gorging themselves silly.

Gerald was very good to us while my dad was away. He came over quite often and would take David and me to the speedway racing at the old West Ham Stadium in Custom House. It was strange that he should react so aggressively to the fact that I appeared to be taking up religion. In fact that was not the case at all. I just wanted to be a Lifeboy. When I told him this one day he reacted by actually taking me to the Baptist Church in his car. He never said a word ... although I knew that he was angry with me.

Sex was not of any importance to me or my school friends at this stage in our lives. Even so, I could not possibly forget the commotion that the *Daily Mirror* caused at our school. A photograph was printed on the centre page, showing a dozen or so female, grass-skirted African tribal dancers parading before our King and Queen. The amazing thing was that the reader could see their naked breasts – ladies' breasts! It was something that we had never seen printed before. Tits were private; they were banned unless they were shown in silhouette form, and for the benefit of art in photography. How could a reputable paper like the *Daily Mirror* publish such an outrageous picture? It was unthinkable, but needless to say the *Mirror* would have sold every copy. It was almost certainly a very profitable day for them.

It was about this time that I began a profitable venture of my own. My best friend, Henry Dillaway, and I had started up in business together. We made a mint. Well, actually we sold mint. Henry and I had an arrangement with an old man at the local allotments behind the Northern Passage, which we called the 'back alley'. We would clear his plot of mint that clogged his patch, then wash it and tie it into little sprigs. This was all dealt with before the Queens Road market opened at eight o'clock on a Saturday morning. We did good business and established quite a few regular customers, sometimes taking over two shillings each, which was not bad at three ha'pence a sprig.

One day Henry could not make it to work and I went out alone. I had not been trading for more than ten minutes when a man grabbed me by the arm and ordered me to take him to my house. He was a West Ham market official and was ready to take action to stop this 'company' from operating without a licence. Bureaucracy and authority has always been a concern to me. I do realize the need for it but I cannot help feeling that there was no need to attack an up and coming enterprise like 'Gold and Dillaway, Purveyors of Mint'.

Henry and I were the best two fighters at Credon Road School. My brother had looked after me while he was there, but when he went up to secondary school, I was left without that support and I had to take care of my own battles. I had only a few minor scraps, but at least the other boys were made to realize that some Jews fight back.

Henry Dillaway, however, was another kettle of fish. We fought many times before we became best friends, and when I heard through the grapevine that he had joined the West Ham Boxing Club, I was horrified. I saw my future standing at Credon Road school declining from equal best fighter to number two, and I was greatly concerned. Without a word to a soul, I packed my old plimsolls and a pair of shorts and went round to the Black Lion Pub in Plaistow which housed the famous boxing club.

I was scared. I knew nothing about boxing, and I had no real inclination to learn, but the fear of losing my joint number one spot at Credon Road School was sufficient incentive. It was two shillings to join, and that meant that my journey could have been in vain because I only had a shilling. However, Mr Myers, the manager of the club took pity on me and let me stay. At first he told me to bring the money when I next came, but later that evening he gave me back the shilling and said that my membership was free. He said that he understood my circumstances. I think he did, and believe he knew here my dad was ... The shame of it followed me around.

Henry did not turn up that night and although I went to nearly every club night he was rarely there. I was quite happy about this because I was starting to show improvement, and with my new skills I felt better about any future confrontation with him.

Sport was in our blood. David was doing very well at football, cricket and athletics. He was in every school first team and as young as he was, the talent spotters were out, and his prospects were good. I could not compete with him at these sports; they just did not happen for me. However, I did swim, and at the age of eleven I was the freestyle junior school champion of West Ham.

When I was awarded my medal by Miss Hall, our headmistress at Credon Road School, she announced that my name was to be the first on the new honours board and that the whole school would have a holiday on Friday afternoon in celebration of my success. I was suddenly a hero. Kids patted me on the back and said, 'Well done,' and I loved every moment of it. I was a star.

My feet came firmly back to earth when the eleven plus exam results were announced. I thought that I would pass and go on to Plaistow Grammar School. This school had its own tennis courts and the pupils actually wore uniform. But it was not to be.

I failed. I cried like a nine year old. Shirley Green sat next to me. She failed too, but she was understanding about my disappointment, and comforted me in a way that belied her tender years. She was plain, poorly dressed and spoke with an accent that was as bad as mine, but she was as soft and kind as any girl I ever knew.

It meant that I was to go to the same school as David – Balaam Street Secondary Modern, better known as 'Burke' Secondary Mod – unquestionably the worst school in Britain. Of course, rumours get out of hand. But if the rumours were only half true, I was in for a bad time.

A Cut Above the Rest

Family life was fairly calm during Dad's last twelve months in prison. There were normal family squabbles. David and I could usually settle them by taking a broom each, and fencing with them until one or the other became tired. At that point it was easier to run one broom down the other until it crashed into the weaker boy's knuckles. We would regularly have plasters and even bandages on our hands, but my mother was unable to stop us from continuing this activity. On one occasion she ran over to Ethel's house to get help. The broom fight was obviously going 'too far' and Mum had to discipline us. This meant sitting for hours in the two old armchairs. These chairs were from the junk shop and were so clumsy they practically filled the living room.

The amazing thing was that David and I remained such good friends. We did so much together. I am only twenty two months younger than he, but in those days that gap was considerable. Regardless, we competed at everything. Reaching the highest point of the poplar tree in our neighbour's garden, how many times we could go around the garden fence without falling off, table tennis played on the dining table. We were so competitive ... Winning was everything.

Today, our competitiveness is the same with tennis, chess, snooker and a variety of other things but competitiveness as a team, against the world outside, is where we really excelled.

Life at 442 Green Street was pleasant. In the evenings we would listen to the Wilfred Pickles programme on the radio or play card games, draughts or Monopoly, while Mum sat and knitted. She often read us letters from Dad. He wrote in such a calm and loving way that we all looked forward to his homecoming, thinking that Mum would have no reason to be lonely or unhappy ever again ... We were wrong.

For the first few months after his release it was wonderful. Dad was never out of work for long and, by hook or by crook, he was soon making enough money for us to escape from the bread line. It was even a time for my brother, sister and me to experience trips to the sea-side. Dad managed to buy a 1936 'Lanchester' motor car. This car, although quite old, was sort of 'posh' and was out of place in Green Street. It had real leather seats and a polished dashboard. Dad would drive us all to Southend-on-Sea for a treat. It was an experience for us and we enjoyed it immensely.

It was not long, however, before my mother and father were quarrelling. Each row was noisy and seemed to last for days at a time. It was so distressing for us children. Thankfully my father was never violent to my mother. One minor exception was when he shoved a slice of bread, covered in jam, into her face. Mum was not hurt, but her appearance gave my sister and me a big scare ... It looked like blood.

Till now Mum had personally cut our hair, but now that Dad was home it was time for me to go to a real barber's shop. 'Mannies' was close to Upton Park station which was less than one hundred yards from my home. I loved the atmosphere of 'Mannies'. There were usually five or six men sitting on wooden chairs waiting for either a shave or a haircut or sometimes for both.

When it was my turn to have my hair cut, Mannie would reach under the chair for a plank of wood. This board went over the arms of the seat and I was picked up and placed in such a position that enabled the job to be done without Mannie needing to bend down. Being perched up on this ledge was embarrassing and I longed for the day when I could sit on the chair like the grown-ups.

Sometimes I would go for a hair cut on my own. The men would chat away, and although I remained silent, I would find the stories that I heard fascinating. They discussed politics and religion for much of the time.

Mannie was Jewish and when he talked to Dad they used a special language. My Nan could speak fluent Yiddish and Dad had acquired many Yiddish sayings which seemed to impress some of Mannie's customers. Dad remarked one day about his recent experience in Shul, to which Mannie retorted, 'Don't tell me, Goddy, that you have been to Shul. The only prayer that you have ever made was for a winner at the races.' Mannie knew more about my dad than I did.

Occasionally the conversation would get around to sex, and because of my presence it would be well and truly watered down. The subject fascinated me. Most men would brag about their conquests, and my dad was no exception. In fact, he'd had more women than the rest of them put together. Well, at least that was how it sounded. He was playing to an audience that were very impressed. There was only one exception ... Me.

I was very suspicious of the number of men that would come through the door and put their mouth to Mannie's ear and whisper a few words. Mannie was quick to understand their requirements and he would pass them a package and take some money. It was a long time before I discovered that they were purchasing either 'Durex' or 'Uno' condoms.

Once again David had to explain to me what they were used for and why. It was very hard for me to take it all in as I was still of the opinion that girls were there to be kissed and I had not yet crossed that bridge.

As the summer holidays went by, the fear of my return to school grew. At Credon Road I had learned to live with the problems of being poor, having an ex-convict for a father and of being Jewish, and now I was worried that it would start all over again. After all, many of the girls and boys moved on to 'Burke' after leaving Credon Road School.

It was the tenth of September, just one day after David's thirteenth birthday, when I dressed to go to my new school. David offered to walk to school with me as it was my first day. As we approached it I saw more and more aggressive-looking boys wearing thick crepe sole shoes. Boys with greasy hair with a big wave pushed over their foreheads, some with tattoos on their arms. They all appeared to be untidy and tough. David was not very big but at least he gave me the impression that he could 'hold his own'. It was not the first time, or the last, that I was glad of his presence.

The first sight of the school unnerved me. It was much bigger than Credon. The boys' and the girls' playgrounds were separated by a wall. I noticed that on top of one section of the wall was barbed wire. It was there clearly to stop the boys from getting over. In those days there was never any fear (or chance) that the girls would make it into our playground. I was to learn that this was a 'hedge' against nature.

The first day of school wasn't too bad. After the first assembly we were informed of the class and teacher that we would have for the whole term. I went into Mr Conn's class, which was to be known as 1A. It was the top class and I was determined to stay there as my dream was to pass my thirteen plus exam and escape from this dreadful place.

The children in my class seemed pleasant enough. A few were from Credon Road School, but no one that I had been close to. There was a girl who sat near me, called Sally, who was so refined. She looked out of place at a school like Burke, and I liked her very much. I had such a 'common' accent that it would have been unthinkable for me to even try to be friendly with her.

The unfortunate thing for her was that she had developed somewhat prematurely and little breasts were pushing against her tunic. To an adult this would be of no significance. To a class of boys approaching twelve years of age, only the removal of sweet rationing could take priority.

The boys seemed to act as though Sally was a bitch on heat. To them it was a sign that Sally was 'experienced', which was absolute nonsense and I hated them for it. These boys were the men of the future and I was already learning about them.

Most fights took place on the bomb site which was less than a hundred yards from the school. It was a kind of ritual. The message was passed round the school and at 4 p.m. the crowds would form. It was not unlike the bare knuckle fighting of the olden days.

The first fight that I was to see on this bomb debris was because of me. I was in the playground when the biggest and the ugliest character that I had ever seen called out to me. 'Hey! Are you Goldie's brother?' I told him that I was. 'Another bloody Jew. Piggy back me across the playground,' he ordered.

'Pardon?'

'You fucking well heard me, you cunt!'

Suddenly two boys grabbed me so that Alan Pike could climb on my back. He was too heavy and I fell, and for this I received the dreaded 'Burke knuckle torture'. One of Pikey's friends admini-stered the punishment. He ground his knuckle into my chest, his middle finger knuckle extended to ensure that the maximum amount of pain was felt by his victim ... me. The pain was excruciating and tears formed. I so much wanted to cry but I knew that it would give them all even more pleasure.

David got to hear about this incident and spoke to Pikey during the afternoon break. He told Pike to be careful because Jews have been known to fight back.

'After school, Goldie,' Pikey said.

I knew nothing of this until I saw David on his way from the school towards the debris. He was as white as a sheet, and I knew that something was wrong. When I heard that he was involved in a fight and that it was with Alan Pike, I trembled. David was as good as dead – well, at best he would be hospitalized.

The traditional 'ring' was formed and Pike, who was pre-maturely hairy, stood ready for my brother. It was truly David and Goliath and I am proud to say that David Gold represented the biblical David. He beat Pike into the ground in what was a tough fight, and from that day on, the 'Gold' name took on a new light. It burned even brighter when the second and, I'm glad to say, last fight of David's took place.

The Moons were a family of villains. With his 'old man' in prison and a couple of brothers in borstal, Derek Moon had quite a reputation. It was only three weeks after the Pike fight when Moony was heard to have said that Goldie would be really hurt if he tangled with the Moonys.

Just like David's fight with Pike I heard of the match by accident, on my way home from school. The crowds were forming themselves into a crude boxing ring and once again David was waiting for 'Goliath'. 'Goliath' this time was not so big, but it was the thought of his family that scared me the most.

As Moony was hustled to the front I was appalled to see that on the middle finger of his right hand, he wore a ring. It had a stone in the centre and was the biggest ring that I had ever seen on a young person. Some of the boys called for him to take it off, but he wasn't able to. At least, that was what he said, and there wasn't a boy there who was prepared to call him a liar.

Within seconds of the fight starting David's face was cut and blood was running down his face. He was to be scarred for life, but from then on it was David who was doing all the punching. It was humiliating for Moony. All of a sudden he stopped fighting. His face was red and it appeared that he was about to cry, which at thirteen years of age would have been unforgivable. David let him off the hook and didn't strike Mooney again. For that matter, David never struck a blow in anger on anyone ever again ... He had made his point.

Buttons Without Bows

In a strange way I was starting to accept and even enjoy being at 'Burke' Secondary Mod. Mr Conn was my regular teacher, and I liked him very much.

After congregating in the assembly hall each morning to say our daily prayers and sing the one obligatory hymn, we would go to our classrooms in order that the register could be taken. There was no more need to put my hand up for free dinners as my parents were now financially in a position to pay the sixpence dinner money. Dad was home now and he was earning an honest living. Well, I liked to think so.

Mr Conn was a good all round teacher, he was very popular and he had strong powers of persuasion. At the last lesson before our first Christmas break from school, we had a 'free' lesson during which Mr Conn decided to hold a class concert.

'You, you, you and you will entertain the rest of the class.' I was one of the 'you's' and was at a loss to know what I would do. The first 'volunteer' sang a song and the next said a poem. Then it was my turn. I had seen the original black and white 'movie' of 'Oliver Twist' at the cinema the evening before and took to the stage and acted out five, ten or was it fifteen minutes of the play. I mimicked Oliver with his 'posh' voice, Fagin the Jew, Bill and Nancy and the Artful Dodger in their strong Cockney accent. I made up the words as I went along and everyone including Mr Conn was in hysterics. The applause lasted for a long time and I was in my element ... Just showing off.

It was ironic that this British film was to cause such furore from the Jewish communities throughout the world, over its portrayal of Fagin. Jews were offended. William Shakespeare had started it all with his portrayal of Shylock, and now Charles Dickens's Fagin was looking very much like the money-grabbing Jews in Hitler's propaganda films ... All three have a lot to answer for.

Dad was home now and, with the aid of a confectionery business he had set up, he was earning an honest living.

We went through a period of really getting on with my father. There were times when he was very generous, but there were times when he was only generous with his promises. These were often linked with a successful night at the 'dogs' and it meant that they rarely materialized.

Christmas had been wonderful. Mum had seen to it that we had lots of presents even though most of them she had made herself. With Dad back at home, we were hopeful of receiving bigger and more exciting gifts that year, and we were not disappointed. Marie had a doll's pram which was to block up the hall-way for years to come. David and I received Monopoly and a table tennis set, and we played on the dining room table till we dropped from exhaustion.

Uncle Gerald fancied himself as a good player but by now both David and I had 'star' quality on the tiny table. We believed Uncle Gerald to be very rich. There was talk that he was earning as much as twenty pounds a week working as a manager of a timber import company. So when he offered to play for money, it seemed fair to relieve him of a small amount of his spare cash. David and I took it in turns to play him. The first game, against David, was for sixpence and he lost. He was so sure that he could beat me that the next game was double or nothing. This went on and on, until the stakes were becoming silly. Twelve pounds sixteen shillings was being staked by us to return twenty five pounds twelve shillings if we won.

David was playing the biggest game of his life and the tension was obviously getting to him. Twenty pounds meant that, if we won, we would both be able to buy new push bikes from 'Bates' bike shop in the Barking Road. The game went to twenty points each and the rules state that the winner must win by two clear points. The game went from twenty to twenty one each, then twenty two all and by then they were soaked in sweat. It was at that point that David hit two of the best shots in his life and won the game. Gerald, to our horror, then said that it was 'best of three' and that he had run out of time.

We were terribly upset but I think we learned a lot that day. We told our Dad about it but he offered no sympathy. He told us the story about the Jewish father who told his son to jump off a wall. He said, 'Jump! I'll catch you, trust me.' The boy jumped only to have his father turn away. As he wiped the blood from his son's knee, he said, 'There you are my boy, lesson number one ... trust nobody.' ... Sound advice.

I arrived home from school one evening and my mother was very excited. She gave me sixpence and sent me straight up to 'Mansfields' the greengrocers near to the Queens Pub in Green Street. It was to buy a bunch of bananas! I had never seen, let alone eaten, a real banana in my whole life and neither had most children in the East End.

The length of the queue took my breath away. It went on for over a quarter of a mile beyond Green Street into Rochester Avenue. It nearly reached my Uncle Nat's house which was at number 82.

This queue was even longer than the one that I was in a few weeks earlier to get into the 'Odeon' at the 'Boleyn', that queue which was formed by cinemagoers went all the way down to my house. They were waiting to see Larry Parks in the *Al Jolson Story*, one of the first films in 'Technicolor' that I had seen.

I queued for both of these 'miracles' and they were both worth it. Each of 'Mansfields' customers was allowed only four bananas. As I walked home I put the bananas to my face just to savour the strong and sensational smell.

My family were sitting at the table waiting for me, the 'Libby's' evaporated milk, still in its small can, was placed on the plastic tablecloth as well as five plates and spoons. Mum carefully divided the four bananas into five dishes. The plates were soon empty ... It was bliss.

Only two weeks later I was to experience yet another gastronomic delight. Dad and Mum had taken all three children to the Odeon to see a more conventional black and white English film, *Passport to Pimlico* which was terrific, certainly the funniest film that I had ever seen. After the show they took us along to 'Nathan's' the pie and mash shop. Pie and mash, with liquor was an East London delicacy.

We loved every second spent in that café, eating at heavy wrought iron tables with marble tops, on which the salt and vinegar were placed in very large containers. The wooden floor was covered in sawdust. We sat there watching the customers coming in carrying their large white basins to take away their purchase of jellied eels, stewed eels or, the most popular of all ... pie, mash and liquor.

Despite all of Dad's efforts poverty never really went away, and the confectionery business eventually folded. The Lanchester was a great luxury and it had to go. It was replaced by a large old van which was more suitable for Dad's wheeling and dealing. He worked very hard and was determined to stay honest. We were proud of him. It was nice to tell my pals at school that my dad was working, even if it wasn't exactly a steady job. He bought and sold manufacturer's overage and 'job' parcels from which he extracted stock to sell in the markets at weekends.

For the next three years I spent most of my weekends with Dad. My main task was to ensure that we paid no vendor fees by helping to keep our pitch and the market inspector apart. First I had to search the area until I found him, and then, once he was sighted, I kept tag until he moved towards Dad's pitch. Then I was off, as fast and inconspicuously as possible, to warn my father. We would move on, only to return minutes later.

Sometimes I saw my dad offer a bribe which was readily accepted ... I was being initiated into the real world.

One day I came home from school to find that our bedroom was full of large cartons, about twenty of them, all filled to the brim with loose buttons; coat buttons, shirt buttons, jacket buttons – there were millions of them. These buttons were to change my life. They changed all of our lives. Dad had swapped them for a parcel of combs, mirrors and plastic wallets that he and I had been selling down the markets for the past six months. Swapping has always been a strategy of traders and I was to put it to good use in future years.

My dad had planned to 'turn' the parcel within the next few days, after which we could have our bedroom back. Even the best of plans go wrong and this was not the best of plans. He could not 'place' the buttons. Mum and Dad decided that he would have a better chance if the buttons were carded, which meant sewing a set of six matching buttons onto a card and the task was put in hand. Mum was an expert with a needle, and we all felt that this would not prove to be too demanding ... we were all wrong.

A week went by and not even one carton had been disposed of. My mother worked with us each night. It was quite pleasurable as the evenings were drawing in and we were able to light the fire in the new fireplace and enjoy ourselves, just like old times. But the job of finding six buttons to go onto a card was becoming increasingly difficult, and eventually we had to give up. My mother came up with the idea of putting a table out in the front of our house to offer the buttons to the public. Dad was not impressed and offered her no encouragement.

On the following Saturday we put the table by the window at the front of the house. Every container that we could find was used to display the different types of buttons. We put out the loose buttons as well as the carded ones.

We had plenty of customers, but the takings for the whole day amounted to less than one pound, which was very disappointing. 'I told you so,' Godfrey told Mum which made her more determined than ever to make it work.

We continued to sort the different styles but we refrained from carding them. The sales went up but very slowly and winter was already upon us. David had built a real stall and we were starting to look more professional but managing it was not easy. The paraffin heater from the air raid shelter was back in use. It was a great help in keeping us warm but a big problem was the rain.

David had not made a cover for the stall. That would have been too expensive, and it was cheaper to cart the stall and the stock indoors each time. Sales kept improving as we served more and more regulars and we were able to get hold of a second-hand tarpaulin sheet to go over the new top that David had constructed. Now the rain could be kept off, but the wind and the rain together was another story and we were still compelled to drag the stock in and out each day.

It was a particularly bad winter and there was plenty of snow. Strangely this did not affect the turnover ... only our fingers. It was sometimes so cold that they would stiffen up and rapid warming would only cause chilblains ... an occupational hazard.

The stall made little impression on the stock that filled our bedroom and we were to live with it for a many years to come. Within the next six months Dad brought home a really large tarpaulin. We were suspicious that it came from the back of a lorry ... literally. We had a saying in those days. 'Ask no questions, hear no lies.' This sheet covered the whole stall and we were to experience the absolute luxury of being able to leave the whole unit, stock and all, on the front over night.

It was a bit of a risk but worth it. After all, the buttons were of little use to potential thieves ... and there were fewer of them in those days.

Marie, now in her eighth year, was changing from being a spoilt child to being a rascal. She came home from school one day with a brilliant idea. If we were to tie an old wallet to a piece of cotton, we could hide behind the stall and pull it every time someone went to pick it up. I must have been mad but I went along with it. Needless to say we got into trouble when an elderly gentleman failed to see the funny side and knocked on the door. Mum let Marie off but I was forced to sit in the dreaded armchair for a full two hours.

Ours wasn't the only small business on Green Street. Between our house and the West Ham football ground there were a number of interesting shops (stalls, really), situated outside regular homes. Next door to us was Mrs Trainer, who sold practically everything. Along from Mrs Trainer's was the book stall. This was a fascinating shop to me because apart from the second hand comics, to which I was addicted, he stocked 'rude' magazines. I was too young to buy them but I was starting to become interested. The covers would nearly always portray a drawing of a pretty girl with her dress well above her knees and, on really good covers, the barest outline of a pair of lace panties would be visible. Items such as these would not even be spoken about in mixed company in those days. This type of book contained about six stories and a few drawings of couples sitting on a settee or on the side of a bed, the woman with her skirt up above her knees and the man with a hand provocatively placed either close to the lady's breast or between her knee and the hem of her skirt.

There were rumours that the owner of the stall could get hold of 'Hank Janson' books and that he kept them under the counter. To many, it was a dreadful thought that such disgusting books were being sold at all, let alone in Green Street!

Little did I realize that one day I would become this 'author's' publisher.

On the famous armchair

Into Business

It was good having Dad at home and I really hoped that he would continue to 'go straight'. The war had been over for five years, and the East End was slowly clearing up and rebuilding. But dreadful things were starting to happen there, and I was always fearful that Dad would in some way get mixed up in them. There were terrible fights taking place at the Queen's pub which was next door to the Upton Park station and only eighty yards from our house. Men were literally carving each other's faces with 'chivs', the recognized word for the open razor.

The most infamous character in Britain at the time was Teddy Machen, better known as 'Scarface' Machen. He was also known as 'the man of a thousand cuts'. Word of his presence in the Queens would spread down the whole length of Green Street, not unlike the arrival of Billy the Kid to a saloon out West.

We continued to operate our button stall although it never looked like taking us out of the poverty trap. A few extra lines were added to the range and this helped a little, but stock had to be paid for and money was in short supply. David and I and even Marie were called upon to help out every evening (and of course Saturdays), but Mum was the real worker. She was not strict with us but we respected her, and none of us shirked from helping out with the business.

The Golds all seemed to be going into business at once. Uncle

David, Mum, me and Marie

Dave was selling books and comics to retailers, helped by Granddad, who was using an ice-cream vendor's tricycle to deliver them for him. Uncle Gerald and Dad were getting closer and there was even talk of them going into business together.

Gerald knew of a transport company that was in financial trouble and was going into receivership. He felt that his brother would be able to do a deal that could get them started without laying out too much money. My father succeeded ... He rarely failed in such things.

In the beginning they would both drive lorries as well as endeavour to find customers. Dad did all of the long runs and Gerald the local ones. This was mainly because Gerald was unable to obtain 'going away clearance' from his wife. So once again Dad was working away from home. Mum was forever suspicious that he was up to something. She had every reason to be, if the stories that I heard were even half true. Mum has told us of how she had come home from Doncaster at one time to find him in bed with another woman. Mind you they did have a chaperon ... A second woman. Dad always managed to talk his way out of these 'difficult' situations.

*

1951 was going to be 'our year'. Dad seemed to be doing well in his transport business, the stall was taking regular money, and David and I had new bikes. The coming 'Festival of Britain' was being talked about and our lives took on an air of excitement. This was my thirteenth year and I had a lot to look forward to. There was the prospect of getting away from 'Burke'; the possibility of starting a paper round and the likelihood of representing West Ham Boxing Club.

The number one priority had to be my education. I realized that, academically, I was at best only mediocre, and it was time for me to put a lot of evening work in. Money was always short and as soon as I was thirteen I planned to start both morning and evening paper rounds. Last, but by no means least, I intended to become an Olympic boxing champion, and I knew that I had to train very hard if this dream was to be realized.

I did train. I ran nearly every morning, either around the block, along the sewer bank, or I would get up at six in the morning to tackle what was to me the marathon to end all marathons, which was to run to the Blackwall Tunnel and back, probably ten miles in all. With all of this, in addition to my work-outs at the gym, I was ready to take on the world. I entered the West Ham School-boy Championships. After winning two preliminary bouts I came up against the eventual champion, Bobbie Kelsey. He won on points after three exciting rounds each of only one and a half minutes' duration. I was bitterly disappointed. But there were to be many bitter disappointments ahead of me.

My boxing was of some significance at school. Even though I had not won many contests, the fact that I was involved in the sport made most of the boys, even the bullies, wary of me. 'Jew baiting', for me at least, was a thing of the past.

I was studying very hard. I began to realize that I had to study that much more than my contemporaries to achieve the same results, but that did not over-concern me. My aim was to get out of 'Burke' Secondary Mod. And if it meant that I had to work through the night then I intended to do so. My mother was always prepared to help and, with her encouragement, I knew that I would succeed. This attitude has helped me through life. I believe that if you convince yourself that you will achieve something, you will succeed. Change that word 'will' for the word 'might' and you cut your prospects down considerably.

I would often think about where I was going in life. I didn't relish the idea of following in my father's footsteps. Market grafting was just that – grafting. I imagined I would be a school teacher, or perhaps an accountant. I would dream about this as I walked home from school, counting the lampposts along the way. Over the years I got to know each one as a number. I even became quite friendly with them: 'Hi, twenty two,' or, 'You need some paint, thirty five.' There were forty two posts in all, and I have since come to see the comparison between them and the passing of my lifetime. Each post represented approximately two years ... The only difference now is that the desire to reach the last post is less intense.

On my thirteenth birthday Granddad asked me to me help him with his comic round at weekends and during the holidays. I was excited because I would be earning money. I did tell him that I would do it for nothing, but he insisted on paying me, which made me very happy because 2/6d was a large amount of money for a day's work. However I was to realize that it was a very long day and I had to earn every penny.

We caught a bus very early one morning to go to Hackney. It was necessary to change buses on two occasions but eventually we arrived at 'L. Miller and Son'. They were the publishers and distributors of big selling comic titles including the ever popular *Captain Marvel*, which outsold every other title by at least three to one. They published a whole range of comics that normally sold for one shilling each.

The titles that Granddad was able to buy were the overstocks which Miller would sell off cheaply after the titles had been on sale for at least three months. Granddad would pick up this line for Uncle David and deliver them to Uncle David's customers.

We would collect fourpence for each comic. Miller charged

Uncle Dave twopence each and he and Granddad split the profit. Sometimes Uncle Dave would pick up and deliver the stock to Granddad, but on this occasion it was not possible. I was called upon to help carry the ten gross of comics from Hackney back to Rixon Road in Manor Park. My fingers seem to hurt whenever I think about that day.

It was fascinating to see Fred, the packer at 'Len Miller's', as he counted out our order, after which Oscar, the manager, would take the money. However, he didn't take a penny before recounting every comic. This double checking was on the boss's instructions. It reduced the possibility of 'fiddles'. After the checking and rechecking, Granddad parted with the twelve pounds and we were on our way. The bundles were tightly strung and it was difficult to squeeze in my small fingers. Once I had managed to place them beneath the string it was then difficult to pull them out again in order to take a rest.

The return journey involved a great deal of walking between bus connections but the final walk from Manor Park Broadway to number seven Rixon Road where Nan lived was more than I could take. However, there was no escape. Granddad was fully laden, so I continued. I crammed my handkerchief between the string and my fingers, which was now possible as the string had slightly slackened. Granddad loaned me his handkerchief for the other hand. By now my shoulders were aching and I was fit to drop, and it was still only eleven o'clock in the morning. This half crown was going to be hard earned.

When we finally made it to Nan's I was exhausted, but after a quick cup of tea, and a buttered 'Matzo', we were back to work. We broke down the stock of comics into smaller parcels and then filled up the ice cream container on the front of Granddad's old bike.

At the end of Rixon Road, Granddad told me to look after his bike as he had something to take care of. I watched him walk away from me and wondered what he was up to. He approached a young man who was standing on the corner of the next road and handed him a slip of paper and some coins. At the same time a policeman approached from the other side of the high street. The young man ran off, but the policeman apprehended Granddad and they stood speaking for some time. When he came back he explained to me that he was worried because in all the panic he didn't collect his betting slip from the bookie's 'runner'. It didn't make much difference because later that day I was told that the horse came last anyway. It seemed that Granddad was a 'block off the old chip' (my dad). His horses and dogs were also followers and not leaders.

Unsung Hero

Things were starting to happen to me both visually and mentally. My face, never attractive and certainly not handsome, was becoming spotty. Hair was starting to grow on my upper lip and beneath my side burns. I was advised to refrain from taking my first shave for as long as I could. It was not the best of advice because it tended to make me even less attractive during those impressionable early years.

Hair was also growing in another part of my anatomy which caused a problem. I had a very embarrassing moment at Balaam Street swimming baths, when my friend Charlie Haynes blurted out in our locker room. 'You've got more 'air round your cock than you've got on your bleedin' 'ead!' The fact that the changing lockers were practically on the edge of the swimming baths did not seem to bother him. It bothered me. I felt that everyone, including the girls we were with, were looking at my private parts.

One of the girls with us was called Vera. She had a pretty face but she was at least three inches taller than me. Charlie reckoned that she liked me but I had no confidence when it came to girls so Charlie did it all for me. Before I knew what was happening, there I was, taking Vera to the 'Century' cinema in West Ham Lane. Charlie had briefed me on what I should do, when I should do it and how I should go about it. 'Don't worry about how tall she is, they're all the same in bed,' he assured me. 'And anyway, you can always take an orange box with you.'

'Very funny,' I thought ... It wasn't funny, not to me anyway.

Vera was so sweet, her face was almost angelic. She spoke beautifully, and I think that there were times when she had difficulty understanding my broad Cockney accent. I had failed to substantially improve my speech, but I hadn't given up. I cannot remember the film that we saw, which is not surprising as I had other things on my mind. Charlie's instructions were to do nothing during the 'B' film, the ads, or the news. I was to wait until the main film was under way then put my arm round her shoulders. If she resisted, I should try again a little later. After five minutes I could start on the top button (if any) of her blouse. I must put my hand down there before even thinking of trying 'down below'. In theory, this was great. In practice it was anything but ...

I made it with the arm and there was no resistance. There was a top button – that would not undo. After three or four minutes I had pins and needles in my arm but I was a little embarrassed to take it away, so it stayed there. After another five minutes it went numb. Then there was no option, I had to take my arm down from her shoulders.

It could be said that the whole afternoon was a success. I took Vera home and gave her a kiss. She had really enjoyed the film and said that she would like to go again with me ... I felt then that I should have persevered with the top button. On the way home I became more conscious of how tall she was compared to me ... I did not take her up on the offer.

Monday morning at school was difficult. I knew that I would see Vera. I had planted that first kiss, but I did not want it to go any further and I knew that she did. She was in another class, so I was able to avoid her for a few days but we did eventually meet up.

'Hello,' I said.

'I've missed you,' she told me.

My market training had helped me to be good with words, but before Vera, I was speechless. The school bell rang, and not for the last time I was literally saved by the bell. But it was the last time that I spoke to her. I continued to think about Vera, reflecting on my complex about my height ... Or more to the point, the lack of it.

Two weeks went by before Mr Welch, the headmaster, called me to his office to tell me that I had failed my thirteen plus exam. I was on the verge of tears when he said that all was not lost. He told me that the North West Ham Technical College, which was only one hundred yards away from Balaam Street, was shortly intending to move to the 'Grove' Central Building in Queens Road which at that time was occupied by the boys from the School of Building.

The boys, and my own brother was among them, were going to a 'posh' up market establishment near Trinity Church in Canning Town. In view of this they might find a few extra places, and I was in strong contention. I couldn't believe my ears, and within a week I was informed that my new school would be North West Ham Technical College for Art and Commerce. I was certainly no artist so I was about to join the commercial side of the academy.

I scraped to earn enough money from my paper rounds to help buy my new uniform, and for the second time in our lives, Mum and I caught the number 40 bus to Canning Town in order to visit 'Graniters'. At least this time we were not dependent on the Relief Office. We bought the basic uniform although I had to look through the 'Goods for Sale' section of the local newspaper in order to obtain a secondhand briefcase.

The six weeks of summer holidays was a time to prepare for my new school. It was compulsory to wear a uniform and money had to be found for this. Mum and Dad were prepared to help but both were finding things tough. Mum worked on the stall for little return and Dad's transport business always seemed to be in trouble. Following last year's discussion, Uncle David pressed Mum again to make Christmas garlands. This was a chance for us to make some money and all of us children were to be involved.

We formed a production line and maintained a regular routine. There were conveniently four procedures that put together our particular version of a Christmas decoration. First we would cut the crepe paper and place it in line onto a clothes horse, next it would be run through the machine with the 'gathering arm' which made it 'crinkle', the third person would cut it off and roll it up, then finally one of us would pack it into a carton and place it in the passage way to await collection and eventually ... payment.

During the summer we could work at our own pace but as the year progressed the workload increased. There were nights when all four of us would work into the small hours and the machine would often become red hot. We were still using the treadle to power the machine but Mum intended to buy an electric motor once we were making money.

I needed to do more than one paper round and I applied to other shops to do an evening round but these jobs were hard to find. I did well in the market and I know that Dad appreciated my help because when we did well he was very generous.

One market day we were selling the monkeys on a string of elastic, when Dad had to go off for the rest of the day. There was a problem at his transport business and I was allowed to stay on at the market alone. I was doing quite well when a stall owner near to where I was working approached me. He asked me to move further away from his toy stall, which I thought was a reasonable request. Before I moved away, I had an idea! I asked him if he was prepared to let me sell some of his toys down at the other end of the market. He thought that it was worth a try but refused to give me credit. He agreed to let me have anything on the stall at a thirty per cent discount. I was not satisfied and finally settled on a discount of thirty three and a third per cent, sale or return.

I could only afford to take a few items at a time but I sold a few and then went back for more. By the end of the day I had taken eighteen pounds and ten shillings on his items alone which earned over six pounds. Dad was pleased with me when he came back but he felt that the stall owner could have given me a better deal. Dad let me keep all of this extra money towards my new uniform. I was more than pleased.

Uncle Nat came round one evening during the holidays and suggested that I should go away with him and his family to Ramsgate. I was so excited, it was beyond belief, why me? Uncle Nat and Auntie Emme lived round the corner to us and I did visit their house from time to time but his offer came as a big surprise. Uncle Nat was a radio mechanic and he was starting to get involved with television although there was such a small demand for this 'eighth wonder of the world', particularly in the East End of London where no one could afford such luxuries. However, he had managed to get hold of a nine inch set to install on a temporary basis at Nan's. Both of Nat and Emme's children, Maureen and Frank, made regular visits to our house and David, Marie and I reciprocated.

My uncle wanted me to go to Ramsgate in place of Frank who had chosen to go on a school camp. Nat had paid for the whole family so at no extra expense I would be company for my cousin, Maureen. It was a wonderful holiday, the weather was perfection and every day was like living in a dream.

One afternoon as the tide was going out, my cousin Maureen wanted to go on the paddle boat. Her parents were not happy as they thought that she was not old enough. They insisted that I took her. It was pure bliss paddling out from the shore. The water was shallow for the first fifty yards then it became very deep. I know this because I had walked out on many occasions at very low tide, then the drop is even more obvious. Holidaymakers paddled alongside us then unexpectedly they would be out of their depth and only swimmers could continue.

We went on for a little way, when suddenly there was a scream of distress from a young lady approximately twenty yards away from our paddle boat. She was waving furiously and I realized that something was seriously wrong. We started to paddle towards her but we were far too slow. I took off my shirt and dived

Picture of me taken in Ramsgate

into the water and swam for all I was worth towards the girl. I presumed that *she* was in some sort of trouble, but I was wrong. Her feet were firmly on the ledge and her head and shoulders were out of the water. She just kept screaming.

'Jenny! Jenny!'. It was her sister who was in trouble and she was nowhere to be seen. I saw a hand appear out of the water just a dozen yards from where I stood. I swam towards it and literally went under the water to grab hold of her body. She kicked and scratched and punched. I was becoming exhausted but I did manage to hold on. Eventually she was in her loving sister's arms, spluttering and crying but at least we had made it to safety. She was no more than ten years old and her sister was about my age. The poor child had swallowed 'half the ocean'. The older girl told me her name was Carol. I took her sister, Jennifer, from her arms and carried her towards the beach. Despite the tears, Carol looked very sweet and she was obviously very grateful.

The little girl clung to me and was still crying which was good news. At least she was alive and I was her 'gallant' saviour. It took less than ten minutes to reach the beach and by now I was madly in love with Carol.

I felt that once I had dealt with the press and the radio interviewers I would ask her to come out with me ... perhaps we could walk along the sea front at sunset, later possibly a moonlight bathe ... When we reached dry land however, the reception was not quite what I had expected. As I put the younger girl down, her mother came over and 'told off' her daughters for being away for so long, then, like a puff of smoke, all three disappeared forever into a crowded beach.

It was with great pride that I walked into the North West Ham Technical College in North Plaistow. My hair had been cut by Mannie only two days earlier. I intentionally did without the hair wave that was worn by the trendier boys of the day, but in order to look the part, I still needed to apply a full dollop of 'Brylcreem'.

I need not have concerned myself. The majority of the students at North West Ham Technical College were artists, albeit technical artists, but nevertheless they were in the main, 'arty' types and their dress was more casual.

In the playground there seemed to be an equal amount of boys and girls (I was to learn that more boys than girls did art and many more girls than boys did commerce). My class was even more disproportionately balanced. Only seven boys against thirty two girls ... it should have been Utopia but the girls in our class were too old for us – or should I say we (all seven of us) were too young for them. Girls approaching fourteen were already looking for boys who could take them out in Daddy's car and show them a good time. We could only take them to West Ham Park on the crossbar of our push bikes. Somehow it was not the same. The 'Magnificent Seven', as we called ourselves, had to remain patient. Our time would come ... Or so I thought.

During assembly one morning I was messing about with a few of the girls when one of them pinched my bottom. I made a screeching sound which did not exactly harmonize with the morning hymn. 'All things bright and beautiful.' At the end of the hymn, the headmaster, Mr Glading told me that I must go to his office straight after assembly.

I was so scared, because I could think of no excuse. I stood before him. He looked up.

'Well, Gold?'

'Sorry about that noise sir,' I said, 'but my voice has gone a bit funny during the last week or so.' His response was like music to my ears.

'Oh, I should have realized. I'm sorry Ralph, of course. These things happen when your voice breaks and you musn't be embarrassed or let it worry you. Now hurry along or you'll be late for your lesson.'

Cheats and liars never prosper, or so I was taught. But I was beginning to learn that there were certain exceptions to most rules ... I had just applied one.

It was a sad day in February when we heard of the death of King George VI. The East End had a particular affinity to King George, and needless to say his death affected all of our lives. We respectfully wore our black arm bands to school the next day, and I continued to wear mine for some time to come. Even selling toy monkeys in the market, although it just didn't seem right, calling out, 'Lovely monkeys, only ten months till Christmas, buy early, get your monkeys now,' while displaying a three inch wide black arm band.

I was always concerned that one day I might bump into one of my school friends while I was selling in the market, especially now that I was at a 'posher' school. At North West Ham Tec I tried to speak a little better. It was not easy, even though my speech had been so bad that any improvement would help. However, in an attempt to improve I would often sound 'h's when they were not needed ... The speech improvement plan was temporarily shelved.

As time went by, new product was added to the display on our stall. Dad had bought some cheap silverware from a salvage company. It had been recovered from a factory fire and the containers and their outer cartons stank from the damp and the smoke. The cutlery and other items were tarnished, but the whole family worked to clean it up and the parcel was soon good enough to display and sell, along with the buttons.

Uncle David was making good progress with his wholesale business. He supplied books, comics, stationery and other odd lines to the newsagents and allied traders. Mum became one of his regular customers. On the stall we started to sell a few paperback books, and there was talk about taking on a few pin-up magazines like 'Spick and Span', which showed photographs of ladies in sexy attire, usually with stockings and suspender belt allowing the occasional glimpse of an inner thigh. Although we eventually sold them, Mum thought that the stall was not really ready yet for that type of thing.

The owner of the secondhand book stall along the road from us was not too happy about this competition. I felt sorry for him in a way – after all he was there first. But it was my first realization

that competition is healthy – you just have to make sure that you are better, as in all business it is surely the survival of the fittest.

I was fourteen and looked nearly seventeen, and by stretching to my full height and not shaving for at least a month, I was able to patronize him in buying the sexy magazine that I had been hankering after for so long. Reading that magazine encouraged me to explore new avenues of pleasure and some mornings, I was left with an embarrassing and obvious stain on my bedclothes. These avenues of pleasure were supposed to be very bad for my boxing but, regardless, I still trained very hard and had managed to win a few more contests. However, I was made to understand that restraint, for the big occasion, was vitally important.

I nevertheless wanted to have companionship with the opposite sex. However, in that direction, I was an utter failure and my excuse was ... boxing.

I did give it a try. I attended the 'Magenta School of Dancing' at Forest Gate. The lessons were costing me two shillings and sixpence a week and I was determined to get my money's worth. My height, or my complex about my height, didn't help. Each time I went, I was the smallest and youngest person there, with the exception of only the instructress. She was only five feet tall and getting on for forty years of age. Because I was always the odd man out she danced with me most of the time and as far as I was concerned was unquestionably ... on offer.

Her technique involved the placing of her thigh between my legs on each beat of the music. She also leaned back before the turn, I leaned forward and there was a movement that induced my penis to increase in size. She was terribly unattractive, and I was concerned that she thought that there was a possibility of this developing into something. I was a hopeless case, my dancing never improved and I did not get my leg over ... Well metaphorically.

David's selection to play for London Boys caused great jubilation in the household. When we heard that he was going to play against Glasgow Boys at the famous Crystal Palace ground at

David's great day at Crystal Palace

Selhurst Park, the excitement rose to fever pitch. David's position was left wing, and he looked so small against his opposing right back. With seven minutes left to go it was one all, and it seemed that both the crowd and the players had settled for a draw.

Then the ball was passed to David, who was some ten yards inside his own half. He dribbled past at least three players and curled the ball in the top right hand corner of the net. It was 'Roy of the Rovers' stuff, but this certainly wasn't Roy ... It was my brother.

Within a week a letter was delivered by hand for the attention of Mr Gold Senior. It was from Ted Fenton, West Ham United's manager. He wanted to interview David, with a view to signing him up for the West Ham Colts, and to offer him a future in football ... David was elated.

The bombshell was dropped by my father who was unhappy about the prospect. He told David to forget about it; after all, football players could only earn, at best, twenty pounds a week, and that only after a long apprenticeship. David had passed his City and Guilds examination, and had already started to work through his own apprenticeship to become a bricklayer, and Dad's opinion was that he had a better future with the building trade. David reluctantly took Dad's advice.

There is an art to bricklaying and David was an artist. He had won several awards, and brought home photographs of his work. You could not fail to see how skilful he was. He and his friend Victor worked for a local firm, and from what I heard the outside world was nothing like school. They were out in all weathers, and suffered. Each evening their hands were blistered and sore. There were lighter moments when the older men would tease the young apprentices, sending them for rubber nails and getting them to carry a hod of bricks to the top floor of a house that was already built. Then they would huddle up during tea breaks to talk about sex. As far as I was concerned, that was still an area I knew little about.

One day I caught the 101 bus to East Ham Broadway and sat upstairs in the front. There were no other passengers until a man got on and sat near to me. I picked up a paper that had been left behind by an earlier passenger and was horrified to read that yet another person had been sentenced to be hanged. This time it was a man by the name of Derek Bentley. The paper said that the murder had taken place in a town called Croydon, which was south of the water. I had never heard of the place. It went on to state that the real killer was a boy called Christopher Craig.

I have always loathed hangings, but this one was more relevant, firstly because Bentley didn't actually do it and secondly, the crime involved a boy who was only the same age as my brother. Thirdly the hanging was to take place at Wandsworth Prison, where I had actually been in to see my dad. It distressed me, and I was glad to see that he would probably get a reprieve.

At this point the man came up to the front of the bus and spoke. 'Damn fog,' he said. 'Looks like it's closing in.' As he said this, he sat down next to me. I was crushed in the corner as he grabbed hold of my thigh. Frightened, I called out and within a moment the bus conductor came up the stairs. He could see that I was distressed and immediately assessed the situation. He threw the man off the bus, calling him a 'dirty bugger'.

Thirty minutes later I was home – still upset, still trembling but home with my mother there to comfort me. She hugged me and soothed me and was very tender but I knew that if she could have got her hands on my assailant she would have been prepared to kill.

She told me that the man was a homosexual and went on to tell me why the conductor used the word 'bugger'. I was horrified and I found it hard to believe that a man could do 'it' to another man. I had thought that there was only one way to do 'it' and that was to lie on top of a woman and put it in, then both the lady and the man made noises like they were on a ghost train ... I had a lot to learn.

Champion

It was a very cold November evening when I arrived home from school. My mother had been crying. I asked if there was anything wrong and she told me there wasn't. There clearly was and I offered to help, after thinking for a few moments, she said, 'I want you to take this note to Billy Ross.' She began writing on a small 'Lions Brand' pad. I looked over her shoulder but she blocked my view. I got the message.

Billy, Dad's old partner in the starch business, had maintained a low key friendship with my parents. He was married but he lived during the week with his mother in Burdett Road in Mile End. Neither of us had telephones, and contact could only be made by a 'runner' … In this case, me.

Mum insisted that I wore a scarf, it was getting even colder and a fog was setting in. I waited at the bus stop just across the street from my house but no buses came. So I walked to the Boleyn and was able to catch a number 15 petrol bus that took me all the way. The journey would normally take less than an hour but I realized that the weather was slowing things down considerably. The fog was becoming thicker and I started to worry about my homeward journey.

It was dark when I arrived at Billy's mother's, and the fog had thickened considerably. It began to look yellow which was a sure sign that a 'pea souper' smog was upon us. I knocked on the door. There was no answer, I knocked again and again but no one was there.

I felt dreadfully alone. I put the sealed envelope, marked confidential, through the letter box and pulled my scarf up over my mouth and nose and took a few short unsatisfying breaths before setting off for home.

The half mile walk to the bus stop was more of a shuffle but I made it. I waited and waited for a bus to come but it seemed to me that the buses had stopped running due to the fog. I started to walk, as I did so I was working out the estimated time of arrival at my house. In normal conditions it would take over three hours and at this pace it would be after midnight before I reached home.

As I walked I suddenly noticed a man in a uniform walking beside me. He was in the road and he was carrying a torch. His pace was a little quicker than mine and he soon moved ahead. To my amazement a double decker bus appeared. I leaped onto its platform to find there were no passengers and no conductor. It took a moment or two for me to realize that the conductor was the man I had just seen walking in front of the bus. I did not see a soul for over an hour. Eventually the conductor jumped on, he wanted to know where it was that I got on the bus. I told him that I did not know ... I didn't.

I was both surprised and delighted to learn that the bus was a number 40 which would eventually pass our front door in Green Street. I say eventually because the journey at that speed would take, at least, four hours. It was close to midnight and not for the first time my mother was worried sick about me.

I learned later that the note was a plea for help. Billy Ross had been my father's partner and friend, and Mum believed that Dad would listen to Billy and hopefully take advice. She felt that Dad was slipping into his old ways. He had renewed his acquaintance with some of his old cronies and Mum knew that he was getting into trouble again. She believed that villainy was a drug to my father and he needed help. Billy did come over and he did speak with my father but I am sure that it was too late ... Dad was already on the downward slide.

*

I helped Granddad over the Christmas period. I was becoming increasingly worried about Nan. She was diabetic and her leg was always hurting her, but I did not realize that this would develop into such a serious problem.

The whole of her family had visited over Christmas and as New Year's Day was Granddad's birthday there was a big family gathering. It turned out to be a depressing affair because Nan was very ill and stayed in her bedroom.

The next day, we heard from Uncle Nat that Nan had been taken into Whipps Cross Hospital. Friday night was the last time that I was to see her because she died within a few days. It was a terrible shock to me, and indeed to the whole family. I loved Nan dearly. It may sound foolish to say this, but I loved her matriarchal dominance. She had undoubtedly been the head of the family and her magnetism had managed to hold us all together. I was beginning to notice that most Jewish people had the same arrogant tone, and yet beneath it all was a heart of gold. Miriam Gold had exactly that, and I was going to miss her. Granddad was devastated. They had quarrelled and she did nag him, but forty five years of marriage was a long time.

She lay in her bleak wood coffin in the front room and my brother, along with other male members of the family sat 'Shiva', which is a Jewish ritual of mourning. Jewish men at all of their religious functions are expected to wear cupules (skull caps). When Gerald checked with David as to whether he had a cupule (pronounced 'couple'), David replied, 'No, I've only got one.' The mourners turned in disbelief ... Our Jewishness was to be seriously questioned.

Granddad's youngest son, Gerald, had already made arrangements to emigrate to Australia. He had realized that working with my father offered no future. The recent incident over the lorries had taken its toll and they agreed to dissolve the partnership.

Dad carried on with the remains of the transport business alone. He still had no car but used one of his lorries to travel to and from work. One morning he went off in a very strange mood.

That was unusual. He would sometimes be argumentative and would make a lot of noise but he was rarely moody.

When he came home that night he spoke to my mother about a special job that he had to do later in the month. It would be late at night and he had to drive one of the lorries. Mum couldn't understand why he was telling her. He had often driven at night and he would not dream of asking permission or even take the trouble, under normal circumstances, to advise her of his plans. He sounded strange, almost nervous, as though he were trying to tell her something, but did not know how.

It was only a few days later that my father told my mother that he would not be home on the following Tuesday. He did not want her to tell a soul. In fact if anyone – and he emphasized the word 'anyone' – were to ask of his whereabouts on that night, she was to say that he was at home safely tucked up in bed ... with her. Mum knew that Dad was getting involved in something dubious, but she was powerless to do a thing about it. I was oblivious to the situation and the fact that Dad had not arrived home that evening did not concern me.

The next morning I awoke early for my paper round and after making myself a cup of tea I put on the radio and listened to some soft music on the Light Programme while I cleared the fireplace and made preparations to light the fire. There was a short break in the programme and the announcer read out a news bulletin. I paid little attention to this and was pleased when the music returned. The news flash had given information about a barge in Silvertown Docks, on which an attempt had been made to steal its cargo comprising £70,000 worth of copper ingots.

Two of the criminals were caught but the remaining six or seven were on the run. This information was of no interest to me, although I did contemplate that £70,000 was an absolute fortune. Thinking no more of it, I carried on with my chores and then went off on my paper round.

When I walked back into the house at around seven fifteen, Mum, David and Marie were all up and about. There was a great deal of agitation. David spoke first.

'Dad's been arrested.'

It was beyond belief, but my father was one of the two 'crooks' who were apprehended at the Silvertown Dockyard. He had been approached by the gang, who had wanted to 'hire' his services, and one of his lorries. Dad knew what they wanted him to take part in was highly illegal, to say the least. But his company was struggling, and he had a wife and three children to support. It wasn't an easy choice, but in the end, knowing the risk, he decided it was an offer he could not really refuse. He was caught, charged and subsequently remanded in custody.

The next day Gerald came over to take Mum and me to Brixton Prison to see Dad. We waited in a room just inside the prison gates for over half an hour. A prison officer motioned us in. Dad looked pathetic as the prison officer brought him into the large meeting place. I noted that he was wearing his own clothes, but apart from that he looked no different from any of the convicts who were in that visiting room.

He looked drawn and pale, and although he was not yet forty he looked much older. Mum and Dad exchanged words of endearment. The only times that I had heard my dad say nice things to Mum were when he was in trouble, and he was certainly in trouble now. His solicitor had told him that there was little that could be done. He had been caught red handed and a plea of guilty with mitigating circumstances was the only route to go. Even then, the solicitor considered five years was the best that Dad could hope for.

There were a number of wooden tables and chairs, which were occupied by other prisoners and their families. My father sat at one end of our table and there was a chair placed at the other end, presumably for a prison officer but I was pleased that no official sat with us.

Dad was on remand for many months, and apart from the occasional visits to see him, life went on normally. His trial was held at the number one court in the 'Old Bailey'. He pleaded guilty and received a four year sentence.

Mum came home in the early afternoon soon after we had

arrived home from school. She had been crying. 'It could have been worse,' she said, but that was no comfort to us. I hugged Mum but I had nothing to say to her as she burst into tears. Marie was crying and it was all that David and I could do to see that we didn't follow suit.

'Four and sixpence,' Mum said. 'That's all I've got.' We were obviously in a bigger mess than I had realized.

I missed Dad terribly. I promised to keep him informed of all of my boxing activities and I also promised to train very hard. He had been a professional boxer himself, and my move into the boxing fraternity had pleased him immensely. I had become the schoolboy champion of West Ham while Dad was on remand, and was more determined than ever to become a 'real' champion. I was on my way to the National Schoolboy Championships and I had a positive outlook ... well, fairly positive. I could not even dream of actually becoming the national champion, that had to be beyond my reach. It was a case of one bout at a time and my next contests were for the 'County' title.

I succeeded in winning both the semi and the final convincingly. I was the new Essex and Southern Counties Champion, which qualified me for the quarter finals of the Nationals. They were to be held at Canning Town, which was my home patch, and I trained harder for this contest than ever before. I was intent on making Dad proud of me. At the West Ham Gymnasium, I was starting to be recognized and was given the opportunity of sparring with up and coming world champions such as Ralph Charles and Terry Spinks. I managed to hold my own against them although I took no chances, always wearing head gear and insisting on large twelve ounce sparring gloves.

The big day drew closer and I became more and more nervous. My weight had to be less than six stone two pounds, which was not too difficult for me to maintain. I went on the bus to Canning Town Public Hall and arrived with plenty of time to spare. There were already some junior preliminary bouts taking place but these were of no interest to me.

In the main dressing room dozens of boys were already getting in line for the weigh-in. A strong smell of 'Liniman's Rub' filled the room. This pleasant odour blended with the smell of sweating bodies of the young boxers who were returning from their ordeals in the boxing ring.

I did not know anyone there and felt quite lonely. It was a little cold, but I felt even colder and recognized that I had goose bumps. Most of the boys were standing in their dressing gowns alongside their fathers. I realized that I had neither and I so desperately wanted both.

My loneliness, my sadness, and most of all my fears, were multiplied tenfold when I saw Peter Montebello, my opponent, undressed and standing on the scales, weighing six stone one and a half pounds. I was shocked. This could not possibly be him. He had muscles like a weightlifter, a head of thick black hair, strikingly handsome and obviously confident as he left the scales and donned a heavy towelling robe. Something was wrong. I approached the scales in my shorts and stockinged feet and looked closely at my opponent. I felt half his size but weighed nearly half a pound more. There was nothing I could do. The match was on and within five hours I would be standing in the same ring as this person ... I was plain scared.

Mum, Marie and David were all there to see the contest. I was not on until the fifteenth bout. It meant that I had even more time to wait and more time to worry. As we climbed into the ring he gave a confident wave to his followers and removed his dressing gown to expose his muscular arms. My arms were already exposed. I only had a towel round my shoulders.

The contest was no contest, and to this day I cannot believe that it happened. My opponent was flat on his back after only one minute of boxing. He did not lay one punch on me as I danced around the ring. I just moved in, slipped into his southpaw lead and landed a blow to his jaw and that was it. The referee stopped the contest and my opponent stood up and left the ring. I had made it to the semi-finals and had not even broken into a sweat.

*

Despite my impressive win in the quarter-finals, I became very nervous when I was notified of the forthcoming semi-finals. My opponent, from Leeds, was the Northern Counties champion, and I thought that this time I would at least meet my match ... I was wrong.

The referee stopped the contest in the first round and raised my arm. I was in the final. It was like a dream. Ralph Gold was to appear at the Royal Albert Hall in front of a huge crowd and television cameras.

All of my family were there ... with the exception of my dad, who I missed. It was strange but, for the first time in my boxing career, I was the man with the reputation, the man to fear. My opponent, Albert Marchant, however, was obviously not impressed. He came at me like a tiger and towards the end of the first round I can remember seeing the huge dome above me as I took a powerful uppercut. It would be corny to say that I saw stars, but my head went back and the huge dome of the Albert Hall was filled with them. I made it through the three rounds and to the great joy of both members of my fan club, I was declared the winner on points ... and the Schoolboy Champion of Great Britain.

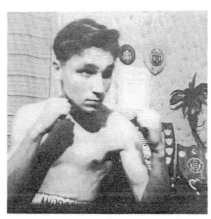

Ralph Gold, national schoolboy champion

I could not wait for Friday to come. In Friday's *Stratford Express* would be the account of the finals and because of the fact that I was a local boy I should, at least, get a mention. I went into the newsagent's to collect the papers for my delivery round. I picked up the *Stratford Express* and there on page forty five was the report: 'Five local boys become Champions of Great Britain.' I was delighted, I leapt on to my bicycle and went about my work.

Out on my round, another paperboy stopped me. 'I saw you in the *Express* this morning,' he said. 'Front page! Congratulations.'

Front page? I delved into my canvas bag and came up with the paper. I had completely ignored the front page, but there it was. It was all about me. 'Now he's the national champion!' it said.

The championships had been sponsored by the *Star*, one of the three London evening papers, and of course they gave good coverage, as well as awarding every winner a watch. Watches were only worn by 'well-off' people and my family were certainly not that. So the watch presented by Reg Pratt, the chairman of West Ham Football Club, was a cherished award.

On the day of the presentation I was down with the flu, so I was unable to attend. The same influenza stopped me from going to school on the following Monday. I did hear that the head-teacher had, in my absence, made an announcement about my victory, but it was not the same. By the time I returned to school, the interest had gone and I didn't feel like the 'champ' any more. There seemed to be, understandably, a lot more interest in the fact that Roger Bannister had broken the four minute mile.

Respect for Your Elders

It was necessary to put my boxing achievements to the back of my mind and to concentrate on the more crucial matters, such as passing my 'GCE' examinations. It was not going to be easy. School work came a poor second to boxing, and I was going to pay for it.

I had hopes of passing my GCE in Commerce but failed miserably; it seemed that there was to be no future for me in the commercial world. History was a different proposition, and there was no prospect of succeeding there whatsoever. However, my mother sat up with me until three thirty in the morning, learning four sheets of precis and notes, parrot fashion and to everyone's amazement ... I passed.

With only one GCE to my name the chances of getting a good job were remote. My first was with one of the largest companies in the world at the time, 'Unesco'. Their head office was a substantial building close to Smithfield Meat Market which meant that I would use the underground railway to go to and from work five full days and a half day on Saturdays.

The first morning was awe-inspiring. I walked through the giant doors, feeling very nervous. I asked at the information desk for the accounts office and they directed me to the first floor. It was eight twenty and I was due to start in ten minutes' time. There were already five or six book-keepers sitting at long benches in a room that was bigger than I had ever seen. It was even bigger than the assembly room at my old school. I wished that I was still there as I stood waiting. I was totally ignored, until an old man wearing bicycle clips came up to me. 'You're nu', aint ya?' he observed. I was astounded; a Cockney accent more pronounced than mine, and in a top class office in the City of London! 'I'm Ernie,' he said. 'How old do you think I am? I'm eighty two.'

I could not believe my ears. He looked no more than sixty. At that moment a man walked through the huge swing doors. He was tall and fat, with long sideburns, and could have walked straight out of a Charles Dickens novel.

'Well, who do we have here?' he asked Ernie.

'I don't know, who do we have 'ere?' Ernie asked me.

'Ralph Gold' I told them.

'Ah!' said the fat gentleman, 'the new book-keeper. You must be the laddie that we intend to train up, to one day take over from me.' He was only joking, of course.

'Follow me, laddie.' He asked me to pick up a ledger as we walked down two or three steps into the main hall. The ledger was heavier than a medicine ball and despite my undeniable fitness I was having difficulty in carrying it.

When we arrived at my seat, which was half way along a bench that seated ten people, he asked the man next to me to explain the credit entries that I was to take care of.

'Mr Craine will take good care of you, laddie, just do as he tells you.'

'I will, thank you sir.'

He left, to seat himself in a position where he could overlook the entire proceedings of the accounts department.

The work was mundane and I spent a lot of my time watching the big clock, which was almost identical to the one at school.

During the six months at 'Unesco' I learned a lot about life, and much of it was from Ernie. I learned that Ernie was indeed eighty two years old, and that he cycled into work each day from

Clerkenwell. He was the company messenger and dogsbody, and everyone loved him. We became close friends.

I was occasionally relieved of my duties as a book-keeper to second as a messenger boy. I went out with Ernie and he would take me to deliver packages to people stationed in huge office blocks in the city ... He had the knowledge and I had the legs.

On those excursions we were allowed to take time for tea and lunch and during that period we talked. Ernie was a Cockney like myself, but he was so articulate. He had had a full life and his success was that he had enjoyed it. He had reached a position of head clerk in the same office that I was in.

Now as a messenger boy he was enjoying his last few years before retirement. He was supposed to make his exit at eighty but they wouldn't let him go – at least that is what he said. He also said that old age is like everything else, if you want to make a success of it then you must start when you're young.

I wanted to be successful, but the main thing that I wanted was to be like him at eighty two ... fit and content.

When we discussed old age he would say that there is one thing to be said in its favour; it is a lot better than being dead. He told me that he disliked the way people would talk to him as if he were senile, they would sometimes shout, as if he were deaf and speak slowly as if he could not understand. But he liked me because I showed respect. I liked him too for the same reason ... How could you not respect an eighty two year old man who could run up the stairs two at a time?

David and me playing the fool

David and I gave Mum one third of our wages, but the stall was still the main means of income, and when we were not at work we would be expected to do our bit to help. It was becoming more of an established business and Mum wanted to change our front downstairs bedroom into a shop. It would involve us all in a lot of work, but David would be the mastermind behind the project.

Mum was building up more and more trade with regular customers and the business was rapidly becoming viable. Jim Cunningham, who worked for Uncle Dave, supplied us with our comics and paperbacks. She had started to buy pin-up books such as *Spick and Span*. These were sexier than *London Life*, *Line and Form*, *Health and Efficiency* and a magazine called *Pin-Up*; publications which were all restricted to showing pictures of bathing beauties and peculiar deformed-looking nudists who were deficient of both hair, or indeed, anything else, between their legs. Parts of their bodies such as genitals and pubic hair were removed by 'experts' in photographic studios. It must have been insufferable for the poor technicians who were exposed to this task on a daily basis.

Spick and Span was breaking barriers by showing more sexually explicit material such as ladies in stockings and garters exposing their thighs. There was even the odd flash of crotch, but the knickers were invariably made of thick cotton fabric and there could be no sign of an offending crack.

These books attracted many amateur photographers to our stall. One chap, Ted, was our best regular customer, he must have taken every new pin-up title. He was a pleasant man and we all got to know him well. He seemed to be happily married and lived in one of the new flats that had been built near 'Mannies' barber shop. Ted even brought his wife with him on occasions to buy his pin-up magazines.

He told Mum about a photography course that he was taking and asked if she would like him to take some pictures of my sister Marie. Marie was nearly thirteen years old and was developing into a very attractive young lady. She had been attending dancing classes and had been chosen to tap dance on stage. Mum was really pleased to be able to have some pictures taken that could be sent to Dad.

Marie spent nearly two hours with Ted on a Saturday afternoon

Marie dressed like a princess

but when she came home she seemed a little quiet. Mum asked if anything was wrong and Marie insisted that I left the room so that she could tell her something. I was already worried about what she had to say to Mum and my suspicions were proved well founded when Mum actually told me later.

Fortunately it was not too serious. Ted had asked Marie to remove her blouse. This upset her and she refused. Ted went about his job but his request changed everything and Mum asked me to tell him that we did not want him to visit the stall again. It was an unpleasant task, but I agreed that it had to be done.

Meanwhile, work on changing the downstairs lounge and bedroom into a shop went on. David built a counter in the front room with the help of his friends Victor and Jim. The room was transformed and started to look something like a 'real' shop. We all joined in with the decorating and I endeavoured to help by trying to put up a few shelves. I began to realize that, with the best will in the world, I lacked the competence to do these jobs, and David was called upon to get me out of trouble. He succeeded, but he had made a 'rod for his own back', because he has been 'called upon' ever since.

Within a week we were ready for the grand opening. Mum had filled the window display with our entire range of products and it looked superb. We put up the 'open' sign on the front door and another sign on the door in the passage that led directly into the front room.

On a cold Monday morning we opened for business. Unfortunately there were no customers and we became quite worried. It took a long time for business to pick up. But it did, and Mum was able to refer to herself as a shopkeeper ... official.

French Letter

I asked Mum if I could go with her on her next monthly visit to see Dad. He was now in Wandsworth Prison and had already served over a year of his sentence.

Mum seemed so much happier of late. She was always attractive but I had noticed that she was recently taking more care in her style of dress and make-up. I felt quite proud sitting beside her on the train to London Bridge. It was rare for me to be able to sit in comfort on the underground. When I travelled to and from work each day there was such a build up of passengers that I invariably gave up my seat before we reached Mile End station which was less than half way.

This day I had the opportunity to sit and read the advertisements at leisure. Normally, during the rush hour I would be pinned into one position and be forced to read one advertisement over and over, usually a boring one which would express the relative merits of using 'Ex-Lax' or 'Andrews Liver Salts'. The underground was filled with advertisements for laxatives. Although some of the advertisements beside the escalators were terrific, they were unbelievably risqué, showing ladies in their underwear applying make up or removing a pair of 'Pretty Polly' stockings, I could not understand how they managed to get away with it. Of course, there were plenty of people constantly complaining to the authorities, and occasionally there was a clamp down which would make our journeys even more boring.

From London Bridge we travelled by bus and eventually arrived in view of the austere prison building in which many murderers, and arguably innocent people had been executed on the gallows over the years.

I felt uncomfortably con- spicuous, as though I were being critically looked at by the people who passed the prison gates going about their day-to- day activities. We rang the bell

Mum

at the side of the small gate that formed a part of the huge, studded prison doors. The gate was opened by a prison officer carrying a huge bunch of keys and a large clip-board. He asked Mum for her name and ticked it off his list, then he led us through the door into an enclosed area.

Standing there, I could see the prisoners within, some in their cells, others going about their daily duties. One prisoner with a red band on his arm was polishing a giant cast iron rose that was situated in the centre of the yard. He had a bald head and I remember thinking that he looked so old and wretched. He worked at his own slow pace and I suspected that no sooner would he have finished the job than it would be time to start all over again.

We went into a side room where other visitors were sitting waiting for permission to go into the main visiting room. They were a scruffy lot with their kids either crying or getting up to mischief. There was a coldness which was largely due to the draughts that were coming under the door and the badly fitted windows. It was all made worse by the dreadful brick walls which were cream and brown, probably last painted when the prison was built more than a hundred years earlier. I hoped that it would not be long before we could go in to see my father.

My wish was granted because the prison warden read a list of names and Gold was among them. Soon we were being greeted by Dad. He hugged Mum for a long time while I stood there not knowing what to do with myself. Then he got round to me and he gave me a kiss. It was probably the last time that I actually kissed my father – after all I was approaching seventeen years of age. But I did love him, and I was pleased that we were still able to be affectionate to one another. I felt so sorry for him at that moment, Mum did not seem to reciprocate his expressed feelings as she had in the past, and I knew that something was wrong.

On the way home I felt that Mum was trying to say something to me, but she was well aware that I did not want to hear it. For the first time since she had met my father I suspected that she was no longer in love with him.

It is not every day that you hear your father on the radio even if his voice is portrayed by an actor. One day David and I were playing cards with our friends while we listened to it. It was the last performance of 'Nick (Chief Inspector Nixon) of the River' in the series. The plays were always good, and knowing that they were based on true cases made them even more interesting. On this particular evening 'Nick' was investigating the theft of a barge which contained seventy tons of copper and it did not take long for me to realize that it was my father's case.

It was the first time that I realized how the media would distort a factual story to satisfy its readers (or in this case listeners). My father came across as a dumb Cockney who was a little aggressive when he was caught. 'Dad' was supposedly fast asleep in his cab while the main crooks were apprehended in the act of loading the copper onto the lorry and they had made a run for it. My 'father' put up a bit of a fight but after many sound effect grunts and groans, he was heard to say. 'Fair cop guv, I done it.' No names were mentioned and our friends were not aware (or at least to save us the embarrassment, pretended as much), and at the end of the programme we carried on playing cards. But I wondered who else

David on his Ariel

had heard the play and might have put two and two together. I suddenly became aware of just how fragile the secret was.

At work, at least, no one was any the wiser. I had left Unesco and, after a spell as a shipping clerk, was now working as a junior tax officer, earning three pounds and fifteen shillings per week. The office, 'Stratford 2', was next door to West Ham Swimming Baths, which was where I had not only won the West Ham swimming championship in 1948 but also the West Ham boxing championship in 1954.

I loved my new job and quickly settled in. Although I was just the office boy, I was given a fair amount of responsibility.

On occasions I was asked to 'man' the office at the end of the building, which was not unlike a prison visiting room. It was a strange experience when one day someone actually called me 'sir.' I did not believe he was being serious, but he was ... I couldn't wait to go home to tell my mum.

Both David and I now had motorbikes, mine a modest 150cc BSA Bantam, David's a more powerful 350cc Ariel. I had passed my test on the second attempt, and in view of my success, I put in for seven days' 'leave' (when in the Civil Service, you do not have 'holidays') so I could join David and his friends, Victor and Jimmy, on a working holiday on a flax farm in Gloucestershire.

For wages of ten shillings a day and full board, we were expected to roll and tie bundles of flax from eight in the morning until six at night, with forty five minutes break for lunch, seven days a week. Although it was called 'flax pulling', the flax had already been 'pulled' from the ground by the wonders of modern machinery.

Our journey by motorbike to Tetbury had its traumas. My BSA was never in good shape, but with only minor mishaps we arrived at the farm. We were escorted by the farmer to our sleeping quarters in order to dispose of the small amount of luggage that we had taken with us, and were far from happy when we first saw the hovel which was to be our home for the next seven days. It was nothing more than a circular cow shed. There were already half a dozen mattresses on the floor but they belonged to workers who were presently in the fields.

We had to go to the big barn and fill our recently acquired palliasse with straw. One blanket was supplied to each worker and in the middle of August it was sufficient. However, a couple of fresh, clean sheets would have been more than just a little acceptable.

We were working within the hour, and after only one more hour we were given a bowl of soup and a piece of bread. The short break was followed by a further four hours of rolling and tying flax. My back ached as we walked wearily back to our shed. Sitting there were another four or five workers. Everyone talked about jacking it in, but after a while it was agreed that we would persevere for at least one more day.

Soon after agreeing to this, a motorbike and attached sidecar drew up alongside us. The driver was an older man, about twenty five years of age, wearing motorcycle gear, including a leather helmet and big round eyed goggles. He looked like Captain Biggles.

His name was Roger Ansel-Higgins. He was a South African but had a British 'RAF' accent. He walked up to David. 'Are you in command here?' David stammered out a reply in the affirmative, although a Boy Scout could have assumed command of this lot.

'What's the score?' asked the South African.

David presumed that he was about to buy the farm, at least. The last thing that anyone would have believed was that he would be 'one of us' ... But he was.

We filled Roger in on 'the form' and went off to bed. There were now about a dozen men who slept around the edge of the shed. Two French youths who arrived later were forced to bed down at everyone's feet, in the centre of the room. They were not too happy about this, I could tell by their tone of voice, although they could not speak a word of English. Conveniently for them, Roger Ansel-Higgins spoke French and was able to sort out any problems they had. Well, almost.

Towards the end of the second day we were out in the field, rolling up the flax, when out of the blue came a beautiful French girl. She was dressed in the most typical French clothes, a black and white ringed T-shirt, a short, tight black skirt that exposed a beautiful pair of legs and, to top it all, a black beret.

The mere fact that she was the only woman we had seen for three days made her special, but a trim waist and small breasts and nipples pushing out from her T-shirt made her exceptionally striking. More so when one considers the fact that there were very few women in those days who would be so daring as to appear in public without a brassière beneath their outer clothing. She greeted her two friends as though each one was a long lost lover. One of them grabbed her round the waist and swung her round. His friend did likewise and they laughed and chatted.

Everyone stopped work to watch every antic and to listen to every word spoken, our inability to make any sense of what was said was of no consequence. There was only one of us that could understand every word ... Roger.

That night we lay in our beds discussing the events of the day and joking about the French threesome when they walked in. One of them spoke to Roger and promptly went about preparing their two beds to accommodate three people. The French girl was going to sleep with us ... Well not with us exactly, but nevertheless in our room.

David, Victor, Jimmy and I were virgins. And not only were we virgins, we had yet to reach 'stage two' in the development of our sexuality. To reach stage three one was expected to actually touch the naked breast of a willing partner. For stage two minimal pressure by one's hand to the covered breast was the only requirement. We hadn't even achieved that.

Now, here we were, not three feet away from a possible three in a bed sex scene. As the three participants discussed the sleeping arrangements, 'possible' was rapidly changing to 'probable.' Within minutes it was 'definite'. Silence at first, then noise, as the straw mattresses signalled movement. It was almost pitch black and impossible to determine exactly what was going on, but intercourse of some kind was under way. The noises continued for over an hour. There was a break as they argued over something. Roger explained the problem to us all. Using the phonetic alphabet, he said. 'November Oscar' and paused, then he went on, 'Delta, Uniform, Romeo, Echo, X-ray.' There was a short pause as we realized that the first letter of every word said it all. A burst of laughter followed, which failed to deter the squeals of delight from the French trio.

Whether the French girl wanted it without a Durex or insisted on one being used, I will never know. All I do know is that they enjoyed themselves, and we were all left with the problem of trying to get to sleep with a hard-on ... we had learned a new meaning to the term 'flax pulling.'

Salvation

Mum had been seeing quite a lot of Jim Cunningham, the man who supplied us with our comics and paperbacks, and on our return I was not only surprised but disappointed to learn that he had moved into our house as a lodger. Marie was now sleeping in the big front bedroom with Mum, and Jim was occupying Marie's old room.

Mum knew how I felt and she tried to explain but I was not ready to listen. Many weeks later Marie and I were talking about the situation when she told me that one night in bed Mum had asked her how she would feel about Jim becoming a sort of new Dad to her. Marie was very upset and Mum got the message ... She said no more.

Jim was nice to me, and I hated it. I did not like him, and I liked him even less when he had been drinking. Drunk or sober he drove his van like a lunatic, and was always trying to impress my mother. He thought that going across red traffic lights was an act of heroism.

In some ways it was nice for Mum. She had never received flowers from Dad, nor had she been shown common courtesies like having the car door opened for her. To Mum it was a new world and Jim was what she wanted. I felt like a killjoy, but I still loved my Dad, despite his arrogance.

Going off to work one morning, I kissed my mother and said

good-bye to her and Jim, who was also about to leave for work. I opened the front door, but as I did so I realized that I had forgotten my wallet. I closed the door and went back upstairs to my room; it was nowhere to be found. I searched every drawer before I realized that I had not removed it from the jacket that I had worn to work the day before.

I checked the time and realized that I was now running very late. As I went down the stairs I could hear bedsprings creaking and grunting noises from Jim's bedroom. I was slow to realize exactly what was happening, but when I did, I was unable to cope. I just wanted them to know that they had been 'caught in the act', and that I disapproved ... I slammed the door violently.

I had great difficulty in coming to terms with the new situation, and I disliked Jim even more. I missed my dad more than ever. Mum was very attentive and thoughtful towards me that evening but I only wanted to be alone. We eventually discussed the situation and I was prepared to accept that Mum was entitled to have feelings of her own. She told me that she was in love with Jim.

'What about Dad?' I asked.

'Well,' she stammered, 'I love him too, but now it's a different kind of love.'

'Does that mean that you'll tell him?'

'Yes,' she replied. 'I'll be honest with him, and I intend to end the marriage.'

When Mum saw me becoming upset she went on. 'Look Ralph, sometimes these things happen. I've spent half my adult life alone. I'm only human after all.'

I knew that she was right and I should have been more understanding. Instead I acted like a spoilt brat. With the benefit of hindsight I am fully aware that my behaviour was inexcusable, but Mum loved me through it ... and there was worse to come.

On her next visit, Mum went to Wandsworth and revealed the whole story to Dad. She told us that he was very upset, but we were to learn that that was an understatement.

*

Jim was a very kind person. He was nice to everyone, but especially my mother. He bought her flowers at least three times a week, and went out of his way to bring things that were needed in the home, not just for Mum but for any of us. When David was unable to obtain a special speedometer lead for his motor bike Jim tracked it down and bought it, telling David that he could pay him when he had the money.

'No rush,' he would say, 'I'm just pleased to be able to help.'

He brought home small presents for us; a writing set for Marie, a paperback biography on the great Joe Louis for me. But although they were expressly the things that we both wanted, we did not want him to be the person who bought them for us.

Mum allowed me to read the letters sent to her by Dad as well as her own letters to him. She was no longer filling the permissible four pages and there was now plenty of space for me to add some words of comfort to him. Dad would plead for Mum to reconsider her decision, and not to take any action which she might later regret. He would finish his own letter with hundreds of kisses. These letters upset us all and we wished that things could be different. Mum had changed. She had hardened-up, and was as determined as ever to go through with it. She wanted a divorce.

It was nearing Christmas. Jim and my mother's brother John, who was also lodging with us once again, were down at the pub. There was a knock at the door and I answered it. Standing on the front porch was an officer from the Salvation Army.

I presumed that he was collecting money, and I asked him to wait while I went in for some coins. He stopped me and asked if he could speak with my mother. My father was in a state close to suicide, the officer told us. He now weighed only six and a half stone and had been put into the prison hospital. We were being advised by a very kind and gentle person, of Dad's terrible plight. He offered no 'commercial' about religion. He was on a mission of mercy and he carried out his task with such skill that no caring person could possibly ignore his advice, which was for Mum to reconsider her plan of action.

The Salvation Army officer and I together were just too much for Mum. She was swayed into staying with Dad, and asked Jim to leave. I was glad, but I was also very much aware of the great sacrifice that Mum was making.

Bubbles

I had started a new career as a lemonade salesman at the 'Corona' soft drinks factory in Silvertown Way, Canning Town. I was delighted, as the pay was ten pounds a week plus commission. The factory was huge, and housed about a dozen lorries, which were parked on the sales side of the complex. The sales manager was Mr Evans, a typical Welshman, with thick black hair and sideburns and an accent that left one in no doubt about his homeland. On my first day he introduced me to the three inspectors and suggested that the youngest one, Colin West, took me out on one of the rounds.

I was both amazed and terrified when I was given the keys of the fully stocked lorry that stood at the loading bay. Colin told me to pick him up at the front gate in the next ten minutes. I made it to the front gate and sat there looking very confident, as though I had driven trucks more than twice as big for the last ten years – which would have been difficult, as I had only passed my test four and a half months ago.

'Right!' said Colin. 'First I'd like to pick up my suit from the cleaners in Canning Town, then on to the café in Barking Road for tea and toast, and then to Dagenham. We should be there by eleven o'clock, complete the round and be back home by seven.'

He was right about one thing. I was home by seven but that was only after going to the hospital to have my arm x-rayed and put into a sling. I had crashed into another vehicle at the very first road junction. The other driver survived although his van was practically written off.

I was ordered by the doctor to go home to rest for at least ten days during which time I intended to visit Mr Evans to collect my cards. I plucked up enough courage to take care of this a week later. Mr Evans welcomed me into his office with a smile. He said that it had been unfortunate but I was not to hurry back to work until I was fully recovered.

'Hurry back?' I could not believe my ears.

On the following Monday there was a brand new lorry waiting for me and another inspector ready to take me out to show me the ropes. After only three days, I was told that as from Thursday I would be on my own. As luck would have it, I did not work alone. A young boy named Tod had been taken on as a spare van boy and he was assigned to me.

I was only fourteen months older than Tod, but he treated me with respect. I believe that he thought that I was much older and that I had been with 'Corona' for a long time. We were to become excellent workmates. We worked all hours, knocking on practically every door in Dagenham. Tod would be the first to say that he was no salesman, but he was so young, frail and vulnerable that the housewives understandably liked him, and most of them would buy whatever it was that he had for sale. I was prepared to work non-stop until we had built a first class round of good customers.

It was a great thrill to see us moving up the 'leader board' of top salesmen at 'Corona' and finally taking the top slot. We took on a round that had been run down, but within a month Tod and I were clearly the top team. I was the number one salesman and my take home pay of more than twenty pounds a week reflected this.

Working for 'Corona' I matured very quickly, and Tod was largely responsible. He needed a father figure and despite the small difference in our ages he truly believed that I was worldly and competent and looked to me for advice in every quarter. I responded by being a good listener and offering support wherever possible. Tod, in return, would do as he was instructed without question. I appreciated his faith in me and never took advantage of it. Except perhaps once...

There was a young girl on the Saturday morning round who was unbelievably besotted by me. She was the daughter of one of the first customers that I normally served. Jenny was not yet sixteen years of age. She came out to the lorry and stayed with us most of the morning, not really saying much but offering to help and obviously just wanting to be near me. I thought that she was very pretty and likeable. But fifteen...!?

Three or four months of this and I was beginning to get feelings that were not proper. One day she invited me in for tea while her parents were out shopping. I spent ten minutes or so talking but I had to get on with my round. I suggested doing the same the following week and perhaps I could spend a little more time. She was delighted and told me so ... I had mixed feelings.

I had been a Boy Scout and I still had not forgotten our motto: 'Be prepared'. Each morning I had driven past the chemist at Barking Broadway with the express intention of buying some of 'those things'. I would not even dream of buying them from Mannie's, nor anywhere else close to home, so Barking Broadway it had to be.

As the week progressed the purchase had to be made and, of course, Tod was instructed to make it. But when we pulled up outside the chemist on the Friday he got 'cold feet'. We did the same on the Saturday and Tod just sat there – he could not do it. I was first reserve, but ... At the counter was a young lady. My face was burning, and it was a battle between my nerves and my loins. My loins won but it was a close thing. 'A packet of Durex, please,' I mumbled. She did not know what they were and called across to the manageress to ask. My legs were like jelly. Finally, I jumped back into the waiting vehicle. 'Piece of cake,' I said to Tod.

Jenny was there at the corner of her road and she actually kissed me on the cheek. Tod looked at me ... I looked at him ... This was it.

Every house on the council estates in Dagenham looked the same. Todd and I had been invited into many of them for tea and we learned that the insides varied very little too. Jenny's home was typical, a lounge suite, a sideboard and a goldfish bowl. In addition though, this lounge displayed a twenty one inch, black and white television set. I was most impressed.

I drank my tea and suggested that we sat on the sofa together. I was thinking back on my early encounters and the advice of Charlie Haynes: 'Top button, hand on breast, take your time ...' The problem was how much time? Firstly, I had a round to do, and secondly I was not sure about how long her parents would take to do the shopping.

We cuddled and kissed as I slowly progressed from the top part, which had gone fine, to the bottom part. I actually felt the softness at the top of her legs, and attempted to pull her panties down little by little. It was at this point that her parents walked through the door. Jenny fell off the sofa with her knickers around her knees. I stayed sitting on the sofa as though I were waiting for my second cup of tea.

After that, Jenny no longer came out to follow the van, and her mother didn't buy any more lemonade. The Durex eventually went beyond the 'use by' date and into the bin.

Take On The Lot

I had been at 'Corona' for over a year when I was called up for National Service. David had been luckier. He had fainted after hitting his finger with a hammer and seemed to be making a big thing of it. The army was not too particular about the condition of its recruits, but men who had giddy spells and a history of fainting were not normally accepted. Fortunately, after failing his medical he never had a dizzy spell again.

I thought that my prominence in the world of boxing would have prompted the army into placing me with the 'crack' Royal Electrical and Mechanical Engineers stationed in Blandford in Dorset. I had heard so much about how the army treated their boxers, and I was hopeful that I would have been among that élite. Unfortunately not. My papers arrived and I was to be stationed at Devizes with the Royal Army Pay Corps.

A few days before my nineteenth birthday I was ordered to report to the White City Coach Station where a coach would be waiting to take me to my new home in Wiltshire.

I had been told that the Pay Corps was for poofs and softies but at White City I met up with a crowd of clearly very tough individuals all heading for Devizes, many dressed in 'Teddy boy' suits, others bearing tattoos and wearing leather gear ... I did not feel comfortable. It would be some time before I was going to feel comfortable again.

We arrived in the early evening and a corporal greeted us as though we were animals and he was an animal tamer.

'Get lined up!' he screamed. 'Look front, don't say a word unless you're spoken to, do you understand?' ... Silence.

'Do you understand?' A few murmurs in the affirmative. He asked once more, before every one replied. 'Yes,' or a few, 'Yes sirs.'

'Yes, corporal!' he screamed.

'Yes, corporal!' we responded en masse.

After being allocated our sleeping quarters, we were sent off to collect our new army clothing, and were instructed to clean the brass buckles, buttons and the toes of our boots until they looked like mirrors. Within the next few days I was to learn the meaning of spit and polish. We were taught to apply a little polish to the cap of our boots, spit on it and then circle a piece of cloth for a couple of hours each day non-stop, spitting every two or three minutes. It was thirsty work and the visit to the NAAFI was like reaching an oasis in the desert.

I'd thought the corporal was the most aggressive person I had ever known, but on the following morning we were to meet a man who was to make the corporal seem like a nursery school teacher. Sergeant Reams was a Scot, five feet one inch tall, with a voice that boomed across the square. He put the fear of God into every man in the newly formed 'Twenty One' Training Platoon of the Royal Army Pay Corps. In a peculiar way we all liked him. He was hard but fair and, after all, his job was to make twenty ordinary young civilian boys into twenty hard, disciplined fighting men within a period of six weeks.

I had the advantage of being a highly conditioned athlete and yet I practically collapsed by the end of the first day. My fellow trainees were a lot worse off with blisters, aching muscles and general fatigue. But at six in the morning, when the corporal yelled out. 'Hands off cocks, put on socks and get on parade!' every soldier was out of bed in a flash, and aches and pains were forgotten.

It was strange to experience the sudden change between youth

Sgt. James, me, Jimmy Parker and John Jobbins

and manhood in everyone. The unhappiness of the first few days was soon behind us and humour was creeping back into our lives. Twenty young men from totally different backgrounds, living under such strenuous conditions in a Nissen hut with cold and lukewarm running water, we were soon to learn a lot about each other's lives.

During the third week we were engaged in a physical training work out when one of the instructors called me to one side. He had heard that I was a 'top' amateur boxer and asked if I would mind helping him to organize the forthcoming boxing tournament. The participants were to be selected from the three new platoons, and having known the men for only two and a half weeks he was in no position to decide who should box whom. My job would be to box for ten seconds or so with each of the sixty men while he took notes. With reservations, I agreed. I was allowed to use conventional boxing gloves while my sixty opponents were expected to don the slightly heavier sparring gloves.

It was an absolute joy. One third of the group were from my own platoon of whom more than half would have considered themselves to be 'streetwise'. But it was quite amazing that not one man was able to last out his short spell in the ring without dropping his guard and leaving himself exposed to be punched at will. That session did a lot for me. I gained a lot of respect from my fellow soldiers, but it also made me realize that my fists were indeed weapons and I had a responsibility to keep them under control.

The boxing tournament was a great success, and at around ten thirty we all made our way back to our sleeping quarters. I was feeling good about myself, but it was not going to last. I approached my bed which was in the far corner of the hut. Thankfully I had made it up before going out that evening. I had not, however done so for the benefit of another occupant. As I pulled the covers back lying there was an enormous (well, quite big) house spider. I yelled and ran to the door. Everyone was staring at me in disbelief. My friend Hugh Jordan, who slept in the next bed, walked over, picked it up and threw it outside and I walked back in like a lamb and went to bed ... my image destroyed.

My image did not improve after my experience on the assault course a few days later; it was there that we were going to be taught, amongst other things, the use of the bayonet. After climbing walls, wading through ditches and crawling through giant pipes we were expected to take on the enemy, in the form of a dozen or so dummies each hung upon a specially erected gallows.

The object of the exercise was to approach the unsuspecting 'adversaries', screaming at the top of our voices, in order to scare the living daylights out of them and then to efficiently and effectively stab the bayonet into the heart whilst calling out. 'In, out and away'. When it came to my turn, the dummy had fallen to the ground and Sergeant Reams was standing there waiting for me to deal with this 'unfortunate', fallen object. I stuck the blade into the appropriate part of its anatomy but to my horror, I was unable to remove it. I tugged and tugged but the sack just lifted and fell.

'Private Gold,' said the sergeant, quite calmly, 'in the act of war you will need both your gun and your bayonet, that is if you intend to stay alive!' Then he roared, 'So shove your fucking boot into his fucking head and then pull.'

'Oh I see, thanks sarge,' I replied sheepishly.

Every two weeks at Devizes station the new recruits stood waiting for the train to take them home. They had cropped hair and berets that stuck out like traffic indicators perched on top of practically bald heads. They were known as 'sprogs' and I was one of them.

I felt very conspicuous as I walked down Green Street from Upton Park station in the early evening, pleased that the light was fading. I was delighted to arrive home where, to my surprise a new (well, nearly new) television set stood in the corner. It had an aerial placed on top and when it was positioned in certain parts of the room we were able to pick up the new third channel which carried adverts rather like 'Radio Luxemburg'. It was great.

It was great being home. David had a new girlfriend, Beryl, and the shop was doing really well. David had built a rack to take the pin-up books which were selling better than ever. In addition to *Spick and Span*, we were selling *Kamara* and *Solo*, two photographic gems produced by George Harrison Marks. He was a very talented photographer who had succeeded in making Pamela Green, his second wife, and June Palmer, another beautiful model, into well-known figures. They were regularly featured in both titles.

These small magazines sold for two and sixpence, and were of great assistance to photographers as most pages detailed the aperture setting that allowed Harrison Marks to outline a perfect nipple against a certain background. Of course, the majority were not the least bit interested in the aperture setting for their camera, only the size and shape of Pamela Green's tits. The sales were so good that Mum was ordering more than a dozen of each every time Uncle Dave's representative called. But probably the best selling pin up book was 'Leslie Carol in 3-D'. Leslie's nipples appeared to come out of the pages when you wore the special glasses.

I did not want to return to barracks, but before I realized it I was standing at the coach station at the White City. It was after ten o'clock at night and I would have given a half of my fortune (about fifty pounds) not to have had to go back. But for Queen and Country I settled onto the coach for the return journey to camp.

Taking Medicine

My father was to be released soon and I wanted to be sure that I was home for the occasion. He had seemed colder in his letters to my mother since her 'affair' with Jim Cunningham. But despite this, I could tell that she was going to make a great effort to revitalize her marriage.

The house, which was always clean, now gleamed. Mum and David decorated nearly every room and there was an air of excitement as Dad's homecoming grew near. Marie was nearly sixteen and she too helped by looking after the shop as well as being the labourer and general dogsbody for the two decorators. Mum spoke with David and me about the need to help Dad with some money when he came home. None of us was particularly affluent but we were able to muster a few hundred pounds to give him a start.

I had managed to take my first week of leave early in November which was the time of his release. Dad's homecoming was by no means as exciting as it had been in the past, but nevertheless it was good to see Mum and Dad back together again.

We gave Dad the two hundred pounds, but I was disappointed by his apparent lack of appreciation. He went off the very next morning and spent every penny on a second-hand van which had been previously used for carrying long dresses and coats. Dad was scheming as always and managed to come to an arrangement with the dealer whereby he overcame the strict law that prevailed regarding credit. The van was a peculiar shape but ideal for what my father wanted.

David was still a bricklayer at this time but Dad asked him to make a wooden rack for the van as it was his intention to go to the market that very weekend to sell comics. I immediately offered to join him.

On the Sunday morning before I was to return to camp, Dad and I went in the new van to 'Club Row Market'. The exit and entrance to the underground railway was via a little passageway and Dad thought that this would be a good place to pitch our stand. I was sent into the market to find the whereabouts of the inspector. Once I had done so I would keep 'tag', and when he was making his way towards our pitch I would run ahead to inform Dad. We would then put our stock back into the van and wait for him to pass on. The stand would then be set up again and we were back in business.

Our pitch soon became established and we had a number of regular customers. One Sunday morning when I was again helping to set things up, a lorry pulled up behind our van as we were unloading the comics. A huge man climbed down from the cab and, towering over Dad he said, in an aggressive tone, 'You're on my fucking pitch, mate.' My dad looked up into his eyes. 'I'm not, you know.'

'You're on my fucking pitch ... And if you don't fuck off, you'll wish you fucking 'ad.'

I was already putting the comics back into the van, but Dad stood his ground.

'Now I've warned you,' the man went on, 'if you don't move, I'm gonna punch your fuckin' 'ead in.'

I went up beside Dad, but the two of us together were no more than half the size of this man. Dad did not move as he repeated, 'You won't you know.'

Another pause, of what seemed to me to be about two lifetimes, before the 'giant' turned and climbed back into his lorry and drove off.

I was more proud of my dad than I had ever been, I knew then that while people could say a lot of bad things about him, no one could ever call Godfrey Gold a coward.

I was given a lot of time off from the army to concentrate on my boxing. I even had my own boxing instructor – a sergeant by the name of Joe Palmer. He was a physical training instructor whose first love was boxing, but in all of his years in the Royal Army Pay Corps. he had never found a boxer who had even a glimmer of hope of making it into the Army team. He realized on my arrival that his luck could have changed, and he intended to put his heart and soul into making me his first success.

He instructed me on the first day to report to him at six in the morning, dressed in my track suit and my army marching boots. He went off on his bicycle while I ran alongside. We started the long climb up the famous Roundway Hill, which has one of the steepest inclines in the whole of the South of England. Less than half way up, Joe ran out of steam and he suggested that I went on to the highest point and he would meet me on the way down. About fifty yards before the top, the road led down the other side, leaving only a narrow path for the benefit of hikers who had the tenacity to go all the way to the top. I tried to keep running but failed.

I made over two hundred attempts at it, but I am proud to say that eventually I got there. I was at the beginning of a fitness campaign that was, to put it mildly, extreme. I ran each morning in all weathers and went to the gym every evening. Joe was nearly always there to drive me on. I learned to skip at speeds that I previously thought impossible, doing 'bumps' (two turns, touching the floor only once) and cross overs. I trained to climb a gymnasium rope without using my feet and ultimately I did it with my legs in front of me at ninety degrees. Joe would make me lie on the floor while he threw a medicine ball at my solar plexus.

These training routines were generating an interest around the camp, and I soon found that I was working out each day before an audience of twenty or so soldiers. This had a tendency to make me train even harder. I was back in the 'show off' mode.

Foremost in my mind was winning the Amateur Boxing Association Championships. I felt that I was in with a chance and intended to put one hundred per cent effort into winning the Bantamweight title, and then to go on to win an Olympic gold medal in Melbourne. But first things first; the preliminary bouts for the Army Championships were to take place in January.

I started out very well, knocking out one opponent after another in the preliminary rounds. Joe was starting to become excited at the prospect of being the trainer of the next Army champion ... but it was not to be.

We went to Aldershot to compete in the quarter-finals, where I took on a tough trooper from the 11th Hussars. I clearly won the contest on points, and the semi-finals were to take place the next evening.

Joe and I went back to our camp in Devizes and although it was a little late he suggested that I did a little skipping, to generally loosen up. As I pounded the floor boards of the gym, I experienced a pain in my jaw and Joe felt that it would be prudent for me to visit the dental officer in order to put my mind at ease.

Within twenty minutes, I was on my way to Tidworth Army Hospital with a suspected broken jaw. The hospital confirmed that it was fractured in two places and the operation to wire it up took place the next morning.

For six weeks I was unable to eat or talk properly as my top and bottom teeth were wired together. I sucked my liquid food through my teeth and endured the misery of being unable to express myself clearly. I stayed in the hospital for over a week before being allowed to go home on medical leave. During that time I met up with a number of other patients who had also received some kind of sporting injury. Many were rugby players with broken noses, arms and legs, and others had muscular strains and sprains. One day the sister on the ward informed me that a new patient was to be admitted and I would be pleased to know that he was from the Royal Army Pay Corps. Why I should be particularly pleased I do not know. I presume that she believed, as others did, that we in the Pay Corps were of soft and gentle nature, but my being a boxer and a truck driver belied that a little. I made some jokes about how they had it wrong and that we were tougher than people realized.

Adrian arrived rather late in the day and as his leg was in plaster he was brought in, in a wheelchair. To my horror his first sentence was made to the sister.

'Sister dear,' he lisped, gesticulating by letting his wrist drop limply, 'will it be at all po'thible for us chaps to watch the ballet on the television this evening?' He pursed his lips and looked around.

'What's it like being in the Pay Corps, Adrian?' asked my rugby pal as he took a dubious glance towards me, grinning along with the rest of his mates.

It was after Easter before I returned back to camp and it was not long before I returned to the old routine. Regular visits were made to the dental officer to check that the healing of the jaw fractures was to his satisfaction. Eventually he sent me to see the specialist at Tidworth hospital to get the Army's full approval for me to resume my boxing activities.

Immediately after receiving the go-ahead I was back into training. Despite my daily run up the Roundway Hill, I was finding it difficult to take off the excess weight that I had put on. For the time being, I would box as a featherweight.

I was selected by West Ham Boxing Club to represent them in a match against the famous 'Sporting Club of Paris' and I managed to secure a few days' leave for the occasion. My opponent was the Olympic featherweight prospect Abdoulaye Faye. The venue was the West Ham Municipal Hall which was next door to the tax office where I had previously worked.

Abdoulaye was the only coloured boxer in either team. I beat him on points but I was not as happy as I should have been because I thought that I had not done enough to secure victory. I loathe prejudice, and I believed, that the judges had taken his colour adversely into consideration when coming to their decision. I also believe that there were times when prejudice had worked against me, but that was no consolation.

It was, however, still a pleasure to tell my friends that I had beaten my first foreign opponent, especially when it was known that he was probably one of the best amateur featherweights in the world at that time.

Books Immediate

While I had been in the army Dad and David had achieved a great deal. Dad was increasing his contacts in the book trade and David, now married to Beryl, had been persuaded to leave the building trade and run a small, 'hole in the wall' science fiction bookshop in John Adam Street which my father had acquired with the help of Uncle Dave. He soon built up a clientele of pin-up customers while still holding on to the 'sci-fi' regulars. Dad was buying a range of paperback westerns, crime and romances under the trade mark of 'Digit Books', and this further enhanced David's range of paperback titles.

The family book business was progressing well. However, while David was confined to the small shop in John Adam Street and Dad was serving his retail customers on a weekly basis, there was no time left for them to expand. And, when I was demobbed, I was welcomed with open arms.

My determination to get to work was understandable. It was automatic that I would immediately take over the round from Dad. This gave him time to concentrate on getting premises from which we could operate efficiently. Dad and David were satisfied that I could hold on to the established customers and keep things ticking over ... But I had other ideas. Ticking over was never my style.

Dad soon found premises to suit our needs and it was not long before we were moving all of the stock from our home in Green Street to 4 East India Dock Road. We decided to call the new 'set-up' in Limehouse, for want of a better name, 'Books Immediate', and without delay a facia sign was erected above the shop frontage.

The property had three floors above a dilapidated shop. At the top there were facilities for a small one bedroom flat. It was situated on one of the major roads that led into the city of London. The traffic was bumper to bumper for three hours each morning and evening. Parking was impossible at those times so I had to load up my stock before seven which meant that my morning run had to take place at the crack of dawn.

My job was to service a hundred or so customers with books, comics and magazines and I was quick to learn that there was a great deal to be gained in beating the opposition to the punch. I had to be friendly, efficient, but most of all I had to be the first supplier to arrive with the new product. The early start helped enormously but planning and knowledge about the trade was essential.

I learned quickly that there were certain titles that the shopkeepers needed to be first with. I could not possibly compete with the supply of the paperback book releases but when it came to the pin-up titles I soon worked out every move that would give me the edge when supplying the big outlets. My takings on the van increased nearly every week and my contribution to the company was such that David and Dad were able to put more of their time into publishing.

Dad had worked out a method of acquiring a complete range of pin-up and 'art' books at a price that enabled us to act as distributors as well as publishers. We printed very small quantities of 'art' books and offered them to smaller wholesalers at special terms. The overage of the three or four thousand print runs was used to swap with other publishers. We accumulated big stocks but at least we had a large selection.

The 'art' or pin-up books were simply an assortment of large-breasted ladies posing provocatively, wearing very little or in some cases nothing. There were still retail shops that would refuse to sell 'that type' of book, not only because of police action, but also because it was a time in history when it seemed society believed that exposed nipples were offensive unless they were on a statue or a woman feeding her baby. Although it was now legal to show the naked breast, anything more than that required the work of the brush-out artist who would remove even the slightest trace of the dreaded pubic hair. If he failed then the publisher was almost certainly in very serious trouble with the police.

As the fifties came to an end our business was expanding. Counting Green Street, we now had three shops, a successful wholesale book service and a recognized publishing house that was by now printing over sixty thousand copies of a range of 'art' books each month.

But our prospects were compromised because although we were printing large quantities of these books, we were only able to sell small amounts of them, and our premises in East India Dock Road were rapidly being filled with the excess stocks.

To print less was not a solution, because the smaller the print run, the higher the cost of each copy. We evaluated the situation and agreed to continue with the over-production – after all we were actually making money even though it did not show in our bank balance. The profit was in the stock. But it was not long before we were bulging at the seams, and my father came up with words of pure genius.

'All we've go' a do' he said, 'is to sell more.'

David and I looked at each other, then David put his hands out from his side and murmured sarcastically, 'Of course, why didn't I think of that?'

Dad was a genius when it came to buying, and it was his idea to go into the 'art' book business in the first place. But when it came to sales he was not very good. His reasoning was a little along the lines of, 'We have the goods, if you want them then come and get them.'

For this to work the 'goods' had to be the best available, and our titles; *Hush, Sensations, Petite*, and the like were far from that. They comprised a number of pictures featuring one or two models who had been photographed in a second class studio by a second class photographer put together by a third class editor ... my father.

The job of the 'editor' was to decide on the pictures that would not contravene the Obscene Publications Act, put them into a pile, shuffle them and then send them off to the printer. One of the great 'shufflers' was Ben Holloway, who was our biggest competitor in the 'art' business. It was this competition that brought about confrontations with the law. Ben was always prepared to go that one step further and he was probably the first man to actually publish a pin-up picture that revealed a flash of pubic hair.

I can remember one day when David displayed the printed copy of our latest *Hush* magazine. After scrutinizing one of the pictures, I said, 'David! What have you done here? Are you mad?'

'What?' he asked.

'You know very well.'

'What?' he asked again.

'There!' I insisted. 'Pubic hair.'

'Ridiculous, Ralph, that is shadow.'

'Shadow? That's pubic hair. I know pubic hair when I see it.'

'You are disgusting,' said David, flippantly. I understood exactly what he was implying. 'Obscenity is in the eye of the beholder.' ... It was pubic hair.

Ben Holloway's magazines *Silky* and *Satin* contained pictures that undoubtedly contravened the Obscene Publications Act of 1959. The photographs that he selected were more provocative, the models' legs were invariably more parted and the panties that they wore were more flimsy, leaving little to the readers' imagination, although pubic hair could still not be clearly seen.

Silky at three shillings and sixpence soon outsold *Hush* at the same price. *Sensations* which was only a two and sixpenny title took a dive. It appeared that the customer actually wanted to pay more for his magazine, probably on the basis that it had to be more raunchy if it cost more. *Satin* at seven and sixpence fitted into that category.

David was needed more and more at 'Books Immediate'. Apart from supervising the shop there, he was largely responsible for the management of the publishing side of our business and was soon to replace Dad as 'shuffler in chief' – although it was becoming obvious that David would soon take a more scientific approach.

Meanwhile, Dad took it upon himself to obtain the best possible pictures. Rumours of his activities with young models on photographic 'shoots' began reaching David and me from various sources. Whether they were true or not, it was becoming more and more obvious that my parents' marriage was having its problems and the 'pin-up' business was not helping.

Dirty, But Nobody Wears Raincoats Anymore

'Hank Janson' was probably the most famous fictional detective in the United Kingdom during the fifties. The stories, which came out monthly, were not written by any one author, but were provided by hack writers. They were always interesting, exciting and sexy. The establishment were not too happy about the latter, as the endings to many of the chapters were very close to the mark. I know because when I was younger I had, on occasions, managed to get hold of a copy (they were like gold dust), and I would turn the pages rapidly to find the so-called 'rude bits'. I was never let down. Hank inevitably met a beautiful woman, and they always finished up in a compromising position. He would invariably find his hand touching her knee. Many times it would creep up her creamy thigh and touch the lace of her panties ... It was typical, at this point, for the reader to be led to the beginning of the next chapter, which would begin, 'The next morning ...'

The original publishers of the Hank Janson titles were Julius and Kirk Reiter, two Jewish immigrants from Germany. They were conscious of the fact that the mention of 'creamy white thighs', the fondling of 'firm-nippled breasts' and other forms of titillation could contravene the obscenity laws. They took the chance and were arrested and eventually sent to the Old Bailey to stand trial.

After they were found guilty the judge elected to impose a harsh prison sentence in the hope that it would discourage others from taking the same path. They were each given twelve months in prison – unquestionably one of the biggest miscarriages of justice in modern times.

The new publisher of Hank Janson, Reg Carter, was forced to tone down endings to each chapter, and satisfy his readers by including innuendoes that allowed the mind to work overtime, but would not offend the law. Reg sold the now 'softer' versions from his premises in Borough High Street, within walking distance of London Bridge. They were printed under a different format, slightly thicker paper, and a cover design that projected an artistic painting of a salacious lady, surrounded by bold red and yellow stripes.

Because of the trial, 'Hank Janson' had become notorious and for a while sales remained high, even when the two shilling cover price went up by sixpence. But inevitably the public caught on to the fact that the stories now lacked 'oomph,' and sales went down.

We 'inherited' Hank Janson when Reg Carter was forced into provisional liquidation. My father, who had dealt with both Reg and the Reiter brothers before him, agreed to take over the lease of his premises at Borough High Street, as well as his remaining stock – mainly 'Hank Janson' paperbacks. The rights were included in the deal.

But if Hank Janson's sex life had been seriously curtailed, becoming his publisher helped mine do just the opposite. The new premises had their own yard, and enabled us to find space for the ever-growing pin-up overage. It also had a self-contained flat on an upper floor. One of my friends suggested that it would make an excellent love nest, a playboy's dream – which is what it stayed ... A dream. However, having said that, one of my dreams did come true. And the flat, with no furniture, was where it all happened.

Pauline was employed to run the shop. She was a nice girl,

nineteen years of age and although a little overweight, she was attractive and good fun. She eventually married David's friend, Jimmy Brown, who also worked for us at that time. Pauline's best friend was Sandra, a small, slim and very attractive girl with the most beautiful and appealing eyes. Pauline suggested that I took Sandra out for a drink, which I did. We fell madly in love and it was not long before I made another purchase of a 'packet of three'. This time I actually used them. The first condom was used in the flat with no furniture, and was an unforgettable moment ... I was finally released from the unbelievable pressure of being a virgin. From then on I bought my condoms in packets of twelve.For three months Sandra and I behaved like rabbits, and my boxing was beginning to be affected. This all happened to me at a time when my boxing career was coming to its prime. I was training harder than ever and despite my move from West Ham Boxing Club to neighbouring East Ham (considered by many to be a bad decision) I was climbing rapidly up the amateur ratings.

I made the decision (again considered by many to be a bad one) to end the affair. With the benefit of hindsight I am sure that it was a bad one. I firmly believe today that my life would have been richer had I developed my sexual prowess as opposed to mastering my boxing skills.

After just two weeks I longed to be back with Sandra, but a late night visit to her home in Brixton left me in no doubt that another man was on the scene ... I had screwed it, metaphorically and quite literally.

I went for a seven-day holiday to Jersey with two friends, John and Ian. We stayed at the Merton hotel in St Helier. It was rumoured that the hotel was a den of iniquity and that at two o'clock every morning, a gong went off and the men were expected to return to their own beds. One part of this rumour was in fact true ... The hotel did have a gong.

We had a wonderful week, but on my return there was bad news waiting for me. Dad had been charged under Section Two of the Obscene Publications Act for publishing six copies of a pin-up magazine called *New Look* which were deemed to be obscene. The case was to be heard before a magistrate at Tower Bridge County Court. My father had the choice of taking this option or going before a jury, probably at the Old Bailey. If found guilty under those circumstances he could have been given a custodial sentence and he was not prepared to take that chance.

The magistrate took only fifteen minutes to find him guilty. He was ordered to pay a fine of fifty pounds, and the six copies of *New Look*, which had been removed from a small retail shop in Southwark, were ordered to be destroyed. Once again justice had been seen to be done and the community were being protected by the strong arm of the law.

My father's conviction meant that if he were brought before another court on a similar charge then the punishment would almost certainly be imprisonment. To avoid this a new company had to be formed and as David now had a wife and family to consider, it was agreed that I should take 'the chair' and the company was accordingly renamed 'Ralph Gold Booksellers Limited'. I was the managing director.

As well as pin-up and 'art' books I sold from the van a range of paperbacks. 'Digits' and 'Badger Books' were important lines for me because not many of the other wholesalers bothered with them. Another publisher that was unable to get a worthwhile distribution was 'Bestseller Library'.

They were specialists in bringing out the old classics with covers that would induce the less well educated readers to buy them thinking that they would find plenty of 'rude' bits. Their most successful titles, as far as we were concerned, were Emile Zola's *Earth* and *Nana*. Both covers displayed sufficient nudity to ensure sales to the well read as well as to the 'dirty old man in the raincoat'

(the description that was used by the media to describe our ordinary customers – I have always taken exception to this view. I believed then, and I know now, that they had it wrong. They thought that they were condemning a minority. Now I am sure that they understand that men who purchase erotica or 'rude' books are regular, every day individuals like themselves. Apart from the religious fanatics and a few 'strange' people, we are all sexually motivated human beings).

One of my best accounts was at Selfridges. The first time I had called there the manager of the book department had been out. But I met his assistant, Margaret, a lady in her sixties who for some reason took an instant liking to me. She had suggested I go back the following week, when they might buy some 'top-up' stock from me.

This time the manager, Mr Martin, was there, and thankfully so was Margaret. She introduced me to him, but he was busy and seemed happy for Margaret to take care of me. To my surprise she offered to come to the van to see my whole range of samples! The thought that 'the range' comprised a variety of sexy pin-up books did not convince me that it would be wise to show it to a sixty year old assistant buyer for Selfridges.

I insisted that I bring the sample box up to her on this occasion, and that I would call again the following week after I had the opportunity for a 'clean up'. She took this to mean that I was about to sweep the inside of the van. I knew different ... The pin-ups had to go.

She spent twenty six pounds with me, taking a few Digit and Bestseller paperbacks. She asked if I carried 'Penguin' titles – I lied when I told her that I did normally and that the range would be back on the van once I had finalised the clean up. There was a lot of work to do before my next visit.

One of our wholesale suppliers for pin-ups was Julius Reiter, the former publisher of 'Hank Janson'. He had completed his eight months in prison and had taken premises close to the Elephant and Castle for the purpose of wholesaling paperback books and magazines. He carried all of the paperbacks including a range of the leading Penguin titles and I needed these books for the Selfridges account.

The next time I visited Margaret, the little wooden cubby holes on my van had been cleared of pin-up books and filled with Penguin, Pan and Corgi titles. Margaret readily came down to my van in the basement, and ordered threes and sixes of almost every title that I had with me. The second invoice that I ever made out to Selfridges exceeded one hundred pounds, and after re-stocking the van I still had another dozen or so customers to serve. Business was good.

It was soon to become even better. One evening I came back to Borough High Street to load the new stock for my book round. David gave me the samples, which I examined and placed into my specially designed sample box.

'Well?' he inquired. 'Did you look through?'

I always looked through, I looked at every pin-up magazine, and not always on a professional basis – I actually liked looking at the pictures. 'Well?' questioned David again. 'What did you think?'

'They're fine,' I replied.

'Ralph, two of our new releases are not new at all. They're re-covers.' I didn't understand what he meant by this. How could you possibly put another cover on to a magazine? I understood that both the Russians and the Americans had put men into space and that was feasible, but to put a new cover on to an old magazine was beyond comprehension.

'*Jade* issue number one, used to be *Sensations* number nine,' he went on. 'Sure, the cover is different and the price is different, but the inside is the same.'

'O.K. So you've reprinted ...'

'No Ralph,' he said again, 'it is a re-cover.'

It took time, but gradually David was disclosing a closely guarded secret. Even Dad had not been put completely in the picture, and now that we knew, we were sworn to secrecy. We were able to sell a bigger percentage of *Jade* at three and sixpence with a 'stronger' cover than we had sold of the original *Sensations*, which was only two and sixpence. This suggested that the customer was happy to pay more. It sounded absurd but after giving it some thought, we came to the conclusion that the customer had discovered from the paperback book trade that the 'sexy' or 'rude' books were traditionally more expensive and he suspected that this rule would apply to all publications ... We did not complain.

The re-covering programme was a resounding success, and we were now turning our stock into money. Even the printer was sworn to secrecy, although we realized that eventually our competitors would latch on.

They did. Within five years the paperback and magazine trade had followed suit.

At the time of the take-over from Reg Carter, my father had spotted a number of samples of very 'sexy' American paperbacks published under the name of Monarch. Reg had made contact with the publishers, a large company in Connecticut named Capital Publishing Incorporation.

These books would sell in Britain, of that there was no doubt. But could they be brought into the country, and if they were, would the police take action? There had recently been a furore in the press about the possibility of American 'trash' coming into our country as ship ballast (ship ballast? I am sure that the press were wrong about this as well). Once in, the reporters prophesied, the moral fibre of our society would be 'brought to its knees'. They urged the government to take immediate and decisive action to ban them.

Now that our cash-flow was improving, Dad decided to take immediate and decisive action of his own, before it was too late. He spoke to Reg (who was now a freelance operator) and offered him cash up front for five hundred of each of a dozen titles that he chose from the sample range. I had scanned through most of them and they were, almost without exception, more sexually stimulating than any British title that I had ever read. One of the titles, *The Sexual Side of Life*, was particularly good. It left nothing to the imagination in explaining ways of improving the reader's sex life. Obviously it was aimed at people with partners, but I was ever the optimist.

Nicky was the best selling title, a brilliant portrayal of the encounters of a promiscuous young lady. I read this book three times, enjoying every word. I knew that it would sell its head off, but I did not believe that we would ever see a copy on sale in Britain. I was wrong.

Six weeks later, five thousand copies of assorted Monarch books came in via Tilbury Docks and were delivered directly to 139 Borough High Street by the local shipping company, Baxter Hoare. Within a day I had put the books on to my van and called on my customers in the West End. Within two days there was not a Monarch book in our warehouse and within four days there was not a Monarch book in the stores and every account was on the phone asking for more supplies. It was a bookseller's dream come true.

Often in business there is a 'leveller' that brings you down to earth. The next parcel of Monarch books was held at customs pending inquiry. Two weeks later we were informed that Her Majesty's Customs had seized our goods pending a court order. We immediately arranged for another shipment but avoided Tilbury Docks. These goods were cleared through Southampton without difficulty and within days we were sold out again.

Somebody had to make the journey to America to tie up a contract for the regular supply of Monarch books. My father decided to go despite his intense fear of flying. He was terrified, but he knew that our business was on the threshold of something really big, and he was unquestionably the man for the job. As it turned out he was. He met Jerry Levine, who was the sales manager for Capital and that contact proved to be of vital importance to the future of our company.

In view of the demise of their existing distributors, Jerry agreed to supply us direct and undertook to bring his principals to England in order to meet us. Dad had told him that we were an established and powerful company and that we were a better prospect for Capital than our competitors, Thorpe and Porter, who were comparatively small and incompetent. Thorpe and Porter just happened to be the largest independent wholesaler in the country, and about one thousand times bigger than Ralph Gold Booksellers Limited.

For the time being we had to do our best to see that the American publishers remained in America.

Paul, I Mean 'Arry

I was more prepared for the 1961 ABA Championships than I had been for anything else in my life. Even though I was working long hours I refused to compromise on my tough training schedule. I was up before six on most mornings to run along the sewer bank, and trained two or three nights a week at the East Ham Boxing Club. I had lived, breathed, eaten and thought about nothing else but the Championship ... Well perhaps with the exception of Joan Bowley.

I'd met Joan through my friends Don and Marie Wagstaff. A group of us had gone swimming, and afterwards Joan and I had our first conversation whilst drinking Bovril and eating toast in the swimming baths' canteen. Despite her spotty face and blue lips she looked wonderful to me, and I wanted to tell her so... but I didn't. My successful sexual encounter with Sandra had not helped me overcome a short lifetime of inferiority as far as women were concerned. The next time I'd seen her had been nothing short of a horror story. After a group outing to Canvey Island, I had to drive while Joan snogged in the back seat with someone else.

Other than my preoccupation with Joan, though, every aspect of my mental and physical conditioning was just right. I stormed through the preliminaries and was declared the North East of London Divisional Champion. Ahead were the awe-inspiring

Outside the Albert Hall

London Championships which were to take place at the Royal Albert Hall. I had already been there to box in the Schoolboy Finals, but this was different. To begin with, I was expected to compete twice in one day. Secondly, if I won the afternoon bout, I would be taking part in my first televised contest.

The *Boxing News* had reported my first opponent Ernie Wiles to be the favourite, but against the odds I came out the clear points winner. The television cameras were unmanned during that bout, so I was not too nervous. But the evening event was very much on my mind. Before the start of the finals the chosen television contestants were each interviewed by Harry Carpenter and I was one of them.

From the start I had difficulty in remembering the young commentator's Christian name. I could only think of Paul, because Paul Carpenter was a film star at the time. Harry was not pleased about me using another name. He retaliated by calling me Larry, the first name of the famous band leader, Larry Gold. This banter went on for some time. When I eventually remembered his name I dropped the 'H'! So he dropped the 'R' and called me Alf ... It was a tough interview.

The fight was sensational. My opponent, Keith Waterhouse, had won the South East Divisional Championships, and came out full of confidence. He clearly won the first round, but I came back aggressively to put myself again in contention by winning the second. In the third, my fitness and sheer determination forced my opponent into submission and the referee stopped the contest ... The underdog was the new London ABA Champion!

It seemed that everyone in the East End had seen the bout. Television boxing had a great following, and after just one televised contest I was already a local sporting personality. People came up to me in the street, patted me on the back and said, 'Great fight last night, Champ!' It was like being in another world.

My successful television debut was the talk of the trade and discussions about the 'fight game' in general, and my prospects in particular, were taking up much of my working days. Most of my customers were newsagents and therefore carried the boxers' weekly bible, the *Boxing News*. For weeks after the championships they published headlines like 'Gold rushes to the top of the ratings' and 'London banks on Gold', so my customers were kept well in the picture. It also held their interest but I was not going to make my fortune by standing around revelling in my achievements in the ring.

Sales of Monarch books were enormous but supplies, due to customs seizures, could not be relied upon. Our main competitor, Ben Holloway, was also experiencing the same problem. He had managed to obtain the exclusive UK rights to sell Midwood Books. These paperbacks were far more erotic than our Monarchs, but nevertheless he managed to import them and they sold like hot cakes.

It was not long before there was an outcry from the tabloid press. The press were the same then as they are today, ready to cash in on 'pornography' in their own way by publishing pictures of a few salacious covers, putting 'stars' or 'censored' strips across the offending parts, and warning their readers of the impending horrors that would befall our society if these books were allowed to proliferate – all of which, of course, increased the newspapers' circulation.

The 'Ben camp' and the 'Gold camp' rivalry did not change, but the stakes were higher, and our main adversaries were still the authorities. Her Majesty's Customs were the first hurdle. The stipulations regarding importation of literature were similar to the postal regulations ... archaic. Everything depended on the view taken by a particular inspector who was on duty at the time when the consignment was to be checked. If he was a bigot then the books would be sent to higher authority and subsequently a seizure notice would be issued. If he was a tolerant and open-minded individual then the books would be automatically released ... It was the toss of a coin.

Before long we were receiving less than half of the consign-ments that had been shipped, and had to increase the price to five shillings to compensate us for the seizures. We liked to think that it was even worse for Ben. Unlike ours, his books were exclusively of a sexual nature.

When the trial of *Lady Chatterley* hit the headlines, I worked full time placing orders for it with every wholesaler I knew, even though I was convinced that the book would be deemed obscene and never released. After all, if the courts found that our silly little 'art' books could corrupt then surely paragraphs expressing the sex act in graphic detail would put the publisher away for life.

Luckily, the defendant – a well-educated, well-respected and well-off man – was unintentionally assisted by both the Judge and the prosecution. The Judge had insisted that Sir Allen Lane need not stand in the dock. The prosecuting council, Mr Mervyn Griffith-Jones, then played an even bigger part in this acquittal when he made his now famous summing up speech to the jury. He asked them if 'this was a book that you would wish your wife or your servant to read'. I ask you!

Within ten days every schoolchild, every adult and every servant either bought, borrowed or stole a copy and was reading, some for the first time in their lives, blatant 'pornography' – and this within the covers of a *Penguin* paperback.

The demand was unbelievable. Customers of mine that had previously been unprepared to even consider stocking a novel with a salacious cover, let alone to purchase any of my 'art' books, were clamouring to stock what could only be seen as 'legalized porn'.

The establishment responded to this natural development of free expression by engaging in a campaign to confiscate so-called 'undesirable' publications from the retailers and to subsequently issue proceedings under Section Three of the Obscene Publications Act.

Section Three demanded that the defendant be required to give reason as to why the offending publications should not be destroyed. Without adequate defence the Magistrate would automatically order that the books or magazines be confiscated. It was pointless for the shopkeeper to oppose the police action because the time, trouble and expense of doing so was simply not cost effective. So in the name of democracy and freedom, books were again being burned. Thankfully this time they were not written by Jewish authors, nor did they condemn minority races. This time they contained pictures of women without clothes, men and women in erotic poses, stories of people engaged in, dare I say it, sexual intercourse.

We had by now moved into larger premises in Long Lane, Bermondsey, and despite the actions of the Customs authorities and the British law, paperback books and magazines came flooding in to the new warehouse.

David, now the proud father of Jacqueline, concentrated on our wholesale and publishing business. A great number of our 'art' books had been re-covered, but there was a long way to go before we could hope to turn the rest into cash.

One day a smartly dressed gentleman walked into our Long

Lane premises. He told us he was the son of the glass millionaire John Pilkington, and that he wanted to buy our entire stock of pin-up magazines. My mouth went dry at the prospect. Overnight there was the possibility of our company – and indeed all three of us – becoming both liquid and rich.

I handed him the inventory which amounted to over six hundred thousand magazines. He didn't flinch.

'How much?' he asked.

'I would not take less than one hundred thousand pounds,' I replied, knowing I would happily settle for a quarter of that.

'Seventy thousand,' he ventured.

'Eighty thousand, cash up front,' I said. He took out his cheque book and started to write.

'I'll collect the stock within a week,' he announced, and left.

Dad, David and I looked at each other in amazement. We didn't know whether to laugh or cry. We spent hours making plans what to do with the money, before we considered the possibility that it might be a hoax or con. Whatever it was, we agreed to put the cheque into the bank for special clearance.

It was not long before our bubble was burst. Eleven o'clock the following morning I received a telephone call from another Mr Pilkington. He informed me that the cheque could not be met because the signatory was not of sound mind. Our fairy-tale customer was on leave from a mental institution ... He was fine, it was us who were mad.

Going Places

My sister Marie was seeing a young man by the name of Ken Mould on a regular basis and I had yet to meet him. Marie and I were always very close and I was disappointed that she had not told me much about him. I came home from work one evening to find Ken in the living room with Marie. He seemed nice enough, but I felt that Marie was concerned that Ken would not be approved of by the family. He was tall, slim and not very handsome. He wore a leather motorcycle outfit, smoked a hand-rolled cigarette, and spoke with a heavy Cockney accent. I felt that he might not be the type of boyfriend that Dad would want his daughter to be going steady with.

I was right. Dad, a Cockney-speaking ex-convict, did not approve. He envisaged better things for his daughter and in his own words he told her as much. ''E ain't the sort you ought 'a be wiv and I intend to see to it that fings go no furver. For a start you ain't stayin' out late wiv 'im.' ... Dad did not exactly have a gentle manner of persuasion.

Marie was even more determined to see Ken and their relationship blossomed. So when I was offered four tickets at half price to attend a social club dinner and dance I took a chance and bought them, then plucked up the courage to ask Joan Bowley to make up a foursome with Marie and Ken. To my surprise she accepted.

The function was held at the Kingfisher Hall in Wanstead, and Joan asked me to pick her up from a first floor flat in East Ham. I had thought that she lived in Basildon in Essex but I discovered that she had recently left home and was now living with her grandmother. I hit it off immediately with her nan, and when Joan finally appeared she looked stunning in a bottle green crimplene dress. I failed to tell her how lovely she looked, I was not well trained in the art of seduction and for some reason I believed it to be terribly un-masculine ... I had a lot to learn.

We arrived a little before Ken and Marie, who came by motor-cycle. Marie was equally stunning in her full skirt and starched net petticoat, but how she had maintained her attractiveness after thirty minutes on Ken's 500cc Triumph, I will never know. Ken also arrived dressed for the occasion in his best suit. After drinks, we sat at the bench-like tables. The place settings were laid out formally and we were unfamiliar with the sight of so much cutlery. Ken and I were really struggling because the girls were looking to us for guidance. Needless to say we used the main knife to butter the bread, put water into the wine glass and finished up eating our peas with the soup spoon ... We lacked class. Nevertheless the evening went well and Joan agreed to see me again.

I loved being with Joan and knew from the start that she was right for me. She was small and pretty, and her voice was distinctly 'up market'. I was constantly ill at ease with my own accent. It was embarrassing for a representative to address me as 'Sir' after I had just asked him to deliver, 'An 'undred assor'id boxes.' David was finding it equally difficult, especially after we began to take on staff at Long Lane. We were determined to improve our speech and to advise each other of errors.

I was beaten in the ABA semi-finals, but despite this disap-pointment I was at my all time peak of fitness. I was ready to take on all-comers, but as my relationship with Joan developed I began to train a little less and I slept a little less. By the time I was selected for the British team in the Maccabi games (otherwise known as the Jewish Olympics) we were head over heels in love.

It was the first time I had fought for Great Britain in an international event, even though it was by no means a full international. Only Jewish sportsmen who were 'Maccabi' club members could take part. The games were to be held in the famous Ben-Gurion Stadium in Tel Aviv. I saw it as an honour although I felt a bit of a cheat, as I was not a practising Jew.

Joan and I were so much in love that the thought of being apart for three whole weeks was purgatory. She would clearly have liked to accompany me but that was out of the question. Before my departure she took me to Basildon to see her parents. Fred, Joan's dad, was a gentle and agreeable man. He was an engine driver and his spoken English was as bad as mine, so we had a lot in common. I loved to listen to stories about his work and the fun that he had with his fireman assistant, Joe Brown. Joe had left Eastern Railway to form a pop group ('Joe Brown and the Bruvvers') and became a household name. I also hit it off with Joan's thirteen year old brother, Bobby. We became friends from the moment we first met.

The same could not be said for Joan's mother and me. I had heard uncomplimentary things about her from Joan's Nan and indeed from Joan herself. It worried me a little because I had very strong views about genetics and I believed that by looking at a girl's mother you could usually see a vision of the daughter in twenty five years' time. When I did eventually meet her, I was horrified at that prospect.

Ethel, who insisted on being called Jo, was a woman who had treated her husband and her daughter with unreasonable aggression, although her son could do no wrong. I found it hard to have any respect for a woman who had once locked my wife-to-be in a coal cellar. We discussed my pending trip to Israel and I felt that Ethel would not be unhappy if I chose to stay there.

On landing at Tel Aviv Airport the heat was unbearable, and I was stunned when the local press seemed to know all about me. They behaved as though I was the reigning heavyweight champion of the world. At the Israeli gymnasiums I was surprised at the number of people who knew of me. Because my weight had risen by a few pounds it was necessary for me to go immediately into vigorous training to get it off. Many came just to see me working out and many wanted my autograph, which made me feel as though I were a film star on set.

When I rode the bus and walked to and from the gymnasium I felt happy about the people around me. There was an unmistakable experience of belonging. I would reflect on my discussions with my grandmother which had taken place ten years earlier. She spoke of her wish for the Jews to eventually succeed in establishing a land of their own, and I would have liked her to have been with me to see it becoming a reality.

My mother and father arrived a few days later with a hand held 8mm camera that took moving pictures. I had never seen one before and became excited at the prospect of actually seeing myself in action. The fact that I had been on television was not helpful because there was no way for me to see the contest in which I was participating. Video machines were not available to the public for another twenty years and hand held video cameras were pure science fiction.

I marched around the stadium following the British flag with great pride. I was not, however very proud of my performance in the ring. I fought the local Israeli boy, a boxer who was barely of intermediate class, in a preliminary round and lost fair and square on points ... Another bubble had burst.

Dad filmed the whole contest, but he had not studied the instruction manual. Apart from the occasional flash from the press cameras the developed film showed nothing.

While I was away, Joan had sent many letters telling me how much she cared and promising that she would love me always. I wrote regularly to her with similar sentiments and our reunion reflected our feelings as we collapsed into each other's arms. I proposed marriage and, apparently without a moment's thought Joan accepted. We were ecstatically happy.

We planned to marry in March of the following year. Despite my unexpected defeat I was still newsworthy and the press gave good coverage to the announcement of our engagement. After my return from Israel I was selected to fight for the London team, and after two successful contests (one of them, against a Polish opponent, televised at the Albert Hall), I was rapidly becoming a boxing celebrity. I received invitations to appear on many of the leading amateur boxing shows in London. Sometimes I would be introduced from the ring even though I was not participating.

The highlight of my entire boxing career was my selection to box for Great Britain in a full international against Nigeria in Lagos. The trip involved a two week goodwill tour of the country, and a few days before departure the whole team were invited to meet the Duke of Devonshire, who was then the parliamentary under secretary to the Commonwealth Relations Office, at his headquarters in Whitehall.

We crowded round his desk to listen to what amounted to a pep talk about our behaviour on tour. This was listened to in good spirit until it became apparent to us that it was being suggested that the British Government saw us as emissaries, and as such it would not be considered a bad thing if we were to lose with dignity. We reached the conclusion that it would be politically beneficial to the relationship between the two nations.

At a nearby coffee shop the team sat and discussed the matter and agreed that we could not even think of entering a boxing ring without giving of our best, and we decided to forget the obvious insinuations.

The trip was wonderful. I lost my first fight but won my second, and had the privilege of meeting a tribal king. He lived in a bungalow which was situated in a normal suburban Nigerian Street in Enugu. As the team coach approached his 'Palace' there stood a parade of men with trumpets, beneath which hung long banners. As we slowly came to a halt alongside the red carpet, they played a fanfare which was dreadfully out of tune. We had been briefed on the protocol and knew exactly what had to be done. We walked into a dingy room where a man was sitting on a throne while other men sat on smaller chairs beside him.

We knew to bow very low, shake hands with the King and his entourage and then collect our memento, which was a statuette of a Nigerian woman. I have treasured it to this very day.

There are many other wonderful memories of my trip to Nigeria but I recall mostly the mad desire to get back to Joan. We had so much to take care of before the wedding, not least of which was finding a home. We found a semi-detached house in Orpington which was not far from David and Beryl's. It was very run down, but we knew that Joan's father, Fred, would help us to improve it.

I still had my doubts about Joan's mother, though. One day I agreed to take her and Joan to the January sales. I walked two paces behind them while Ethel made firm suggestions about the items that we would need for the new home. Like a fool, I said yes to practically everything. I kept looking at Joan and then at her mother and thinking, 'Am I doing the right thing?' If my theory about genetics was correct then the answer was 'no', but I knew there was no turning back.

Joan noticed my apprehension and as I dropped them off in East Ham, she walked back to the car. 'Ralph, I know what's going through your mind, and if you want to think again, I'll understand,' she said, and gave me a kiss on the cheek before joining her mother.

I was in a quandary. My theory about women and their mothers was worrying me and I looked to my father for guidance and, in his infinite wisdom, he suggested that I bought a one way ticket to Australia. When I considered the genetic link between men and their fathers as well as women and their mothers, I realized that our marriage had no chance. I didn't take his advice, and the marriage went ahead.

The wedding was not exactly a flop, but it never came up to expectations either. We had arranged to marry at the Caxton Hall register office because it had a reputation of being both different and special. On the big day the hall was under repair, and the large entrance was covered in scaffolding, which created a depressing atmosphere. The weather was dreadful, the cold March wind was intense and waiting outside the register office were a few windswept reporters and one solitary well wisher, Mum's neighbour Mrs Trainer. She had travelled up from Green Street carrying a box of confetti, which the Council had forbidden anyone to use.

The reception took place in the neighbouring St Ermine's Hotel and all fourteen guests had to walk the fifty yards holding on to their hats. I invited Mrs Trainer to join us. David was my best man, and he would be the first to admit that he was the worst best man since weddings were invented. He had not prepared a speech and just stammered a few words. Joan's Dad was no better.

But despite the speeches it was a happy enough occasion. I was happy to get on with the more important side of the proceedings ... like consummating our marriage.

Real Pornography

As I walked past the newspaper stand on my way into the office I saw on the billboards that Nelson Mandela had been incarcerated. It was of little significance to me at the time.

Our first police raid took place on that very day at Long Lane, Bermondsey. I was terrified. I had not previously experienced any involvement with the law. As a youngster, if I needed to know the time or directions I would address a policeman as 'sir'. Now, at twenty four years of age, they were on the doorstep of my warehouse, addressing me as 'sir', but despite this I knew that we were in trouble when they produced a warrant to search the premises.

I welcomed them in to our carpeted main office and arranged for Grace, the cleaner, to make tea for everyone. The police officers were so polite and friendly that my concerns melted away.

By lunch time three large trucks had been loaded with pin-up books and our entire stock of American books that had a sexy cover. They offered me no breakdown of the stock that they had taken and I was afraid to ask. I informed our solicitor, Alan Bray, who told me that he would get in touch with them. I had read in the newspapers that there was a great deal of bribery and corruption in the vice squad and I wondered if these officers were expecting a 'pay-off.' If they did it was just too bad, because I was incapable of making such an approach.

Although we were publishers, distributors, wholesalers and retailers of 'art' books and erotic books from America, the majority of the literature that we sold was more conventional.

I have never had anything to do with product that could remotely be considered by any normal healthy adult to be 'hardcore' pornography. In the early sixties there were a number of 'pornographic' book shops in the West End of London, although I had never been into one. It was generally understood that these shops were allowed to stay open to sell their publications to consenting adults providing that they made a payment to certain people in authority. Police officers who took bribes unofficially warned 'their' shops of pending raids. Some of them were brought to justice and sent to prison, but others took their place knowing that they now needed to be more careful.

We were receiving a number of orders from new customers in the Soho area of London for romance and adventure magazines as well as selections of our remainder paperback books. They were not fussy about the titles, the authors, or the age of the product. It was needed just to fill the front part of their shops and it did not matter whether it sold or not as the main business was in the back room.

George Harrison Marks, the photographer and publisher of *Kamara* and *Solo*, had a studio in Gerrard Street above a bookshop. One morning I received a phone call from the owner, who asked me if I would supply him with a selection of magazines and books for which he was prepared to pay up to two hundred and fifty pounds, cash on delivery.

I sorted out the product that I knew would be suitable and packed it into cartons. Ken, who was now married to Marie, had been employed by the company to take care of the shops as well as make various deliveries, so I asked him to drive me to Soho. I had arranged to meet the owner in a pub and offered to shake hands as I told him that my driver was making the delivery (which wasn't true – Ken was waiting for me to inform him that I had the money before he parted with the stock). The shop owner ignored my hand and put his own hand into his trouser pocket to pull out a wad of large, white five pound notes. He counted out fifty of them and handed them to me.

'Check it,' he insisted. I had done so already as he was passing the money from hand to hand.

'Thank you,' I said, 'I'll go and see if my driver's finished.'

I left the pub, impressed that he trusted me to complete the delivery, and returned to the van. But Ken wasn't there. He had put sixpence into one of the parking meters that had been recently installed and had gone into the shop to look around. I walked into the store to find Ken standing at a counter that was openly displaying packets of black and white, six inch by four inch photographs of men, women, animals and children engaged in disgusting acts.

It was my first experience of real obscenity. I knew that this sort of thing existed, but seeing it for the first time was a real shock. I have always held strong views about pornography. I firmly believe that the word is used in the wrong context when it is linked with normal (non aggressive) sexual activities and erotica, but as I glanced down at this filth, my knees sagged and I trembled. I had never seen anything so obnoxious in my life.

We delivered the goods and got away from that shop as fast as we could ... This was not a place for decent people.

Our shop in Shaftesbury Avenue, off Piccadilly, had been open for about a year when the police raided it and seized one hundred and seventy one copies of John Cleland's famous erotic novel, *Fanny Hill*. The fact that it was in the centre of town meant that the police kept a very close watch on the type of publications that were sold there. On more than one occasion they took our publications and issued 'seizure' proceedings to destroy them under Section Three of the Obscene Publications Act. It was never worth contesting these confiscations because, although the stock was automatically destroyed, no further discipline ensued.

Mayflower Books, the publishers of *Fanny Hill*, however, insisted on defending the allegations made under Section Three. In view of the fact that I was the official defendant, to do so, they needed my co-operation and I agreed to help them.

The case was to be heard at the number three court at Bow Street, and as the managing director of the company, I was obliged to attend. There was no possibility of my receiving a fine or of going to prison as the prosecution were seeking only to destroy the one hundred and seventy one seized books on the grounds that they were obscene. Mayflower Books had provided a top counsel in Jeremy Hutchinson to represent me.

Speaking for the defence, author and book critic Peter Quennell, stated that '*Fanny Hill* is an advocate of the pleasures of straight sex, and when she describes sexual deviations she makes it clear that she does not approve of them. She uses no four letter words to describe her adventures and I think that Fanny would have been horrified at *Lady Chatterley*.' He also upheld that the book had historical as well as literary merit. It was literature as distinct from pornography.

At an appropriate moment during this cross examination the magistrate adjourned the hearing for seven days. This delighted us, because we were in the process of capitalizing on the enormous amount of media coverage of the proceedings. Only two weeks earlier, we had obtained a manuscript of another book by John Cleland which he had written nearly forty years after *Fanny Hill*. This second book was called *Memoirs of a Coxcomb*, but since Cleland had been sentenced to be put into the stocks for publishing an obscene work after writing the first novel, the second, despite the title, was considerably less titillating.

As the author had been dead for hundreds of years, his work was in the public domain and we were free to publish it. We saw the opportunity to capitalize on the present furore over *Fanny Hill* by creating a similar cover design for *Coxcomb*. The content had not yet been printed, but thanks to the postponement of the hearing we received the newly printed cover in time to stick it onto a dummy book. This enabled me to walk along Bow Street exhibiting a copy before dozens of newspaper photographers and television cameramen who were recording my arrival at court.

Memoirs of a Coxcomb received full media exposure, and within

Displaying Memoirs of a Coxcomb

a week of publication we realized that the fifty thousand print run was insufficient. We went back to press on two occasions, and at five shillings per copy we made a substantial profit. The remainder of the *Fanny Hill* case was dealt with in a few days. The prosecution called no witnesses, but in summing up they undermined the expert defence witnesses' claim that the story had literary merits by insisting that 'good literature' was hardly of any interest to the type of customers that frequented the defendant's shop in Piccadilly. The magistrate clearly accepted this view and ordered all one hundred and seventy one copies of *Fanny Hill* to be destroyed.

Once again I was 'guilty' of selling 'obscene' books, but at least this time there was no significant punishment. Mayflower Books continued to publish *Fanny Hill*, and the rest of the book trade ignored the decision of the court and continued to sell it. If it wasn't for the success of *Memoirs of a Coxcomb* I would have been the only loser.

Return To the Dock

Joan and I loved our little home in Orpington but we had still failed to find many friends in the area. The recent publicity over the *Fanny Hill* case had not helped. We were both aware of the attitude of most people in those days regarding 'rude' books and we feared that many of our so-called friends and neighbours were purposely avoiding us.

The timing may not have been right but we decided to start a family. Our plan was to have two or possibly three children, very early in our marriage. I was a great believer in making plans.

It was a great relief for me to dispense with the using of Durex 'Gossamer' condoms. It had been like wearing a space suit to sunbathe, and without them making love took on a new meaning. Joan missed her next period and the doctor assured us both that our baby was on its way. It was due to be born in the autumn, so we decided to book an early summer holiday in Jersey well in advance of its arrival.

Only a few days after making the arrangements we had a visit at our Long Lane warehouse from Chief Inspector Ernest Webb of the vice squad. Like those before him, he was very friendly. He wanted to look through our stock with the intention of taking away any publications that, in his opinion, could contravene the Obscene Publications Act. It would then be left to the Director of Public Prosecutions to decide on the necessary action.

After countless cups of tea and hours of searching the police had collected at least four van loads of books and magazines. I have always had a high regard for the police force, but I could not come to terms with their involvement regarding 'titillating' reading material. Many of the regular 'coppers' buy, read and enjoy our publications, and they must have found it almost embarrassing to be called upon to seize the so-called offensive material via operations 'Moose' or 'Find the Lady'. There was never any need for such Machiavellian methods to achieve results, as most dealers would willingly co-operate and willingly responded to reasonable guidelines.

Instead, the full enforcement of the law was used, and needless months and months of reading, storing and preparation were spent before the courts had the final say as to what was and what was not likely to corrupt.

Within months we heard that the DPP intended to take action under Section Two of the Obscene Publications Act against eleven of the books that had been taken from our premises. It was a dreadful shock because Section Two carried the threat of both a criminal record and imprisonment. I have spent my life in fear of losing its greatest asset ... Freedom. Now here I was going on holiday with my lovely pregnant wife, knowing that my freedom was now under threat.

I was determined to see that our holiday would not be spoilt and the two weeks spent in a hotel that literally backed on to the beach at St Ouen Bay was truly magnificent. The sun shone from dawn till dusk on every one of the fourteen days, and Joan and I had a wonderful time. We were never happier or more in love.

But when I phoned David on my return to Gatwick airport on the following Sunday evening I was brought back down to earth. The court case had been brought forward and the jury was to be sworn in at nine o'clock on the following day at the Old Bailey.

I met up with my counsel, James Burge, at eight the next morning. Mr Burge, a large and quite assertive barrister, informed me that he had not fully prepared the defence of this case in view of the newly arranged time and he would do his best to postpone the hearing. He was of the view that, under the circumstances, I ought to consider making a plea of guilty.

'What circumstances, sir?' I asked. I still called anybody who wore a tie 'sir'.

'Well,' he replied, 'firstly, the present climate is not good and it will be hard to find a jury to acquit. Secondly, the judge will not be too pleased that we take up the court's time by delaying the proceedings.'

'... And thirdly,' I thought, 'you haven't done your homework!' Mr Burge was working by the seat of his pants, and I knew it.

He said that he might be able to strike a deal with the judge whereby he could guarantee that I would not go to prison. Until he had used the word 'prison', I had considered that to be no more than the remotest of possibilities. However, I would not have been the first innocent man to be found guilty, and I happened to know of lots of people that would be happy to see a man jailed for selling 'rude' books. To them anything 'rude' was liable to corrupt someone ... but not them, of course.

It was approaching mid-day before I stood in the dock, with my knees shaking and my mouth dryer than a desert sand dune. The clerk of the court read out the charges and asked, 'Ralph Gold, how do you plead, guilty or not guilty?'

He seemed to linger on, 'guilty'. I knew that I could not plead honestly as I had 'done the deal'. I looked down at Joan and then timidly let out the word, 'Guilty!'

The judge glanced at the huge courtroom clock and decided that he would sentence me after the court had recessed for lunch. My counsel requested that I might be released for the short period but to my horror and total disbelief the judge refused.

I was pointed by two burly police officers in the direction of the basement cells. 'This cannot be happening,' I thought to myself, 'Something has gone dreadfully wrong.' I turned my attention towards Joan. She was holding a screwed up handkerchief in her hands. Tears were running down her cheeks and I longed to hold her, but that was impossible ... I was no longer a free man.

There were dozens of other detainees down there but they all seemed to know and understand the procedures. I didn't. I felt like a fish out of water and I was both despondent and downright scared. One of the detainees spoke to me. 'Right fuckin' mess doun 'ere, ennit? These fuckers have bin doin' dis furever an ney still don't know their arse from their fucking elbow.'

'I know what you mean,' I responded pathetically. Then I walked away from him, only to be checked by an officer wearing a peaked cap and carrying a large bunch of keys. He led me into a cell that was not much bigger than the average bathroom. A wooden table and a bench stood at the far end beneath the bars. If I had stood on the table I probably could have seen the thousands of office workers walking along Old Bailey, going about their daily routines, enjoying, but probably not appreciating, their freedom.

I felt more and more concerned that my counsel had screwed up on his so-called 'deal'. Dad and David arranged for food to be sent to my cell but I could not eat a thing. I just sat on the wooden bench willing away the time. The eighty six minutes felt like a hundred years, and I reflected on what I would do if the 'deal' was not to be honoured and I found myself literally serving time. It was a dreadful thought, but it was by no means inconceivable.

One thing I did not do was reflect on the 'crime' I had committed, because there wasn't one. I firmly believed then (and I now know) that the law was an ass and I was about to be kicked by it.

I returned to the dock, just as many murderers, thieves, perverts and villains had done before me, to receive my sentence. My knees trembled as I stood there waiting for the judge to return from his chambers. I am sure to this day that he took his time. He was one of many who had a particular aversion to people who were in my kind of business.

Fortunately Mr Burge was true to his word and the punishment was indeed only a fine of two hundred and fifty pounds, although the Recorder, Sir Anthony Hawke, took pains to announce that if I failed to pay it within three months then the alternative was a nine months' prison sentence. My company was given a stiffer penalty, a fine of fifteen hundred pounds. He went on to say that

I (Ralph Gold) had taken full responsibility for the distribution of this 'pornographic' literature and that it was a pretty shoddy trade.

Thirty years later I can inform Sir Anthony that he was wrong. Nobody in his right mind would have called those books 'pornographic', and nobody in his right mind would have sent an innocent man to jail for selling them. In modern times those same books would not be sold on the cheap book counter of Woolworths, not because of their content but because there is now no market for them. Readers today would expect far more explicit detail.

This whole affair had set back our business by more than five thousand pounds and the British taxpayer by a similar amount ... What a waste.

Not To Be

Joan and I were very excited about the prospect of becoming parents. The pregnancy had gone very well and we had started to convert the small room into a nursery.

Early one evening, however, Joan asked me to call for the doctor. She felt a few twinges in her tummy and expressed concern for the baby. The doctor arrived very quickly, but it was too late. Joan was haemorrhaging. She lost the baby. It was a great shock to us both, but naturally Joan suffered a great deal more than I. She had actually seen parts of what would have been our son.

Her attitude was tremendous: 'It won't be long before I'll be ready to try again,' she told me and she was true to her word. Only four months later she was pregnant again. I was delighted and so was her mother, and she was determined to see that this time nothing went wrong. She insisted that Joan was treated with kid gloves, and if it meant that she had to be there to hand out the treatment then so be it ... and who was I to argue?

I agreed with this single-mindedness as it enabled me to pursue the sport that I loved with the intensity of the past. I had officially 'retired' from boxing, but my retirement had only lasted six months. I was boxing for the London team again, and still had the dream that I would one day become a great champion, although with the passing of years it was becoming less and less likely.

At the age of twenty five I was becoming known as a 'veteran' boxer. I was still at the top of the tree but I was beginning to experience problems. It was difficult to maintain my weight and I did not enjoy the training as much. Nevertheless, I was as determined as ever that I would win the one title that had eluded me, the National ABA Championship, so I never relaxed my training routines.

I never let up on my determination to sell more books, either. We were becoming very large stock holders of cheap, remainder books and I set about the task of selling them at the highest possible price to customers who were selling on to the really big outlets.

With both my father and I convicted publishers of obscene books, it had been necessary for David to take over as the publishing director of our companies ... Two down and one to go. We were all aware of the strong possibility that any future successful prosecutions against either Dad or me could well result in a custodial sentence. We had felt this was an appropriate time to change our company name. 'Ralph Gold Booksellers Ltd' became 'Gold Star Publications'.

Dad had tied up deals with various American publishers. We were soon importing adventure and romance magazines, as well as a larger range of paperback books. The adventure magazines contained a number of pin-up pictures, and it wasn't long before the American publishers realized that their customers were far more interested in the pictures of girls than they were in the rest of the publication. This brought about the birth of the 'girlie'.

The police in America endeavoured without success to restrict the sale of many of these titles. The British Customs had similar problems, and finally the British vice squad were put to work as censors. Dad, in the meantime, was buying from the Americans faster than we were selling, and as well as payment difficulties we were experiencing a lack of warehouse space.

A meeting of directors to discuss the stock situation, which was causing cash-flow problems, was called by my brother David. As well as my father and myself, it was to be attended by David

Warburton, who along with Derek Vinter supervised our paperback publishing company, Compact Books (formerly Roberts and Vinter). This was probably the first serious meeting to be held, and my father's opening statement to my brother David and me was, 'Okay tycoons. Wha's this all about then?'

My father had a way of changing a discussion into a lecture by speaking louder than everyone else. In this case he had the perfect solution to the problem. 'Firs'ly,' he stated with conviction, 'we gotta sell more.'

David and I glanced at each other and raised our eyebrows in despair at the well-worn phrase.

'Thanks Dad,' I said, with a note of sarcasm. 'We should give that some thought.'

The meeting was productive, but the main problem was far from solved. And other situations were developing that concerned David and me, and we needed to clear the air. After the meeting, David Warburton excused himself and left, but Dad, David and I stayed on.

Without consulting either David or myself, Dad had been involving himself in other businesses. One of these, a bingo hall, was marginally successful and required his attention primarily in the evenings. But his latest venture was manufacturing cheap perfume to sell to the market trade. It would take up a great deal of his working day, which we felt would distract him from the main enterprise of Gold Star Publications.

Some years before, Dad had been very ill with meningitis. He had made a full recovery, but since the illness, David and I found it even more difficult to communicate with him. He tried to win arguments by shouting down everyone else, and this occasion was no different. He took offence at our objections, and we realized for the first time that he seemed to think he owned the whole show, and was consequently imposing his will.

'I will do what I like,' he yelled, 'and you will do as you are told!'

David and I realized that there was no point in challenging this statement. We quietly picked up our papers and left Dad there alone. Most days, we drove home together and on this particular evening we welcomed each other's company more than ever. We have always been good friends but the fracas with Dad had brought us even closer.

We had operated the company as partners. Dad had insisted that we were the 'Three Musketeers'. He would put his arms around our shoulders and tell us we were in this together, that it was, 'One for all and all for one.'

'With Dad in this frame of mind I am not feeling comfortable,' David said.

'You're right, we should pick a moment when he's in a more agreeable mood to broach the subject of the shareholding,' I suggested. 'I'll feel better when the whole matter's brought out into the open. I know I shouldn't feel this way but we're becoming vulnerable and I don't like it. There has to be a distribution of share capital sooner rather than later, and I'm worried that there's going to be a problem. I've got a nasty feeling Dad may not honour his word.'

'Never!' David protested.

'I'm glad you said that,' I told him. 'But I wish I were as confident as you are.'

We rarely listened to the radio on our journey as we had so much business to discuss. But on that evening the Light Programme was tuned in for background music, and as we were talking the announcer interrupted the programme to inform listeners that John F Kennedy had been assassinated in Dallas. It took us a long time to get over the shock and return to our more trivial concerns.

Mum and Dad's relationship had been deteriorating for some time. Dad now had a young girl, Denise, helping him at the bingo hall, and Mum worked there less and less ... The end was nigh.

It came as no surprise to receive a phone call from Mum's friend and neighbour, Ethel Jude. She wanted me to come to Green Street as soon as possible because my mother was in a terrible state ... Godfrey had left.

Joan was heavily pregnant but she insisted on coming with me.

It was only nine in the evening when I opened the door with my own key and went through the shop. The house was in darkness. 'Mum,' I called out. 'Is anybody home?' I held Joan's hand tightly.

A moan came from the bedroom and we rushed up the stairs to find an old lady lying in the bed. It was my dear mother. She was only fifty years of age but she looked eighty. Her teeth were lying on the bedside cabinet, her hair was uncombed. She had been lying in bed crying for more than five hours after Dad had told her that his bags were packed and he was leaving her for good.

All of her children were now married. Godfrey, for the first time in his life, had a reasonably high and honest income and, as far as she was concerned, they were on the threshold of an exciting life together. But now, after thirty years of marriage, she found herself to be dreadfully alone.

I have always loved my mother dearly and to see her in this state was very painful. The fact that there was nothing that I could do for her made it even worse. Joan and I comforted Mum till the early hours, but in the final analysis we had to leave her to come to terms with her plight.

For the time being Dad had 'shacked up' with his young girl friend, Denise, in the flat above the shop at 'Books Immediate'. She continued to work with him as his personal assistant, although her work load was small because Dad was not one for dictating letters or documenting transactions. Her services were called upon from time to time by David and myself. This felt strange in view of our loyalty to Mum, but the business had to be the priority, and using Denise meant that we needed one less on the payroll.

There was a lot to be said to my father's credit. His abilities to make contacts with both suppliers and customers had given the business a great start. It was his idea to publish the pin-up books and to put into effect the practice of swapping them for more variety. He was without doubt an outstanding innovator, but now the business was moving towards bigger things, Dad had little time for them. He had always joked about doing his invoices on the back of his cigarette packets because he believed, at least, that he was in control. He saw our push towards mechanization for various aspects of the business as a danger and a threat.

David, on the other hand, seemed to come up with a new idea to improve the business nearly every day, although he had a way of keeping his ideas to himself until the time was right. We rarely trod on each others toes, because we each had our own 'niche' in the company; David was an incomparable administrator, while I was the 'deal maker'. To avoid confusion, we were now known as 'Mr David' and 'Mr Ralph', and Dad constantly made references to David and me as 'tycoons'.

We enjoyed our travels together, and discussed over and over again the various aspects of the business, particularly the need to resolve the question of share holdings. Occasionally we discussed our marital situations. David was never very happy about his relationship with Beryl, and always seemed pleased to hear that Joan and I were getting on very well. We often joked about who was in control of whom and which one of us was more under the 'cosh'.

One day on the way home we put each other to the test. I stopped the car outside a shop while David went in to buy something. When he came out, I had moved the car forward by thirty yards or so as I had seen a better spot to park. David waited by the kerb expecting me to reverse but I made out that I had not seen him. We played this silly game for more than ten minutes, each knowing that our wives were expecting us home sooner rather than later. It was I who eventually gave in, and reversed to where he stood. I wondered how long he would have remained there in the rain ... just to prove his point.

Protection

It was inconceivable that an ordinary man like me could actually be present at the birth of his child but I had read somewhere that it was being allowed and even encouraged. I talked with Joan about it and she was delighted with the idea. Her doctor at Farnborough Hospital raised no objection; in fact he was pleased too.

Less than a week later, I received a phone call to say that Joan's waters had broken and she had been admitted to hospital. I raced there feeling more than a little apprehensive. Joan was lying in bed looking absolutely wonderful. There were no signs of any labour pains and according to the nurses, it could well be some days before we became parents. I sat with Joan till very late in the evening, but eventually the nurse sent me home. She said that nothing would happen for some time and it would be better for me to get some sleep. It was the same the following day. I sat with Joan, but took time off to walk along Orpington High Street, where I bought a huge white furry teddy bear with a blue ribbon collar ... I also bought eighteen inches of pink ribbon, just in case.

I stayed till ten that evening and went home to bed. At five o'clock on the Friday morning I received a phone call to say that the baby was on its way. I dressed, picked up the teddy (as well as the pieces of ribbon) and was in the car in ten minutes flat.

As I went past the parade of shops close to my house I saw a big

Fair swap – Joan and Teddy Bear

sign which read, 'A Sun is born. Don't miss the new 'Sun' newspaper.' I saw this as an omen. I didn't know it then but my own son was already five minutes old.

I was proud when I arrived at the hospital, a short time after the birth of my son. I stuffed the pink ribbon into my pocket and after putting on my overalls and mask, I was shown into the delivery room. Joan looked tired but so happy to see me. We swapped babies; I held my son and Joan hugged the silent teddy. We named our son Bradley. He was beautiful ... Just like his mum.

Now Joan and I had Bradley, we decided it was time to move to a bigger house. Even so, how we finished up in Chingford I do not know. I was happy to live nearer to my place of work in Bermondsey, and Joan wanted to be nearer to her parents in Essex so Chingford seemed a good compromise. Joan was not unhappy about moving away from Orpington or from David's wife, Beryl. They had still not managed to get along, even for the sake of their respective husbands.

We found a detached house that stood alone in Marlborough Road, where most of the other houses were terraced. Both David and I had taken delivery of two new white Vauxhall 'Viscounts'. With power steering, power brakes, electric windows and stereo hi-fi systems, they were distinctly more impressive than the Ford 'Zodiacs' we had driven before, and it was wonderful to drive down Marlborough Road in my new car and pull up outside what was unquestionably the best house in the road.

Joan had found it easier to find friends there. We got along well with Joan's hairdresser, Sylvia and her husband, Archie, who lived less than one hundred yards away. Archie was a very talkative man and among other things he told me that one of his neighbours was an auntie of the infamous Kray Twins.

We found ourselves being invited out to dinner and to parties which was something that we had not enjoyed since before we were married. I knew the basics of conventional ballroom dancing, but the new dance craze involved a lot more movement and a lot less touch. Nevertheless, we thoroughly enjoyed 'twisting' to Chubby Checker or 'rocking and rolling' to just about anything else.

Joan naturally wanted to reciprocate, and so we began to organize a house-warming party of our own. It was held in the main lounge and the new cocktail bar I'd had built looked spectacular. The guests arrived wearing their mini dresses and drainpipe trousers, and soon the music was at full blast and the party was under way. I had prepared a special reel to reel tape recording, taping all of the pop records from the radio hit parade. It had taken several days to prepare what I considered to be the right selection with plenty of Beatles and Rolling Stones records. The only problem was the odd interference from Alan Freeman, the disc jockey, who had somehow managed to appear despite the erase button or the phasing knob.

At about nine thirty there was a ring at the front door, which was surprising as all of my guests had arrived. Stood there were four men. One was particularly tall and large in build and another was very small, probably four inches less than me. The other two

Joan at the bar in our lounge

were identical height, and I thought that they could be twins. At that moment Freddie King, a friend who trained at the same gymnasium as me, appeared alongside me and greeted the lookalikes.

'Ronnie, Reggie, it's good to see you,' he enthused. 'You know Ralph, it's his party.'

I could hardly say, 'I don't know them and I like it that way.' I shook hands with them and had no option but to invite them in.

I had only ever seen them in the newspapers, and in view of what I had read, I was very concerned for my guests as well as for myself. The other two, carrying about six bottles of spirit, walked past me into the room where the party was in full swing.

Freddie put me somewhat at ease because he seemed to know them, as did Sylvia and Archie, but the rest of my friends sensed the tension and the atmosphere became strained. I did not know who had invited them, although I suspected that it was Sylvia.

The music continued to play and the partygoers continued to dance but the party itself went flat. The four gangsters stood by the wall for at least ten minutes but it was obvious that they were bored. They had expected a different sort of 'rave' and I was pleased when one of the twins came up to me and politely told me that they had to go and thanked me for inviting them. I hadn't, but I didn't say so. I was very angry that a so-called friend had done this to me, and I hoped that the Krays would never come into my life again.

They didn't, but an adversary of theirs did. His name was George Cornell. Dad, David and I were working at our new premises in Dock Street when Dad took the phone call that threw us all into a state of panic.

'Hello Goddy.' I could hear the faint male voice from Dad's earpiece.

'Hello, who's that?' my father queried.

'My name's Cornell, George Cornell,' the man said. My father knew of him, although David and I didn't. 'We've got to meet,' he told my father.

'I 'aven't *got* to do anything,' came my father's unwavering reply. They spoke for another three or four minutes before Dad said, 'I'll be there,' and placed the phone back in its cradle. He sat for a while, thinking. We knew that something was wrong, badly wrong. We waited impatiently for Dad to tell us what was going on.

'That phone call,' he said, 'was from George Cornell, a fully paid up member of the Richardson gang. He's a gangster and a racketeer and he wants to speak to me.'

Dad was obviously concerned and it quickly rubbed off on David and me. Just hearing the word racketeer was enough. Thoughts of Al Capone and 'Legs' Diamond rushed through my mind as I remembered the films that I had seen about the protection rackets in America; of the little shopkeepers who were told, 'Pay up and we'll look after you; don't and we can't be held responsible if your shop's burned down or your kids don't make it to school.' What were we to do?

There were few options. The police could not possibly assist. Just making an approach to them could mean that one of us or our family would end up in the River Thames wearing concrete boots. I asked Dad if he had a number to get hold of Cornell.

'Phone him back and tell him that you can't see him until Monday week,' I suggested. 'You don't have to give a reason, just play for time.'

Dad ignored my advice. He had arranged to meet George Cornell outside Bloom's, the Jewish restaurant in Whitechapel High Street, in three days time and made it clear that he would run away from nobody. I thought back to the day in 'Club Row' Market and of how Dad stood his ground on our 'pitch'. I was proud of him then and I was proud of his reaction to the threat that was at hand. He made it clear to us that there was no running away from the likes of George Cornell.

David and I discussed the problem until very late, but settled nothing as Dad clearly intended to attend the meeting. It was ten o'clock before we left the office to go home in our separate cars. I played my favourite tape recording of Beethoven's Fifth but hardly heard a note as I continued to worry about the situation.

It was five minutes past midnight when Joan and I were woken by the telephone. It was David. 'Did you hear the news? He's dead.'

He sounded excited and relieved, as though he was talking about the death of a Fidel Castro. 'Cornell, Cornell is dead. I've just heard it on the news. Shot through the head. Taken to the Maida Vale Hospital and found dead on arrival.'

For the first time in days I slept through the night. I am not a religious man, but I believed that somebody 'up there' was taking care of my family and me. Cornell's death was the final solution to our problem, and it could not have been timed better.

Whitewash

Bradley was twenty months old before my daughter was born. Almost every night during that time he had woken up, and it became so bad that when he didn't cry Joan would wake me up to ask what was wrong.

During the latter stages of Joan's pregnancy, her mother and father came over to Chingford to look after her and at the same time Fred took it upon himself to decorate the dining room and the kitchen. Bradley, during their stay, was an absolute angel. He slept like a baby, not once did he wake in the night. We had told everyone of the horrors of his sleeplessness, which made Joan and me seem less than honest. We did not care a bit. It was just wonderful to know that if he did wake up, somebody was there to take over.

Fred was working wonders with the decorating. He had finished the kitchen and intended to start on the dining room on the following evening when Joan signalled that something was happening, and perhaps I had better call the midwife. It was eight o'clock and Bradley was still up, although he was ready for bed and was playing with his Nan on our brand new royal blue fitted carpet.

My mother-in-law immediately took her daughter's arm and guided her toward the dining room door, but first Joan insisted on giving her only child a big hug before leaving him momentarily unattended. I picked up the phone and started to dial, I gazed into the large mirror above the fireplace which reflected the perfect scene. As the midwife's phone began to ring, Bradley stood up and held on to the lip of the dining room table. Standing on the table, for only the next few seconds, was an unopened tin of 'Dulux' brilliant white gloss paint. Joan turned to blow kisses all round as she made for her bedroom, only to see the can of paint falling to the floor. As it landed the lid came off and the carpet became a sea of white paint. I thought that Joan had produced the baby right there and then, but it was her waters that had broken.

Tina, weighing in at six pounds, arrived shortly after the midwife. Fred and Jo were terrific. We took it in turns to leave the job of removing the paint from the carpet, to make our individual visits to the delivery room. Tina's arrival was dramatic, her brother had seen to that. We named her Tina because she was so tiny and the name fitted perfectly ... Tiny Tina.

Rose and Godfrey were now totally apart. My father would annoy David and me by continually speaking of my mother in unnecessarily aggressive terms, almost as though it were she who had gone off with someone else. David and I felt that he still harboured thoughts of his time in prison, when Mum had succumbed to the affections of another man. But his present behaviour was nonetheless extreme. The sympathies of Marie, David and myself were totally with Mum.

However, at last the issue of stock options seemed to have been resolved. Until recently, Dad had pretty much held the purse strings of the companies, and although David and I had participated on equal terms, Dad had always assumed that any major decisions were his to make. But as Dad became more involved with his perfume company, he took less and less interest in book and magazine matters, which, to all intents and purposes, David and I now had control of. Finally, David had spoken to Dad about the dangers of the business falling out of our hands, painting a worst case scenario of Mum's imaginary new husband taking over if Dad died leaving Mum in control.

The share capital was to be split equally into three portions and put into a holding company, and so Dad arranged with the accountant for the necessary share transfer documents to be sent to us. On arrival they were duly signed and hastily returned. I was totally unaware that I had signed one more document than David.

Our business was constantly being impeded by the actions of both the customs authorities and the police. Most of the people in high office were against the proliferation of our type of product, and we suffered as a consequence. Consignments were regularly seized at the docks and publications taken from shop premises, and court actions would usually follow. People who were prepared to lobby in our defence were few and far between.

I am of the opinion that many of the judgements reached by those in authority have been hypocritical. I was not shocked to read that the Secretary of State for war, John Profumo, resigned from office, nor was I shocked twenty nine years later when the Director for Public Prosecutions, Sir Ernest Green, resigned either. I learned at a very early age that countries were run on the basis of, 'Don't do as I do, do as I say'.

But pressure was not just coming from the establishment. Peter Hill, founder of the 'Festival of Light', with the help of the Bishop of Stepney, Trevor Huddleston, spoke regularly through television interviews of the moral decline of our society. In their opinion, this was largely due to the increase in shops openly selling 'pornographic material'.

Mary Whitehouse's campaign to 'clean up' television had established a sizeable following. It was suggested that she had the support of half a million viewers. I believe that even greater support would have been achieved by the anti-porn brigade if they had focused their efforts against the proliferation of material portraying violence. There was vehement representation from them about sex and violence, as though the two were inextricably linked. We were never in the business of selling anything of a violent nature, and Mary Whitehouse's error, in my opinion, was to imply that adult viewers should not have the freedom to watch clean, healthy sex. After all, they always had the option to use the 'off' switch.

The views of the establishment were not dissimilar to those of Mrs Whitehouse. But to their credit, the establishment had banned cigarette advertising on television which, in my view, was a move in the right direction. People – especially children – should not be encouraged to indulge in something that was clearly killing hundreds of thousands of people in Britain every year. But good old-fashioned sex never hurt anybody.

Despite these drawbacks, our business was still expanding. We had established ourselves in the larger premises in Dock Street, near Tower Bridge on the north side of the Thames. Before we had cleared out the warehouse at Long Lane we had a visit from another team of police officers. They were unaware that we were about to move and I was certainly not going to tell them.

The 'raid' process was put into effect. Morning tea for all, followed by a walk through the building during which they selected product that in their opinion could be deemed to be obscene. They arranged for my staff to place it in the despatch area while a number of five-ton police trucks were ordered to come and collect the so called 'offending publications'.

The annoying thing about this 'raid' was that books and magazines were seized that had recently been released, after inspection, by HM Customs. The whole thing was becoming confusing and ridiculous for all concerned. Despite this the authorities were not prepared to accept our offers of co-operation. We proposed that by sending samples to both the police and the customs in advance of shipment, we could obtain clearance from them before making any financial commitment that would subsequently affect both sides. They refused point blank, stating that they were not censors, and censorship was a court matter and therefore not for them to decide. This attitude must have cost the nation millions of pounds over the years to say nothing of the cost to us ... Pathetic.

Information about the raid was given by the police to the media. They obviously had good reason to do this because it informed the public that they were taking the appropriate action to stem the growth of so-called 'obscene literature' in Britain. There seemed to be a great need to appease the likes of Mary Whitehouse.

The news reached the ears of Adrian Brown, the presenter of a current affairs programme for BBC Television, and he made a telephone call to me at my Long Lane office. He was most insistent that we met as he needed the co-operation of David and me to put together a programme about the 'pros and cons' of erotica and its effect on the new sexual revolution. He made it very clear from the outset that he intended to put forward an unbiased view and like a fool I believed him.

Our first meeting was planned to be at Long Lane, where he proposed to give to us an outline of his intentions after which he would listen to our views. Then, between us, we would decide whether there was value in holding the proposed television interview. I was too young to be aware of the 'golden rule'... reporters should be trusted only at your peril.

The uninvited camera crew arrived five minutes before Adrian Brown. They had instructions to set up their lighting but I refused to give them permission and asked them politely to wait.

Just like the police, we offered them tea and made them all very comfortable ... I had a lot to learn.

Adrian Brown was so convincing and David and I were so naïve that we accepted his apology for prematurely bringing along the film crew. 'But,' he told me, 'I thought that it might save time if we could do the interview sooner rather than later.' That was not our deal but like two lambs we were being led to slaughter. The crew set up their equipment in the main office, which now looked bare because of the ongoing move to Dock Street. This suited the presenter because it gave an appearance of being sleazy.

Neither David nor I were dressed for the occasion. Our hair was a little too long with sideburns to match, and we wore kipper ties and flared trousers. It was the accepted fashion but to be seen on television and to be discussing our particular subject, we would under normal circumstances have dressed with a little more propriety.

We did as well as could be expected for two young company directors who were not particularly eloquent, and with only an East End education at Burke Secondary school to fall back on. Adrian gave the impression that he was a fair man. He did not appear to be condescending and asked questions to which we had the answers. The answers were there in our heads but, in truth, we were incapable of articulating them. However, at the back of our minds was Adrian's agreement that we could edit out anything with which we were not happy, and that gave us comfort.

Three days later we were invited to the BBC Offices in Aldwych where we were taken to the preview room on the second floor. Adrian was there and he greeted us saying that the interview was a complete success and that we would be pleased. We knew that we would not be ... And we were right.

It could have been a lot worse, but we really wanted to scrap it. We had a signed document that gave us the necessary authority. Adrian, however, was a very persuasive man and he suggested that we were incorrect in our view that we would be portrayed as anything other than two regular, decent, young men putting across a responsible view, and he suggested that my remark, that 'there is nothing wrong with good, honest, clean sex,' was a 'gem' and in his opinion said it all. David and I were not so sure, but in view of the time and trouble that all concerned had gone to, and all of the money that had been spent on the programme, we were persuaded to allow it be broadcast with only minor cuts.

Tricks of the trade were used and even the small cuts were not made. The programme appeared on our screens within two weeks and David and I were horrified and embarrassed by what we saw. It did nothing to improve our image, but convinced us to keep a low profile in the future.

Part Two

FROM MY SIDE

Depression

Joan was going through what we had thought was post-natal depression. But we were to discover that it was far more serious than that. I arranged for a private appointment to see Dr Vere, a specialist at Guy's Hospital. Our own doctor had told us that he was considered to be one of the best psychiatrists in the country but after meeting him, I was not impressed. He was originally from Eastern Europe and his English was not good. There was a constant need for him to repeat the last sentence and after an hour with him, Joan was even more depressed.

Day by day her illness became worse, I was in no doubt that it was really serious and I so much wanted to do something constructive about it. Nobody was able to help and nobody seemed to care. The general consensus of opinion was, 'Give it time, it will go away.' For us it did not. Joan was so low at times, she would sit through an entire evening without speaking a friendly word or without the trace of a smile.

We saw other psychiatrists and eventually she was advised to have shock treatment. As all else had failed, she decided to give it a try. It was archaic, it was ugly and it was unnecessary but Joan felt that she had to go through with it. We went to a private clinic in Highgate which was run by the Catholic Church. Joan was nursed by nuns who treated her well, but they were not as tolerant as one would have expected.

Joan told me later about the horrors of the treatment that she had experienced. I could not help but believe that they were using a sledgehammer to crack a nut, but the real horror was that it was all to no avail. The whole episode turned into a nightmare.

After six months nothing had changed. I began to believe that the real cause was me. Perhaps I was not right for Joan, perhaps she was no longer in love with me, perhaps we were no longer compatible. These thoughts went through my mind and I found it hard to completely dispense with them. Simultaneous orgasm was something that we rarely achieved and it was clear that I was no great lover. We were young and we could well have benefited from good counsel. (I say 'we' because, in my opinion, the onus to overcome sexual difficulties rests invariably with both partners.)

I eventually spoke to David Ryde, a doctor who had been with the British team in Israel and we had become friends. He asked me to bring Joan along for a chat. I was pleased that she agreed and we visited him on a number of occasions enjoying his outspoken attitude to sexual matters. I was envious of his relationship with his own wife whom we met. They had been married for more than ten years, twice as long as us, and they appeared to be twice as happy. I knew that communication was the key and Joan and I were lacking in that area, certainly in bed. Thankfully, the 'give it time' advisers were partially correct and Joan gradually went back to being her old, wonderful self. Life for me returned to relative normality and our sex life too showed signs of improvement.

This was not a particularly happy time in my life. My boxing career was coming to an inconclusive end. My 'comeback' had resulted in the first knockout of my career (albeit a technical one) and a points defeat to a seventeen year old; my brother's marriage to Beryl was clearly coming to an end and the business was in a very bad way after the collapse of one of our main rivals, Thorpe and Porter. They had gone broke owing us £260,000 and the tragedy was that we had not even lost a competitor, because Thorpe and Porter continued to trade under new ownership.

In addition to this, I was about to learn of something that was to totally destroy the relationship between the so called 'Three Musketeers'. One morning when I arrived at work, David was sitting alone in the main downstairs office at Dock Street.

'Sit down, Ralph,' he told me, in a depressing tone. 'We have to talk.'

He told me of an argument that had taken place between Dad and himself prior to my arrival. My father had been looking at the cash-flow figures and was understandably concerned. The bank statement showed that we had an exceedingly large overdraft on the 'Gold Star' account, and he acted as though David was to blame. David had looked at him as though he was mad.

'Surely he can't fail to realize that the bank overdraft is directly related to the enormousness of our stock,' David said to me. 'He must know that the overstocks were due to the commitments that he had made to the American supplier!'

However, Godfrey was convinced that the whole thing was brought about by his so-called 'tycoon' sons who had involved themselves in a number of 'high-falutin' schemes that were bleeding the company dry. That was ridiculous and David had told him so. The course of action which we had to take was obvious. We needed to reduce the American purchases, even if it meant that we broke our commitments with our suppliers. This was a matter of survival.

'You'll do nothing of the sort!' Dad had told him, to which David had responded by suggesting that they should not discuss it until I arrived.

'Let Ralph have the casting vote,' David proposed.

'Vote! 'e gets no vote!' Godfrey had shouted, 'he's got no fucking vote, so he can go and fuck himself, and come to that, so can you!'

'But he holds three shares, the same as you and me,' David insisted.

'Well that is where you are wrong, Mr Tycoon!' Godfrey snapped. 'Two of your brother's shares are controlled by me, I hold a signed transfer, so for the second time you can go and fuck yourself!' With that he had stormed out of the room.

'And that is where we are at,' David told me.

I was dumbstruck and felt weak at the knees. Everything I had worked for seemed to be falling apart at the seams.

'Is it true? Do you believe him?' I asked eventually.

'Yes, I'm afraid I do.'

'But it's not possible,' I stammered, 'I couldn't be that stupid ...' I trailed off, and then asked in a pathetic, resigned way, 'could I?'

David said to me in a calming and sympathetic manner, 'It was a long time ago and I think that Dad was too clever for us by far. We'd better take some professional advice.'

We went to see our accountant. On the way there, David and I talked about our future. We were convinced that Godfrey was right about the signed transfer and, if it were true, he had successfully cheated us out of our rightful positions in the business. We therefore needed to make contingency plans for our future. It would certainly mean that we would split up from Godfrey and start up on our own. It was a daunting prospect in view of the fact that we would be without the foundation of the group of companies that we had helped to build.

Malcolm Harris was the person who dealt primarily with our account at 'Harris Kafton', but he was not able to see us on this occasion. Our appointment was with his partner, Eric Kafton, the more forthright of the two, who normally dealt with Godfrey. Eric invited us into his plush office in Albemarle Street and arranged for coffee. After the normal courtesies we settled down and I told him the whole story. It took some time but as I wound up, I noticed that Eric had a wry smile on his face. When I had finished he said, 'I personally arranged for those transfers to be drawn up. Strictly on your father's instructions, mind you, and I believed that I was acting with your full knowledge and approval. I told your father at the time that he would also need to call an extraordinary meeting, and that you would each need to sign the minutes. He didn't listen to me. The meeting was never called and the transfers are not valid until it is.'

David and I looked at each other, overcome with joy. 'Do you mean the transfers are valueless?' I asked.

'They are not worth the paper they are written on. Your father took advice and disregarded it.'

Once outside David and I hugged each other in total relief ... We were still in business.

We had been seeing less and less of Godfrey during the last few months, as his time had been increasingly taken up with 'Fame Perfume'. Now it was obvious that he no longer wanted to speak to either David or me. It was not hard to follow my father's reasoning. He must have believed all along that we were his employees. However, having been there from the beginning, we had always understood ourselves to be equal partners.

His pride had been hurt, and to him that was everything. The relationship between Godfrey and us was never the same again.

Porn Run

We were living in exciting times. Most women were now on the pill. They wore mini-skirts and kaftans, men wore beads and long hair, and everyone seemed to be smoking pot and enjoying a new sexual freedom ... Not me, I hasten to add. This freedom was also experienced in the theatre. Shows such as *Oh Calcutta* and *Hair* exploited the acceptance of nudity on stage. However, in publishing, there was a call for much more control, even though books such as *Last Exit to Brooklyn*, Henry Miller's *Plexus*, the unexpurgated editions of *Kama Sutra* and *The Perfumed Garden* were given the all clear. The police continued in their pursuit of the retailer, wholesaler or publisher of other 'wicked' books and magazines. Seizures, confiscations and more serious punishments such as imprisonment were common.

Paul Raymond had established a market for girlie magazines in Britain when he published *King*. It was a new concept, far more sophisticated than any other publication produced specifically to be read by the adult male. It cost five shillings and was printed on high grade paper, the quality of the pictures was better, and it contained articles on motor cars, famous buildings and any other subject that would cause the establishment to see the magazine as less offensive and thereby give it a free rein. With a title like *King* this helped. 'Gold Star Publications' and Ben Holloway had imported a range of titles from the United States, but the authorities had seen to it that there was no continuity of supply. They either confiscated the product at the docks or sent in the police to seize it from our warehouses.

King, followed by *Penthouse*, was published and printed in this country. These magazines were far more erotic than anything that we were able to import due to the inconsistencies between the law governing internal publishing, and those controlling importation. Home published magazines outsold our American titles on a scale of over ten to one. We were fighting with one arm tied behind our back.

The Customs at Tilbury Docks had held the photographic negatives to three titles that we intended to publish: *The Single Girl* (an innocuous sex instruction book, with a hint of humour), *Sex and Spice* (a sexy joke book) and *Political Capers* (which was just about the softest girlie available in the whole world). A letter from Tony Hoffman, our lawyer, requesting the solicitor's office at King's Beam House (the Customs & Excise head office) to permit us to censor the film, and remove the offending items, fell on deaf ears.

David was determined to see that we did not lose out entirely

and with the help of Jerry Levine, linked up with an American publisher to print their title, *Nugget* in this country. We called it *Golden Nugget* and planned to launch it as soon as possible to take advantage of the interest that was being shown for home produced magazines.

Once again the authorities intervened. The film which was sent by post, addressed personally to David Gold, care of 'Gold Star Publications', was seized on entry and we were confronted with six months of litigation. It was ironic that any one of the British publications contained articles and photographs that were much more explicit than anything on the film. But this did not interest the censors. They issued a destruction notice. We suspected that the authorities, with the help of the developing computer, were able to keep tabs on us and were blocking us at every avenue. We went ahead with the publication, making our own film directly from the imported magazines. The result was appalling and *Golden Nugget* never did better than break even. We were selling more than ten thousand copies of each issue, but we needed the help of advertising revenue, which was not forthcoming. The only advertisements ever to appear in the magazine were in-house.

If *Golden Nugget* had succeeded then we would, no doubt, have built a successful mail order operation on the back of it, but it did not. Someone once said, 'To be a success in publishing, be daring, be first and be different.' He forgot to say, 'Be lucky.' We did not stand a chance. Our new title fell between two stools. We were too sexy to be sold as an interest magazine, but not sexy enough to compete with our rivals in the girlie field. Within six months we discontinued the title.

However, we were delighted to hear that the courts had deemed as 'disgusting', but not 'obscene' the stock of magazines which had been taken from Long Lane during the previous year, and it came as a bonus to us that the returned merchandise could be delivered directly into our new premises at Dock Street. We saved both the time and the expense of doing it ourselves. In the final analysis, however, we were fast running out of space and some of it had to go into storage.

As these items were being returned we heard news that our main competitor, Ben Holloway, was being raided. It proved beyond doubt that there was no consistency in the behaviour of the authorities, and both Ben's company and ours were obliged to take contingency action. We decided that we would store product that was likely to offend the authorities away from our regular warehouses.

Ben was a lovable rogue who refused to be intimidated by the police, and while we chose to be co-operative, he was determined to tell them to (in his own words), 'Go fuck yourselves,' which did nothing to secure a better relationship with them. On the other hand, David and I as a matter of policy would act with a reasonable degree of respectability and responsibility. It has undoubtedly 'paid off', although not without a great number of knocks along the way.

We were always keen to learn about the various aspects of our industry and we decided that we should be familiar with the activities of the so called 'porn' shops in London. I had only been into one 'porn' shop so far in my life and I felt that David and I could learn more if we spent a few hours in Soho.

We walked into the first shop that we could find and browsed around the racks, only to find that they were selling similar merchandise to that sold in our own shops in Piccadilly, John Adam Street and Archer Street. We were about to leave when a voice came from the far corner of the shop and a man's face emerged through a hatch that had previously appeared to be a normal mirror. It was in fact a two-way mirror and he had been watching us for a full five minutes.

'Would you like to see more?' he inquired.

David hesitated, looked at me for guidance and we walked towards the hatch. A door opened, which had been camouflaged by the books and magazines hanging from it ... We felt like Aladdin and his Genie walking into the cave. On the other side were piles and piles of pornographic literature, much of it sealed in cellophane wrapping. We picked a few of these books up and noticed that there was nothing in the shop that sold for less than seven pounds ten shillings.

There was no way that I was going to spend that amount of money, even for the benefit of our research, so we edged our way towards the door. The shop manager appeared from his office, having kept an eye on us for the whole time. I told him that we wanted to go back to the regular shop to buy some adventure magazines.

He was big and looked aggressive but he opened the door. We pretended to browse for a few moments more before edging towards the exit. Once outside we ran like a couple of kids playing 'knock down ginger'. Our research was complete ... Compared to that stuff, we were selling hymn books.

My dreaded thirtieth birthday came and went. It was difficult to come to terms with being so old. I was still training every day and I was involved in the occasional contest but selection for a representative match was now out of the question. Not only was I a veteran in boxing terms but I was the oldest amateur boxer of that period, and the newspaper reports would not let me forget it. Remarks like, 'His get up and go has got up and gone,' and, 'He won't see twenty five again, he would not even recognize it,' were in good humour, but they made me realize that my boxing days were rapidly coming to an end.

Meanwhile, the business was still expanding. We had acquired premises in Manchester from one of our customers who had gone into liquidation owing us money. This was to become known as our Northern Depot, and before we even had it up and running the Manchester police had raided it.

Once again the police dithered about what to do and finished up taking away a selection of magazines and 'art' books – some of which had previously been cleared by the London police. Initially, they were there looking for pornography but they soon realized that here was a company dealing solely in conventional paperbacks and magazines which were available from regular newsagents throughout the country. However, once on the scene they were obliged to seize something to make it appear that they were doing a worthwhile job, and a selection from what they saw as 'marginal' product would suffice.

The girlie magazines that were generally on sale in WH Smith were rarely taken by the police but any magazines with photographs showing even a trace of pubic hair were seized and as such titles were stored in the Manchester depot, the raid went ahead. As a consequence, it was publicized through the media, and the likes of Mary Whitehouse were satisfied that at least some action was being taken to stem the growth of the so-called porn industry.

Britain was soon to become a fully fledged member of the Common Market and, encouraged by Harold Wilson's drive for new exports, we had started exporting goods as well as importing them. Unfortunately, we were not the only ones to move our attention overseas. Mary Whitehouse had expanded on her desire to 'clean up' Britain, and was channelling her energy towards Europe by helping to form a 'Keep the Continent Clean Association'.

The fact that Denmark, a pornography exporter, had been invited to join the EEC, meant that she had much to say on the subject: 'A flood of filth would wash across the world,' she told reporters. 'I have learned about the significance of pornography on an international level. The deep implications of its spread are fantastically far reaching.' Very emotive stuff, but with the benefit of hindsight we know now that Mary Whitehouse had got it wrong. We know now that a lot of people got it wrong, but that wasn't much consolation at the time.

My business with Woolworth was growing, and on one occasion I made a four o'clock appointment with their remainder book buyer on the same day of my return from the Frankfurt Book Fair. My flight landed at two and I intended to go direct to Woolworth from the airport.

At the Book Fair, I had filled my case with a collection of samples from British publishers. Frankfurt was a long way to go but it was the one time when I was able to see all the paperback publishers in one place at the same time. Corgi Books were about to publish *The Story of O* which was yet another big sex title on the lines of *Fanny Hill* and they were intending to test the censors in the same way ... publish and be damned.

They presented me with a promotional booklet about the novel which contained excerpts from the text. On my return, I was stopped by a customs officer who treated this booklet as though it was some secret and dangerous document. I was taken to a bleak room to await a special investigations officer and was kept there for more than thirty minutes. I began to realize that I would not now make my appointment at Woolworth. It seems ridiculous that I attached so much importance to the meeting, but the pressure was immense and I am sure that I aged a few years whilst waiting.

When the officer finally arrived I was closely questioned. A smuggler of drugs would not have had to go through a stiffer interrogation. Needless to say, I was released although many of the samples were confiscated including *The Story of O* promotional leaflet which had contained paragraphs such as the following:

> ... at the same instant, her legs were spread apart and her lips gently worked open – hair grazed the inner surface of her thighs ...

> ... One of the men gripped her buttocks and sank himself into her womb. When he was done, he ceded his place to a second.

> The third wanted to drive his way into the narrower passage and wrung a scream of pleasure from her lips ...

After all of the indignities that I had suffered, the unexpurgated paperback edition of Pauline Reage's book was published less than three months later by Corgi Books (Transworld Publishers Limited) and no action was taken by the authorities.

Even so, it was a long time before I was able to get another appointment with Woolworth.

Breakthrough

David and I tried hard to make things work with Godfrey, although it was hard to forgive and forget. David and I, however, were more than ready to. For Dad, though, it was more difficult. We were even selling his perfume along with our books through a franchise scheme, and I hoped that this would at least keep us in touch and that in time the wound would heal. I dreaded the prospect of the business falling apart as a result of the recent confrontation, and I was determined to ensure that a solution would be found. I was pleased when I learned that David and Dad had discussed the current cash-flow problem, and that Dad had finally agreed that we should reduce supplies wherever possible to ease the overdraft situation, which was something that David had urgently recommended more than a year earlier.

However, the main dispute between us was still festering into something very serious. It seemed there was no solution, unless Dad came to terms with the fact that he was senior only because of his age and for no other reason.

We had recently acquired an ideal new warehouse premises in Whyteleafe, Surrey. Dad had approved the move, albeit reluctantly, and David and I had no hesitation in offering the most prestigious office to him. But Godfrey showed no interest. He said he doubted he would move from the old site at Dock Street, and made it clear that he did not give our side of the business another six months. In his opinion we were due to fail, and on that basis both the move, and the huge commitment, would be academic.

When Dad's brother, Gerald, visited England for the first time since emigrating to Australia, it created a great deal of excitement in the family. I naturally insisted that he stayed with Joan and me, and Joan prepared the guest room while I went to London Airport to meet him.

Gerald had been making marvellous progress in Australia. He too had set up in the book trade, and we were receiving substantial orders from him, mainly for paperbacks, which would fill twenty foot containers. Gerald was now supplying our paperback imprint, Knight Books, to milk-bar outlets throughout Australia.

He arranged to see his brother Godfrey but first agreed to have dinner with David and me at our favourite restaurant. We spent hours discussing the 'break up' and Gerald wanted to do all that he could to bring about a reconciliation. David and I were pleased about this and we put forward ideas, hoping that Gerald could convey the right message.

Gerald hired a car and phoned me from Dock Street to tell me that he was going to collect some papers from Whyteleafe. 'And by the way,' he whispered into the phone, 'Goddy will be with me.'

'I don't know if I'm pleased or not,' I said to David. 'I wonder how he will behave with the staff – after all he hardly knows them and he is so unpredictable. I hope he likes his office....'

'Ralph,' David interjected, 'don't worry. What will be, will be,' he said, and went on with what he was doing.

Less than an hour later, Gerald pulled up in the car park outside my first floor office. I was a little nervous as I walked out to greet them. It had been nearly a year since I had seen or spoken to my father. Gerald was getting out of the car as I went around to Godfrey's side to open the door for him. As I did so I put my hand before him and said, 'Hi, Dad.' Gerald was smiling and seemed happy that he had brought about this meeting. Two seconds later the smile left his lips as Godfrey forcefully slammed the door, missing my arm by a whisker. The door was closed ... literally.

I was walking back to my office feeling very despondent when David appeared in the passageway. He had seen the whole incident from his office window. He put his arm round my shoulder. 'Ralph, forget it. You did your best and you could have done no more.'

David was right, of course, but I hated it. I knew then that Dad would hold out forever. I reflected on my mixed feelings for him. When I was young, I had been ashamed of him because he was nearly always in prison, but still I loved him and each time I wanted him to come home so much. Later, I was so proud of his guts, determination and even the occasional show of affection. I knew that my mother could have been happier with someone else and I knew that because I had loved my father so much, she was now alone ... It's a tough old world.

Her Majesty's Customs at Tilbury Dock had seized another large consignment of magazines. There had been a period when both the police and the Customs had allowed us to get on with our business, but now they were again giving in to the pressures forced upon them by the likes of Mary Whitehouse and Lord Longford, another character who was making himself known as the saviour of public morality.

Both the Customs authorities and the police would speak to us 'off the record' to say that they were in the hands of the 'powers that be', and they were only 'doing their job'. It was a case of appeasing the establishment by getting the numbers right; when they raided a dealer in hard-core pornography they would seize perhaps only 500 copies of indisputably illegal product, but the street value would be less than £5000. When they raided us, however, they would boost their seizure figures by taking away at least 500,000 girlie magazines and sexy paperbacks with a full sale value of over £1 million. This would help to justify the huge amounts that they were to spend on storage, filing, documentation and manpower. The figures would be submitted to the Home Office who would publish them knowing that Mary Whitehouse and other bigots would be placated.

*

When the newspapers reported that there was going to be a six day 'Sex Fair' in Copenhagen I could not believe it. The fact that they had abolished all censorship there, two years earlier, made no difference. I was stunned to read that the general public were free to walk around a hall in which live sex shows and continuous pornographic movies were being exhibited. The general view according to an authoritative report was that it was a good idea and that such things were very much needed.

In addition to the 'all action' shows there were displays of sex products and marital aids. The general public were allowed in for only the last two days as the exhibition was primarily for the benefit of the sex wholesalers and retailers. I was surprised to learn of the high number of sex shops trading in Europe.

A German company called 'Beate Uhse' was making a name for itself in this field. Hundreds of their shops throughout Europe sold sex products while their head office, comprising nearly one hundred thousand square feet of floor space in Flensburg, conducted a mail order service unparalleled throughout the world. Their success was staggering.

We obtained one of their catalogues and were surprised to see the type of product that was being sold openly; battery-powered massagers which had the appearance of a penis, condoms of every colour, shape and size, rubber and leather clothing and a variety of lotions and potions. David was confident that it would not be long before this type of merchandise would be on open sale in Great Britain ... but I had my doubts.

I had started visiting the various remainder dealers in London and Manchester because many of them would buy remainder paperbacks and product that I could use in franchise schemes or sell to Uncle Gerald in Australia. It was from one of these dealers that I heard about a 'parcel' of sex aids he had rejected on the grounds that it was too risqué. Following this tip-off, I went to see the 'parcel' for myself.

The salvaged goods were laid out in a riverside building close to Tower Bridge where I went to view them. Feeling like a character from a Charles Dickens book, I climbed the stone stairway into a huge warehouse where piles of salvaged stock were laid out in lines ready for inspection. A tall thin man with a goatee beard came over to me and asked what I was looking for. I told him that I understood that he had a parcel of adult product to sell. He responded with a big smile and pointed me to an area in the far corner.

As I came closer I saw hundreds of artificial penises, vibrators and funny little things for which I could not perceive a use. Nevertheless I found it difficult to turn my back on a bargain. The asking price was £20,000 and I finally agreed to pay £6550 cash on collection, which I arranged to take effect the very next morning. This was a parcel that I did not want to lose.

A Shadow

I do not think that under normal circumstances more than three days ever go by when I do not speak to my mother. Even before my father left home, Mum looked to me for support and I have always responded. I cared about her shop, her relationships, but most of all her health.

One autumn morning she phoned me to say that she was worried following a visit to a mass radiography unit. She had subsequently received a letter suggesting that she consult her doctor within the next few days. 'There is nothing to worry about,' I assured her, 'but of course you must go sooner rather than later.'

I telephoned the medical director who advised me to make an appointment for my mother to attend a clinic close to the docks in Beckton. They had the necessary equipment and no doubt could deal with any problems on the spot. I offered to take Mum to the clinic but she insisted on going alone. Not wanting to dramatize the event, I agreed, but I sat by the phone all of the following morning just waiting for news. Before midday it rang and Dr Lawless's secretary told me that the doctor wanted to speak to me, and I knew then that there was a problem. 'I will be there in less than an hour,' I informed him, and I was in my car within minutes.

As I sped along the Barking Road I was forced to slow down

behind a bus which displayed two large advertisements showing on the left hand side an x-ray picture of a healthy lung, and on the right hand side, a lung distorted by a cancer as big as an apple. These posters were part of a 'stop smoking' campaign. 'Mum smokes over fifty cigarettes a day,' I reflected, 'and now she may be paying the price!'

Mum greeted me close to tears. She knew that something was wrong but she was more than ready to leave it to me to make things right again. I asked her to wait outside while I spoke to the doctor. The news was bad; the picture that he displayed on the screen was no different from the one that I had seen on the back of the bus.

'What's your prognosis?' I asked. He remained silent for a few moments, then without looking into my eyes, he said, 'I'm afraid that it is almost certainly cancer and I can offer no more than a small chance that your mother will live for very long. I have given her an antibiotic, although the possibility of that,' he said as he pointed at the screen, 'being an infection is very small indeed. I have arranged for her to see a specialist in a month's time.'

'Doctor,' I suggested, 'for the moment forget that's my mother,' I said, referring to the screen. 'That's your wife, or the person that you love most in the whole world. Now what would you do?'

He paused for a moment. 'The same,' he said. 'Only I would arrange for her to see the same consultant, Mr Flavell, without delay.' Before the words were out of his mouth I told him that I wanted Mum and me to see Mr Flavell the next day, if possible.

I called David at the office and asked him to meet me at my house in an hour. Then I spoke to Mum and told her the situation without implying that it was more than an infection which might have to be removed from her lung. Mum smiled, put her hand on my arm and said, 'Thanks for coming. I know that everything will be alright now.'

David was at home sitting with Joan when I arrived. I needed to be alone with him and I asked Joan to excuse us while I took David into the garage which was accessed directly through the kitchen.

'David,' I blurted out, the moment we were alone, 'Mum has cancer and there's little that they can do.' My brother burst into tears and this somehow released a tension that had built up in me for hours, and I cried too. It was some time before we were able to talk again but eventually I told him the facts. When we had composed ourselves sufficiently we informed Joan of the bad news. We had a cup of tea and it took time for us to find the strength to tell Marie.

I took Mum to see Mr Flavell at the London Hospital. She was very nervous but he put her at ease while he arranged for more x-rays and tests. He told me that he would admit her within the next few weeks for major surgery. I pleaded with him to operate as soon as possible, as I somehow knew there wasn't a moment to lose.

After deliberation he arranged for her to come in on Sunday which was only three days later. I was delighted, I knew that Mum could not cope with a delay ... she was not the only one.

The operation took place on a Monday. When Marie, David and I arrived she had been in surgery for nearly four hours and was still there. All three of us sat in the waiting room, until I elected to take a walk along the corridor. It was there that I greeted the surgeon, Mr Flavell. He was still wearing his theatre gown. After removing his mask he told me that my mother might not live through the day. He had removed most of her lung and then found it necessary to take tissue from her heart. Only time would tell whether he had removed the whole of the cancer – assuming she survived the operation.

It was a miserable day in November 1970 when David and I went to Kensal Rise in north west London to see an old friend in the business, Russell Gaye. Russell had been a friendly competitor of ours since the early days when we were establishing ourselves as publishers and distributors of books and magazines.

The meeting was not particularly successful. Nevertheless, our visit to Kensal Rise proved to be one of the most exciting and inspiring days of our business lives. On the return journey, driving down Edgware Road towards Marble Arch, David mentioned to me that we had dealings with a customer in this area, and he was sure that he owed us money. He could not remember the principal's name. However, he did remember the name of one of his shops. It was 'Ann Summers'.

'Isn't that the new sex shop?' I asked. I had read about a shop which had caused an unbelievable commotion when it had recently opened. Evidently, the sales had been sensational and the press had reported that queues were being formed around the block at Marble Arch causing confusion because they mixed with people queuing to see *Mary Poppins* at the Odeon cinema. I wanted to see what all the fuss was about, so I asked David to pull over and park the car.

The Ann Summers shop was very busy and there was even a line of people queuing at the pay desk. I was pleased to see that some of them were female. Previously, marital aids had been offered for sale exclusively by post, with the promise of absolute discretion, in brown sealed envelopes and packages. Here they were being openly sold in a huge high street shop. I was happy to see that Britain appeared to be 'growing up', although I found it hard to accept that this 'freedom' would last for very long.

For more than ten years I had been selling magazines and books which referred to sexual intimacy – publications that showed men and women in the most erotic poses. I firmly believed that selling them was for the public good and I was sure that there was even more of a public need for marital aids. However, I found it hard to come to terms with the fact that they were being openly sold in a high street shop.

Walking through the door, I hesitate to say, I was embarrassed in case someone I knew saw me – something of an irony, but we were living in times when men would not have thought about, or admitted to needing help with their sex lives.

Once inside we found ourselves looking around an expensively fitted shop that displayed a variety of vibrators, dildos, lotions, potions, novelties and books which mainly offered advice on sex. It was these books that had in the main been supplied to Ann

Summers by our company, and it was for these books that the owner was reluctant to make payment.

'Why?' I asked David.

'Why indeed?' He shrugged. 'This place is packed out, he must be making a fortune.'

We each picked out a few items and took our place in the long queue. We waited for at least fifteen minutes before we were served by the young lady assistant who did a calculation on her modern till, and asked for seven pounds and twenty pence.

'That's seven pounds four shillings,' she informed me, as though I were incapable of working out the new money.

I looked at what I had bought and could not believe the figure. 'Sorry?' I questioned, as though she had spoken to me in another language.

'Seven pounds twenty pence,' she repeated.

I opened the plastic bag which had a picture of a big red apple displayed under the name, Ann Summers, and peered in at the four items that I was about to purchase. Two of them (according to the labels) were clitoral stimulators, the third was a delay spray and the fourth a massager (vibrator) which was in a blister pack topped by a picture of a lady who for some reason had the object laid provocatively against her cheek.

I reluctantly paid the money, and David and I agreed that we should return to the office ... we had a lot to discuss. We had put only sixpence into the parking meter outside the shop, but we had overrun the thirty minutes and sure enough a policeman was placing a ticket on the screen of my new white Rover 2000. Despite the fact that I apologized profusely, he still left the ticket and walked away.

I was livid. I had just spent over seven pounds for a few bits and pieces, and here I was being expected to pay another two pounds in addition to the original sixpence which I had put into the parking meter. David consoled me by saying, 'Never mind Ralph we will put it down to 'R and D'.'

'What's that, ripped off and done over?' I asked.

'No Research and Development, you fool.' I knew very well

what 'R and D' meant, and we certainly had a great deal of research to do before we could develop into the sex market.

I began my own research at home. I didn't talk it through with Joan. I just removed the items from the Ann Summers bag and put them into my bedside drawer, and when we made love I put on the 'Romeo', one of the three types of clitoral stimulators. These were supposed to be fitted onto the base of the penis, and as the brush-like tips were pushed at the clitoris it enhanced the whole proceedings. But this just did not happen for me. The 'Romeo' had a pronged rubber tongue protruding from a rubber ring that was supposed to hold it firm against the base of my penis, but the ring rolled round and round and the tongue stuck down instead of up. Not only that, it went up and down the shaft, making a nuisance of itself. We had no alternative but to interrupt the proceedings and talk ... which in itself was a marital aid.

I did achieve a great deal from the delay spray. It had set me back nearly three pounds but was worth every penny. I was learning that the commodities on sale in a sex shop were no different from any other leisure products – the true value was indefinable. I knew that I wanted to be part of that business in the knowledge that I could make a great deal of money ... If in the meantime I made some people happy, then that was a bonus.

From then on, David and I left no stone unturned in our determination to learn more about the sex business in general, and Ann Summers in particular. This apparently highly successful company owed us money and something did not add up. How did a shop that was purported to take over four thousand pounds a week have difficulty in paying a four hundred and fifty pound invoice?

I first discovered that Ann Summers was the brainchild of a man referred to as 'Dandy Kim' although his real name was Michael Waterfield.

Kim had had some success with 'Variations on a Sexual Theme', and was determined to establish himself in the sex industry. He had heard of the enormous breakthrough of 'Beate Uhse' into the

German mail order and sex shop business and hoped to emulate them. He decided to investigate their activities and he contrived a scheme that would enable him to get right into the heart of the organization. He hired a Rolls-Royce and chauffeur and he approached Dirk Rottermond, the managing director, with a view to interviewing him for a British magazine. He took with him an expensive camera which he had hired for effect. Herr Rottermond allowed him to go around his factory and some of his shops to take pictures. Kim Waterfield spent four days there after which he had obtained enough information on suppliers and their approach to retailing to consider opening the first sex shop in Britain.

After his fact-finding tour at 'Beate Uhse' in Flensburg he had discovered Doctor Manfred Volbrecht, a leading manufacturer of sex creams, lotions and potions who was prepared to supply the British company on good discount and credit terms.

Kim Waterfield was in a 'go' position, but he first needed a good shop in a prime site. He discovered a property at Marble Arch which was owned by the Church Commission who needed only to be assured that Kim Waterfield was potentially a good tenant before they would give him a lease. How he succeeded in achieving that I will never know, but he did, and the Church Commission were the landlords of Britain's first sex shop.

Next he had needed a high quality name which, according to him, would portray a good image for the new sex industry. The success of the German company, using the name 'Beate' prompted him to choose a female name. He decided on Ann Summers believing that it typified an English rose.

He had engaged Caroline Teague as his secretary. Caroline was twenty nine years old and had been the manageress of his country estate at 'Sedgehill' Manor in Dorset during a time when Kim Waterfield was affluent. He then owned a helicopter as well as a stable of fine horses and his lifestyle and mode of dress had been visibly extravagant. It was said that he bragged of a relationship with a member of the Royal Family with whom he shared a 'love nest' in Wapping, although there was never any proof of this.

Kim re-established contact with Caroline, who had also been

his mistress, and put a number of proposals to her. First, that she should change her name by deed poll and become officially 'Ann Summers'. After that she would be given a directorship and a salary of £10,000 per annum. From then on she would front the whole enterprise. Kim had changed his outlook about press coverage. He loved being the playboy lord of the manor and he encouraged the gossip columnists to publicize his activities (no matter how outrageous). But, because of his Catholic upbringing, he was embarrassed about his involvement in the sex trade. Even his own published book, *Variations on a Sexual Theme* was written under the pseudonym of Terence Hendrickson.

The grand opening of the shop in Marble Arch was sensational. David Wynne Morgan and Guy Knowles were taken on as public relations consultants and with the help of Klaus Uhse (son of Beate) they succeeded in achieving maximum media attention. Every tabloid and even some of the more serious newspapers carried stories on the grand opening of Britain's first 'sex supermarket'.

The newly named Ann Summers was interviewed on television and radio as well as for magazines and newspapers. She was beautiful and articulate and readers of the London *Evening Standard* acclaimed her as 'The Woman of the Year' in 1971.

What more could Kim Waterfield ask for? There was only one thing that she did not have in abundance ... And that was money. Despite his early success with the Marble Arch shop and his expansion into Bristol he was soon back in financial difficulty. His extravagance, flamboyance and his showmanship meant that he could not possibly survive.

We were keen to meet Kim Waterfield as soon as possible, and arranged to have lunch with him in the Waldorf Hotel. Waterfield wanted to meet for dinner, but David and I insisted on lunch as it was only a preliminary meeting. Over lunch he told us the reason why the company had failed. He explained that after establishing a booming mail order business, it had been ruined by a postal strike that lasted for months. No money came in while his commitments, such as staff and salary continued to burn up the profits from the shop in Marble Arch. He failed to tell us that the biggest commitment was his own extraordinarily high salary. His wage bill was high, but with an annual turnover close to a quarter of a million pounds and a very high mark up on his product, he thought that it was a bottomless pit ... Kim Waterfield would be the first to admit that he was incapable of balancing the books, and his business was doomed.

According to the appointed liquidator, Bernard Phillips, these extraordinary overheads had led to a deficit of £78,000. Ann Summers and her fiancé, David Jones, a public relations consultant, attended the initial meeting of creditors where Ann agreed with the accusation that too much money had been taken out of the company but insisted that none of it had gone to her.

All fingers were pointed in one direction, but nothing untoward could be proven and a normal winding up was to go ahead.

Bernard Phillips asked for tenders to purchase the assets which comprised the two existing leasehold shops and the Ann Summers name and logo ... We were to make a bid.

An English Rose
and Its Thorn

My brother and I have traded on the principle that our business should be run within the confines of the law. We have tried wherever possible to reach a working arrangement with the police and customs, but they were never prepared to listen to us. One person who did listen was Lord Longford. An ageing father of nine children who had spent his life being good (presumably in bed as well) and self righteous, he was now in the throes of producing his controversial report on pornography. David and I wrote to him and suggested that we could help with research for his report, and were invited to his office. We felt that our input would be of great value to him and at the same time we would gain by presenting a case for better control over the 'hard core' pornography market. But our promise to help was to backfire.

I was able to express my own view about what constituted pornography. It was certainly not pictures of the human body, no matter how explicit. Pornography in my eyes is the portrayal of any form of violence, sexual or otherwise. Lord Longford appeared to listen intently ... although with the benefit of hindsight, I now know that he had not taken in one word of what had been said.

He showed David and me a selection of magazines that he had

brought back from the continent. They were so horrifying that I felt sick and could not even satisfy my curiosity by taking more than a cursory glance through them. They were appalling to me, but strangely His Lordship had by now seen so much of this filth that he was no longer affected by it.

We took along a selection of our own publications which we presented to him in the belief that our range was clearly within the bounds of accepta-bility. *New Direction* had now been established as an interesting monthly magazine about sex and its sister magazine, *In Depth* was about to prove that there was a place for a magazine that was exclusively aimed at solving sexual problems.

We had already sold over 150,000 copies of a booklet of sex positions called *Intercourse*, and another 'one-off' magazine, *Ways of Loving*, was already a bestseller. Lord Longford was a long way from being impressed, and once again David and I were bemused by the fact that he could see little difference between the horrendous pornography which he had shown to us and the magazines and books that we were responsible for publishing.

Lord Longford was a very strange man. He was pleasant enough but seemed totally biased and his forthcoming report could not possibly be of any value. He was seen as a weird individual by most of the industry ... He even wore a dirty raincoat.

The last straw was the statement that he made to the press after visiting a 'live show' in Amsterdam, when he quoted, 'I have seen enough for science and more than enough for pleasure.' I believe that everyone had seen more than enough of him. We had come forward with a genuine desire to help him to see the other side of the argument but we were about to be hoisted by our own petard.

We waited patiently for the publication of the Longford report and so it seemed did the police. There had been no seizures from our warehouse in Whyteleafe for nearly a year, at which time they had taken away the remaining stock of a 'one shot' magazine called *Brutus*. We anticipated no further action regarding it. The magazine was no more than a fictitious, albeit historically correct, story about Brutus, the games master of the Colosseum. The activities were portrayed by the author, David Gray and the brilliant Italian artist, Angelo Angellini. The orgy scenes and the evils of the games were titillating and some of it horrifying ... but obscene? Never!

The lull in police activities enabled us to get on and progress our publishing and distribution enterprises. Since acquiring the 'salvaged' marital aid stock we had added a marital aid range to our mail order line. Mail order was becoming a significant part of our business, and a new company was formed to handle it, originally named 'Elixir Marital Aids', and then renamed 'Lydcare'.

We were not the only people interested in talking with Kim Waterfield. His former printer, Karl Slack, had not been paid for producing his catalogues and in view of the fact that payment was becoming less likely by the day, he had accepted a range of marital aids in lieu. In order to dispose of this stock he had formed a partnership with Harry Rogers who owned a number of West End bookshops, trading as 'Lovecraft'.

We were living in an age when people had been starved of sex product, and only now was it available in a 'normal' shop where almost anything of a sexual nature could be sold. Even if, at times, it was absolute rubbish. There was talk that in one of Karl and Harry's shops they sold jars of vaseline with a label stating that it was some weird and wonderful ointment, which when applied to the penis would guarantee the 'smoothest ride of all time'. For this the gullible customer would pay as much as five pounds. Yeast tablets were relabelled as 'Spanish Fly Tablets' and vitamin pills were sold as 'Go Go' tablets. Karl Slack told me that a shoplifter actually brought back one of his vibrators and said 'I'm returning this. I'm a shoplifter and if you think that I'm going to risk my liberty for this rubbish, you're mistaken.'

The amazing thing was that these obvious 'cons' were no different from the doctor supplying sugar tablets for a headache or perfumeries offering scents to drive your man wild – if they work, they work! And more often than not they did.

I knew I was not easily going to deter Karl Slack and Harry Rogers from making a bid for Ann Summers, but it was paramount to avoid a 'Dutch' auction, with us bidding blind against each other, that would have been stupid. After several meetings, we agreed with Harry and Karl that we would each present a sealed envelope containing the figure which reflected the highest amount we were prepared to pay for the assets. The difference between the two figures would be paid to the loser by the winning party – on that basis the loser would at least receive some compensation for stepping down.

David, Ron and I agreed to offer the sum of £20,110. We believed that they would put forward a bid of £20,000, which had been mentioned during our earlier discussions. Our extra £110 bid was a hedge against the other side's possible £20,100 bid which we felt they might have been considering.

When we finally met for the envelope-opening formality, there was a great deal of tension in the air. We were immensely relieved when Harry and Karl's offer of £15,101 was revealed – £5,009 less than ours. Harry and Karl were magnanimous in defeat, although I wondered if they had actually lost as I paid them the difference between the two bids. We now had no known competition in our endeavour to take over Ann Summers. Within a week it was ours.

In Depth and *New Direction* were now regular monthly publications. We were publishing a number of other magazine titles as well as a range of popular sex instruction books. We needed to make space for a bigger 'art department' and David made arrangements for a mezzanine floor to be erected in the Whyteleafe warehouse to accommodate it.

Many of the photographic shoots for our publications took place in rented studios or rented homes, but it was suggested one day that an outdoor location was needed. And where better than the woodland close to the Whyteleafe head office?

The books *The Adventures of Fanny Hill in Pictures* and *Sappho of Lesbos* required the models to dress and undress in appropriate 'costume'. The sessions were to last for a few days, and suitcases of Roman and period clothing were carried up through the wooded area to a piece of common ground which provided the ideal setting.

The photographer, Horace Ward, later reported back to me details of the farce that had taken place. The models changed into their costumes behind a little clump of trees, and as they walked back towards Horace and the art director, Bernie Rickman, they heard someone chipping away with a hammer at some rocks. They put down their cases and walked over to a middle-aged man and tapped him on the shoulder.

'Excuse us, but are we on the right track for Rome?'

The man dropped his chisel, his mouth opened and stayed that way for some time. Then he spluttered, 'I don't know, I'm only here looking for fossils!'

The chances of meeting one man in the middle of Whyteleafe Hills during the week is remote, but as they were actually filming another man arrived. He was dressed in a suit and said that he represented the City of London Corporation, and showed them his credentials. The models in the meantime were lying in the grass with hardly any clothes on, which made it awkward for them to move. The man was insistent that they did just that, because use of the common ground for commercial purposes was not permitted without prior consent ... *He* was on common ground but he was without common sense. They waited until the man was out of sight before continuing with the filming.

The photographers were always on low budgets, and when

Horace asked me if he could use my office for a shoot at the weekend rather than hire one, I had to agree. I have been in the business for more than thirty years and I have never attended a photographic shoot, but that Saturday I was tempted to do a little weekend overtime. But still I resisted ... Shmuck.

David and I were not at the Whyteleafe premises on the day the police called for the second time since we had moved into them, but Ron Coleman, our chief executive, made them welcome, in accordance with our policy. David Pritchard, the warehouse manager, assisted them in every way, and even supplied the fork lift truck and its driver to stack their 'booty' onto five lorries. Amongst the stock taken were big quantities of the early editions of *New Direction* and *In Depth*, and Sue Caron's successful book, *A Woman's Look at Oral Love* (Sue had originally been my secretary before her writing and editorial talents became apparent). A detective inspector led the 'raid'. He told Ron, over a cup of tea, that this time things were more serious as the DPP was looking for a 'Section Two' prosecution which he was confident of winning. In addition, he would also be seeking the maximum sentence of two years in prison.

When David and I returned, Ron told us exactly what had happened including the remarks made by the detective inspector. We were both very concerned about this new development. Weeks went by, but without any sign of the usual seizure notice and destruction order. There had been a lot of talk in the press that the Director of Public Prosecutions should be taking stronger action against the 'porn barons'. David and I would not have been unhappy if he had. But instead he chose to take action against us.

Out of the blue we received a summons to appear at Croydon Court to defend the publishing of *Brutus*, which had been seized in the earlier raid. To our amazement the case was to be heard under 'Section Two' of the Obscene Publications Act. This was of particular concern because we were anticipating a summons on the more recent raid, and in view of the remarks made by the officer in charge, the DPP was leaving no stone unturned. If David were to be found guilty ('found' was the operative word –

there was no way that he could, in fact, be guilty) then prison was a strong possibility. If he 'got off', then the DPP had another trial up his sleeve. David was undaunted. He used his well-worn phrase, 'It is what it is and we are what we are.' He went on, 'If I have to go to jail then I will cope, but I refuse to capitulate to these bigots.'

In the meantime, the 'porn barons' continued to sell publications depicting violence, and involving children and animals. The tobacco manufacturers went about their business, too, despite the latest report from the Royal College of Physicians on smoking and health. Thousands of people were dying each year as a direct result of smoking. The tobacco 'barons' were in agreement with the government that they should print on their cigarette packets a statement that, 'Smoking can cause lung cancer.' David and I thought about printing on our cover a statement: 'Beware! Reading this magazine can cause an erection which may result in masturbation, or even fornication.'

The comparison says it all. Punishment for causing said erection – eight months in jail; punishment for causing cancer and heart disease – a knighthood.

Longford Report

The *Longford Report* was due out at any time and the press were having a field day. Lord Longford was featured throughout the media usually as a fumbling old fool. The newspapers were 'cashing in' by informing their readers of revelations of the full-frontal world of 'nudes, sex and smut'. Even the *Daily Mirror* was prepared to publish pictures of the participants of a live show; one centre page picture showed a naked woman with her breasts exposed and by implication, she was using a vibrator 'down below'. In the same picture, members of the Longford Committee were clearly enjoying themselves.

Lord Longford's objective was to denounce porn and to bury forever the suggestion that pornography could act as a safety valve, and even lead to a decrease in sexual crimes. He became a laughing stock, and it reached its peak when he walked out of a live sex show in Copenhagen with the manager protesting, 'But sir, you haven't seen the intercourse yet!' On his return he posed the question, 'Why are people laughing at me?' ... I wasn't laughing. I knew that it was Lord Longford who would have the last laugh! His expenses had been met by a substantial grant from the 'Will's Tobacco' Family Trust and his book was a bestseller ... In his own way he had cashed in on porn.

Our solicitor, David Offenbach, was said to be the best solicitor in Britain for dealing with obscenity cases. To my amazement he was no older than me, but he was extremely competent and already had a number of successes under his belt. We were confident that he had made the right choice when he informed us that he had engaged John Mortimer QC to act for us. We had never heard of him but David Offenbach would not have risked his ever growing reputation by taking on anyone but the best. John Mortimer's junior, Geoffrey Robertson, was appointed to assist. He was full of enthusiasm and believed passionately in our innocence; we were well aware of being in capable hands.

I had always been in awe of barristers. My mind drifted back to the few court cases, such as the *Fanny Hill* trial and my own ridiculous guilty plea at the Old Bailey more than eight years earlier. It was all history, but for me the bitter memory would live forever. The counsel then were aloof and arrogant. John Mortimer and Geoffrey Robertson, on the other hand, were friendly and approachable. This case should never have been brought before the magistrates and in the absence of a jury things could easily have gone wrong ... Thankfully they didn't. John Mortimer's summing up lasted for more than an hour, during which time I noticed him characteristically twiddling with a piece of string behind his back. He has strong personal views on the subject of censorship and has frequently stated that 'all life is the writer's subject'. On this day he put his feelings across with great eloquence and after two long hours the magistrates decided that the book was not obscene and David was released from the dock.

But David's ordeal was far from over. John Mortimer and Geoffrey Robertson were on standby for the forthcoming Old Bailey trial involving *New Direction* and *In Depth* magazines, in addition to two paperback books, *Lesbian Lovers* and *A Woman's Look at Oral Love*. They gave us a lot of confidence, but the thought of David standing before judge and jury yet again, and the possibility of a two year prison sentence, was awesome.

As the early copies of the *Longford Report* were released to the media, David and I suddenly became public figures. Lord Longford, surprisingly, had treated us quite fairly, indicating that we were genuinely seeking guidance and that we would accept any reasonable line drawn. He wrote of our loathing of the portrayal of violence, animal sex and the abuse of children.

He went on to say that we abhorred live sex shows which was not true – neither David nor I had given him our view on the subject. It was obvious that Lord Longford had not been a good listener.

He wrote that our distribution comprising more than 20,000 outlets all over the country, three London bookshops, and the recently acquired Ann Summers sex shops, showed us to be the leaders in the field of pornography, albeit soft. But in the report, that was inconsequential; pornography was still pornography. The implication that we were the market leaders was picked up by the *Sunday Telegraph*, and their reporter and a team of photographers were waiting on our doorstep at 'Gadoline House' (the name given to our Whyteleafe head office). He was so pleasant that one could almost believe that he had come over to interview Ralph and David Gold, the publishers of *The Life and Times of Mother Theresa*, instead of the Gold Brothers, Britain's so-called leading publishers of pornography.

Our first thought was to refuse to see him, and he waited in reception while David and I deliberated. Eventually we agreed to invite him up, although we were well aware that we might once again be putting our heads into the lion's mouth. We immediately made it clear that we wanted no publicity, that our connections with the media had not been favourable in the past, and we were not prepared to give him an interview. He only wanted to photograph us and to write a small article which would give us the chance to refute Lord Longford's implications. 'Trust me,' he said, 'I'm a reporter and I'm here to help you,' which was as corny as the line, 'Take your clothes off and lie down – trust me, I'm a doctor.'

David told him directly that we were not confident about his sincerity and at that moment we noticed the change from Doctor Jekyll to Mr Hyde, as he told us that if we were not prepared to co-operate, then we would be a great deal worse off as he could not project our side of the 'story' without hearing it. He made it clear that if we did not allow him to photograph us in the comfort of our own office then he intended to catch us in a furtive shot as we left it. He advised us that we would finish up in the *Telegraph* come what may. We were trapped, and not for the first or last time forced to give in to a form of blackmail.

A day or two later, a phone call from a neighbour alerted me to the front page article:

BROTHERS HEAD BOOK TRADE

Two brothers, Mr David Gold 36, and Mr Ralph Gold, 34 are named by the Earl of Longford among the chiefs of the pornographic book trade in Britain...

Despite our protestations, fairly printed in the article, the damage had already been done. The inaccurate implications were there. We were deemed to be pornographers which was untrue, but it had been quoted by a 'respectable' newspaper, and on that basis the mud would stick.

We were advised to issue a libel writ immediately, which we did. We also demanded an apology which was not forthcoming. A period of time lapsed and after consultation with leading counsel, we realized it was unlikely that we would win damages. In fact, proceedings would only serve to make things worse.

As a direct consequence of the article Wendy, our sweet and gentle baby minder, informed us that she could no longer sit for us. It could have been coincidental but Joann (pronounced Jo-ann as she now liked to be called) and I knew otherwise. The time was right to start afresh and look for a new house, but I realized that life would never be the same again for me or my family.

I read my own magazines each month and, not just from a professional point of view, I liked them, especially *New Direction* which I felt was informative and could well help me to overcome my own inhibitions. Unfortunately womenfolk, Joann included, had not yet emerged from their 'shells', and magazines of this sort were rarely even looked at by them. I am firmly of the opinion that had we studied together the sex manuals and magazines of the time, then Joann and I would be happily married to this day.

In the early seventies, Thomas Main, a doctor who trained colleagues to deal with psychological problems of sex, published a report in which he claimed that women were desperately in need of help to enjoy their sex lives. He claimed that over fifty per cent of women who went to him for birth control advice were shyly hoping to find a solution to their sex problems. Their 'shyness' equally prevented them from reading our magazines.

In view of the pending court case I had looked out for newspaper items about us. One very profound letter that I discovered was a published in the *Sutton and Cheam Herald*;

> GSP's magazines are in part informative and educational... They are, in large measure, sexually titillating. But who is to deny that many, and not only the lonely and unattractive, at times have a need for such stimulation. May I say that they have every right, within the law, to publish magazines to meet a need. I feel strongly that we would all be better engaged fighting our real and common enemy, hatred and violence in our society. ...

Few could disagree with him.

Other family doctors were making statements in support of sex aids. Many were in favour of them being obtainable on the national health. 'These things are not just kinky but of medical value,' it was stated in an article in the *General Practitioner* ... Few would disagree with that either.

Not a moment went by when I did not think about the impending court case. The possibility of David winning was very slim. He had attended Croydon Court for the formality of being committed to the Old Bailey to defend the publishing of the offending titles 'for gain'. The court made it sound as though 'for gain' was in itself an evil for which serious punishment was due.

I had faith in our jury system, but obscenity was such an

emotive subject that I expected even the most honest of citizens to be swayed by a judge whose bias would undoubtedly be in favour of a conviction. The possibility was horrifying. The company had just made a large commitment in moving to Whyteleafe, and without David it was doubtful that I could successfully run the business.

In the meantime, we had to continue as normal. It was necessary for both David and me to visit New York to see our suppliers, so for the first time ever, we left the company without one of us directly in charge. Our trust in Ron Coleman was such that we made the trip, confident that the business was in safe hands.

We stayed with Vera and Jerry Levine, in their pleasant detached home in Westchester County. Jerry worked for Capital, the publishers of Monarch. Each morning we travelled to his office in New York which we used as a base. Most evenings we went out to dinner and I could never come to terms with the size of the meals ... Such a waste.

One evening we went with Jerry to see the New York equivalent of London's Soho. The sex shops there were sleazy and we learned nothing from that particular exercise. The adult book centres were no better, but I was interested to observe that each shop had a number of 'porn' movie booths which were in constant use. Men would go into them on their way home from work, or on a night out, and spend fifty cents for five minutes' viewing in total privacy. There was a market for this sort of thing in Britain and David and I were already considering the possibility of placing the equipment in our own retail outlets in the West End using erotic films produced by Harrison Marks and Russell Gaye.

Jerry took us to see *Deep Throat*, which was probably the most famous 'porno' film of all time. My experience in such matters was limited. I had not seen a blue movie until I was twenty five. I remember walking into the boardroom at Long Lane late one evening to find my father and a few other people watching a black and white film. An 8mm projector was set up and the room was practically in darkness. I was told that it was Christine Keeler, of the infamous Profumo scandal, who was squirming above a skinny individual who still had his socks on. It was dreadfully out of focus, and the participants jumped both voluntarily and involuntarily as the old film missed the sprockets. I was not in the least 'turned on' by this film, although I did in a way enjoy it, and hoped that I would be able to see something similar again, perhaps in more comfortable surroundings.

Deep Throat was terrific at first, but after ten minutes of the same old thing I became bored. I literally fell asleep and David and Jerry fell about laughing. While the actors on the screen were grunting and making slurping noises, I was snoring my head off. 'Porno' films are great, but in my opinion they are best saved for those magical moments with a female partner.

On our return to the office we were greeted with news of yet another raid. Ron had dealt well with the police, who were now familiar with the structure of our company at Whyteleafe, and they knew and got on well with our staff. Ron had told them of our impending court case and that it seemed ridiculous to be taking yet more stock without any judgement being made on the earlier raid. The police officers shrugged their shoulders, agreeing with everything that Ron had said, but what could they do? The hierarchy had spoken and they were there only to do its bidding, even if it was stupid, unreasonable and costly to the tax payer.

Only A Judge Has Control

A date had been set for the trial and from that moment on the tension increased. The crown had appointed Jeremiah Harman QC, who was a prosecutor of high repute, and David and I were unhappy to learn that John Mortimer was unable to act for us due to prior commitments. David Offenbach recommended Montague Waters QC as an alternative. He was relatively unknown and, as far as we knew, had not been involved with obscenity cases before. We were feeling vulnerable, despite David Offenbach's assurances.

The morning of the trial was rather like visiting someone prior to a major operation. It was early on a cold and miserable day in late October, 1972 when David and I climbed the steps of the Old Bailey, not knowing where to go or what to do. Inside people were congregated in little groups and we stood alone feeling very anxious.

The arrival of David Offenbach and Geoffrey Robertson was like a breath of fresh air. They spoke highly of Montague Waters and assured us that we were a long way from certain defeat, in fact, Geoffrey reminded us of the high number of expert witnesses who had agreed to come to speak in our defence.

Before the case began David was required to surrender his bail which meant that during the trial he was to be in the custody of the court. Later, we were pleased to hear that the judge had agreed for him to be released each lunch time and evening for the duration of the trial.

After going through the formalities of a 'not guilty' plea, David was taken down to the cells while David Offenbach undertook the lengthy procedure of choosing a jury. Prior to the Criminal Justice Act of 1991, both the defence and prosecution lawyers were allowed to challenge the acceptability of potential members of a jury. There was no requirement to specify a reason and David Offenbach jokingly told me that he challenged a man for carrying a copy of the *Daily Express*, 'You just can't trust them,' he said with a smile. 'Now *Guardian* readers ...'

Taking into account the recent heavy publicity in the wake of the *Longford Report*, the judge warned the jury about serving if they had any preconceived views on the matter to be discussed. In response one man asked to be excused. He later explained that he had two children and was totally opposed to pornography, so could not listen to the evidence with an open mind.

After nineteen rejections, the jury was established and included a stockbroker, a teacher, a research chemist and two engineers. 'As far as juries go, this is an intelligent mix,' Geoffrey Robertson told us, and if he was satisfied, who were we to argue?

David was not allowed in the courtroom during these proceedings, but once a jury had been selected, he was brought into the dock where he sat in the company of two burly police officers. During the trial, Joann, knowing how worried I was, made a fuss of me and I appreciated it. She wanted to come to the court to offer her support and I welcomed it.

Although David had now totally split from his wife Beryl, she also came. There had never been any real trauma between them, even though they were obviously incompatible, and again I was pleased that the jury saw David and me as everyday, happily married men and not playboys accompanied by 'dollybirds'. That would have been fatal.

As the hearing continued we all began to appreciate the qualities of Montague Waters. He was not only a brilliant lawyer but he had a wonderful sense of humour, whilst the prosecutor,

Jeremiah Harman QC was a totally dedicated, deadpan, professional. It was going to be a hard battle and the verdict was always in the balance.

My confidence soared as our counsel introduced expert witness after expert witness, culminating in perhaps the most qualified man in the world to speak on sexual matters – Dr Eustace Chesser. He was a consultant psychiatrist who had spent much of his life lecturing on matters relating to human sexuality. He had written twenty seven books on the subject and was the honorary secretary of the Society for Sex Education and Guidance, executive member of the International Union of Family Organization, the research director of the Research Council into Marriage ... The list went on and on.

He had nothing but praise for our publications and believed that the free dissemination of such items was in the public interest because they tended to lower the threshold at which guilt and shame attached itself to normal sexual practices. Our publications, in particular *In Depth* and *New Direction*, were ideal media to relate the undisputed facts about sexual practices and matters of personal hygiene. He was of the opinion that *In Depth* was most helpful as it provided an outlet for people with sexual problems by making them feel that there was, at least, someone with whom they could communicate.

When questioned by the prosecution about anal sex (which had been the subject of one of the *In Depth* articles), he replied to the effect that it could not be characterized as a 'perversion' in any morally derisive sense. His own researches in Manchester revealed that at least 20 per cent of the married women that he studied engaged in this form of sex and he was of the opinion that in recent years this percentage was increasing and that it did no physical or mental harm when performed by consenting adults. Oral sex is practised much more widely than anal sex and his support for *A Woman's Look at Oral Love* was clearly expressed when he told the court that Sue Caron's account of the subject was a good one, gracefully written and highly informative.

For the second time during the questioning of Dr Eustace

Chesser, the Judge – Lord King-Hamilton – threw his pencil down in disgust when the doctor revealed that in his studies he had discovered that 99.4 per cent of men over thirteen years of age engage or have engaged in masturbation on a regular basis. He peered over the top of his glasses, and the whole courtroom waited on his every word as he paused for effect ... The hush was deafening.

Then he spoke very slowly and said, '... Whatever happened to self control?'

There was silence for a few moments before some of us could contain our laughter no longer. It was probably the most stupid remark I had ever heard, and to this day, I believe that it swayed the jury in our favour. His remark proved beyond doubt that the so-called establishment was clearly out of touch with reality. It was evident that the judge was in favour of a conviction which seemed to annoy the jury.

David agreed to speak in his own defence, even though he knew that it was a big gamble, because the prosecution would have the opportunity to 'tear him to pieces'. Lesser men would have crumbled under the attack from Jeremiah Harman QC, but David stood his ground, although the prosecutor had him on the ropes when he read a passage from one of the magazines.

'Are you telling me Mister Gold, that the line, "...Cock smothered in honey was about to be sucked dry. As I plunged it into her mouth my semen gushed down her throat" ... is not obscene?'

'No, it's not obscene,' David replied, sheepishly.

'Would you accept that this is filth?'

'Objection!' Mr Waters leapt to his feet. 'Totally irrelevant.'

'Overruled, you may answer the question,' said the judge.

'No sir,' David answered.

Jeremiah Harman taunted David with a barrage of questions along similar lines but David stood firm. I believed, however, that the jury felt it had heard enough lewdness to sway it back towards a conviction.

By lunchtime we were feeling pretty low and welcomed the

recess. But after lunch there was no respite. The judge summed up the evidence of the expert witnesses for the defence (he made no reference to the fact that the prosecution had failed to put forward even one expert witness). He made the word 'expert' sound as though there was only one expert in the land on the subject of sex ... him.

Judge King-Hamilton continued. 'Dr Chesser has said that, with reference to homosexuality, reading these publications will do more good than harm. He thought that the publications would not make people practise what they had not practised before, it would only make them more understanding of them.' A pause. 'Well that...' he glanced over his spectacles, '..is a matter upon which you may or may not have your own view.'

Another point on which he suggested that the jury might form a different view to the professor of sexology, was in regard to the doctor's evidence that these publications would assist in helping an impotent man to get an erection. Judge King-Hamilton again paused for effect and to the astonishment of everyone in the court room, he said, 'If this sort of publication is shown by a psychiatrist to a man who is impotent in the hope that it will stimulate him sexually, then what effect do you think it will have upon somebody who is not impotent?'

Finally, the members of the jury retired to consider their verdict. The whole of our business future rested in their hands. Three hours later they returned to inform us all that they were unable to reach a verdict on two of the six counts. The judge was then prepared to give them further direction which allowed for a majority verdict of eleven to one or ten to two.

I was sick with worry. How David must have felt waiting in the area of the cells I will never know. We sat in the Old Bailey canteen drinking coffee. I could not eat a thing because the tension was unbearable.

Less than an hour later we were called back into the courtroom. The jury filed in and moments later the judge came in and took his seat.

'Are you agreed on your verdict?' the clerk of the court asked.

'Yes sir.'

'And is your verdict unanimous?'

'Yes sir, it is,' replied the foreman, an older man wearing thick horn rimmed spectacles. It was unlikely that he was one who had held out for a 'not guilty verdict', I thought, negatively.

'On count one, how do you find David Gold ... guilty or not guilty?'

The gap of less than two seconds seemed like an eternity as the foreman said, 'Not guilty ...'

'Count two?'

'Not guilty...' Another four to go but we knew then that it was unlikely that we would lose.

We didn't, and the relief that we felt is impossible to explain. David was released from custody and everyone gathered round to congratulate him. It was possibly the happiest moment of my life.

Montague Waters then addressed the Bench regarding costs. His clients had been found not guilty and were perfectly entitled to seek complete recompense from the court. But Judge Alan King-Hamilton would have none of it.

'Those who publish this kind of material know the risks they run. They know they are liable to be prosecuted, starkly emphasized by the fact that the defendants are awaiting trial on another similar indictment.'

Montague Waters tried again, but the judge was not interested. He decided that we should not receive any payment of costs. We didn't pursue the matter. It was enough that we had won the day. It was a case of 'two down, one to go'. We were fairly sure that the impending indictment would be dropped. If it were, then the police would live to fight another day. But if they chose to fight again after two bloody defeats, surely failure would bring about a public outcry!

Only a few days later a call from David Offenbach brought us back to earth.

'They're going ahead with the second indictment,' he told me.

'That's impossible! I don't believe it!' I protested, but it was true. The papers were in the post and the trial was going to take place early in the new year ... David was still not a free man. It was back to the drawing board, more witnesses, more costs, and more time away from our business. It was starting to hurt, and the bank balance reflected this.

Back To Business

Weatherwise, 1973 got off to a bad start. It was so wet and cold and each morning the roads were icy making the drive to work quite hazardous. I had time to reflect on the dreadful traffic jams that would be building up on the way to London and how David and I, once upon a time, would spend up to four hours of our day stuck in them. Here on the Kent-Surrey border, our problem was snow and this year it had been particularly bad.When it fell during the day, my trip home was exceedingly dangerous and returning from work was often a nightmare.

It was wonderful when I arrived home to a roaring fire and a hot dinner. It has been said that happiness is not something you

experience, it is something you remember ... I remember it well.

At the office we were concerned about the 'follow-up' court proceedings. Each day we expected the matter to be dropped and each day we were informed that there was not even the slightest move in that direction, so the tension remained, and whilst David put on a brave face I knew that he was a worried man.

Paul Raymond published only quality magazines but even he suffered at the hands of the law. Tony Power, his editor, alleged victimisation when 170,000 copies of *Men Only* were seized. This happened only a month after 26,000 copies had been judged obscene and ordered to be destroyed by chairman of the Bench at Watford.

The publisher of *Mayfair* was killed in a dreadful car accident and his widow took charge of his highly successful magazine, which was already accepted by the establishment. Another magazine, *Playboy*, failed in the United Kingdom because it went too far 'up market' in an effort to gain the extra income from advertisers.

It was implied by a number of retailers that the police had drawn up an inventory of publications that was recognized as the 'porn list'. These publications had not been before the courts and it was clear that the police were acting as judge, jury and executioner by seizing and eventually destroying stock of the titles. It was never worthwhile for a retailer to mount a defence. For a while, Gold Star Publications undertook to meet the cost of defending the seizures. But even if we won the case, while we might have proved a point, it was far from cost-effective. In the meantime, we had learned the difference between unlawful and illegal. Unlawful was acting against the law and illegal is a sick bird! ... Our bird was more a parrot than an eagle.

The pending third trial was very much on David's mind, even though David Offenbach had assured him that a custodial sentence, following the recent acquittal, was practically out of the question – especially as the next proceedings were to adjudge the obscenity or otherwise of near identical titles to those which had already been given the all-clear by a jury only weeks earlier. We remained convinced that the prosecutor was desperate for a conviction at any cost.

The second visit to the Old Bailey was a farce. We were again represented by Montague Waters but a new judge, Bernard Gilis, was appointed to see that fairness prevailed. David Offenbach took pains to tell us that if we thought that Judge King-Hamilton was against our publications and was liable to hand out excessive punishment, well, 'we ain't seen nothin' yet' ... We had drawn a short straw for the second time around, and this time it was even shorter.

On the basis of fairness, the newly sworn jury were asked to leave the room while Judge Gilis informed the participants of the trial that there was to be no reference to the previous case. It was a point in law but I was stunned – after all, they were the same titles and practically the same product. The fact that they had previously been cleared, in my opinion, *was* relevant.

Throughout my life I have often found myself in a cinema or at a sporting function, evaluating the cost of the show and measuring this against the approximate takings. I found myself engaged in exactly the same exercise for the second time at the Old Bailey. I estimated the wages of the staff, from the judge to the cleaner, and the value of the prime space in the city of London. The overall costs were clearly enormous. Generally, for the sake of justice, it could be considered to be cost-effective but this so-called 'test case' was a disgraceful waste of money ... Public money as well as ours.

The all male jury were, once again, out for a long time and once again the verdict was 'not guilty' on all counts. We practically cried with relief. This time the judge was obliged, albeit reluctantly, to give in to our request for costs. He nevertheless fought hard to save the state a few thousand pounds and knocked down the asking figure accordingly. We did not have the strength to protest.

David had spent another ten days of his life within the jurisdiction of the court, applying for bail in order to leave it. He remained in the custody of the court officers during the proceedings. While the jury was out he was allowed to stay close to the courtroom where he played chess with his warden. This helped to ease the tension for David and he was naturally pleased to win the game, but when the verdict was announced that particular victory paled into insignificance.

David was not one to be emotional but on this occasion we hugged each other as he sobbed with joy in my arms. He looked ill and had lost weight, but I knew now that he would in time be his old self again. The result proved once and for all that we were trading within the law.

During the same week, David Offenbach and Ron Coleman had attended an appeal at Old Street County Court against a recent decision to impose a destruction order on more than fifty thousand magazines which had been taken from the Whyteleafe warehouse. This time the magistrates referred to the publications as 'titillating' but not obscene ... This was indeed a time for celebration.

Despite our victories, the media showed no interest. Had we lost, then the headlines might well have read, 'Jail for Porn Baron', or 'Peddler of Filth Caged'. But we were proven to be innocent and the press chose to ignore the fact. They saw no mileage in informing their readers that the people had spoken and at last the silent majority had its chance to say in two words what it really thought: not guilty!

Over the past few months the press had given chapter and verse to Lord Longford's views. They had milked every aspect of his visits to sex dens, porn cinemas and live sex shows which was their way of cashing in on pornography, whilst reporting on our third acquittal in a row, would have sold no extra papers.

Milton Shulman for the *Evening Standard* was the only reporter to put forward our case regarding costs: 'Could not a series of such prosecutions – involving a series of acquittals – become an indirect way of imposing heavy fines upon citizens that the court has found innocent of any crimes?' he asked. In his article he informed his readers that the police had seized 871,468 suspected obscene items in four months. 'What are the police to do?' he went on. 'Should they confine their attention to only the more aggressive samples of hard-core pornography?' The answer was clearly 'yes', but it took more than ten years before the establishment came to their senses.

The Home Secretary, Robert Carr, made a brilliant speech at the Tory Party Conference when he stressed that he was not a prude and that he believed that adults could decide for themselves about porn. (He used the all embracing word, 'porn' which I find irritating. Pornography is ugly and illegal while erotica, for adults, can be both entertaining and fulfilling ... They are like chalk and cheese.) In the light of Lord Longford's Report he was not going to push for more censorship or for a re-definition of the law. The proposed new laws were being brought in to remove squalid sex displays from shop windows, outside cinemas and from poster hoardings. No right thinking person could object to that, but as the 'Public Displays Act' came into force we were again singled out. Our shop in Piccadilly Circus was the first to receive attention from the authorities. The company was charged and received a £100 fine, despite the fact that to support our case, we had shown photographs of many cinemas and competing shops in the area to prove that we were well within the accepted level. We were being treated unfairly. But we were getting used to it.

On A Wing and
A Prayer

It was a miracle, but my mother had survived her operation. I began making regular visits with her to the chest clinic in London, where she underwent examinations and x-rays. Each time we waited patiently for Mr Flavell to inform us that he was satisfied with her condition and I would have the pleasurable task of passing on the good news to Marie and David. Her wounds from the operation were now completely healed. There were no signs of any recurrence of her illness, and she was able to work full time in the shop, which was so important to her. She had obtained permission from the council to remove the normal frontage and have a regular shop window installed. It had taken her a long time to get over the break-up from my father, but now she was rebuilding her own life and personality and became more and more loved by her family, friends, and customers. We were proud of her.

Mum had amazed us all with her determination to remain independent. Despite her illness she had worked six days a week in her shop, personally taking care of every aspect from dressing the window and buying the stock to doing the books. She had worked very hard to successfully keep our home together when Godfrey was in trouble, and now that he had abandoned her she was clearly entitled to a reasonable settlement. After lengthy

Mum in her shop

negotiations, she accepted his pathetic offer of £10,000.

Soon after our showdown with Godfrey he had bought a bungalow in Selsdon which was not far from our warehouse in Whyteleafe. David and I were surprised about his choice of location and even saw it as a sign that he too was hoping that one day there would be a reconciliation. In that event, he would be within easy reach of the office we had allocated to him at Whyteleafe, but it was not to be.

Godfrey travelled into the city each day to run his perfume and publishing business, marketing highly erotic paperbacks which, we understood, were selling well. He was now in his mid fifties but he continued to be at his office very early each morning and did not leave until well after seven in the evening.

His affair with Denise was long over, and he had developed a relationship with Janet, a young girl who packed perfume for him. She had reached the grand old age of sixteen and rumour had it that they were 'getting it together'. Janet was very attractive and, it must be said, she looked older. He invited her to live with him after she became noticeably pregnant with his child.

Janet soon delivered, in my opinion, the only real love in my father's life, his son Mark. He was thirty two years my junior but I was informed by my sister that he was my living image. In a strange way I was pleased. Oddly, I was pleased for my father too. He now had another opportunity to become a dependable father and, in fairness to him, he did not do so badly this time.

David was a keen flier. He had passed his General Flying Test, and had taken me up once, along with his friend from the club, Cliff, better known as 'Boo', Marwood. Boo was a tall, dark and, I suppose, fairly handsome man with a very friendly, outgoing personality, although just a little too pushy for my liking.

I too had been bitten by the flying bug, but before I told David I was taking it up, I wanted to be sure that this time it was for real. This was actually my second attempt. The first time the plane had flown into turbulence, and I'd decided it wasn't for me. But, having resolved to try again, I went to the airfield alone and parked my car alongside the Biggin Hill Flying Club, which was less than fifty yards from the Flairavia Club of which David and Boo were members.

I was nervous as I walked inside, where I was greeted by an instructor who was the temporary receptionist. I told him of my three hours of flying experience and he said that he could arrange for an immediate lesson. I was not prepared for it but I agreed, and within five minutes I was approaching a Cessna 150 with Mick Ronayne, the club's chief flying instructor who was wearing an RAF blazer and displaying a typical Air Force pilot's moustache. He spoke rather well and instilled confidence in me.

The weather was not very good and after fifty minutes' flying we called it a day and we went back to the club room. There, over a cup of coffee, he presented me with 'Flight Briefing for Pilots, Volume One', and explained the basic fundamentals of flight, after which I was satisfied that it was safer than it looked and I was well on my way to becoming a fully fledged flying ace.

After completing more than fifteen hours of intensive flying tuition with instructors, the prospect of my first solo flight was getting closer. I had told Joann that I had taken up flying but I was determined to keep it a secret from David and Boo until I had accomplished this epic circuit. I was, however, suspicious that my secret was out. We went out together regularly on boxing dinners, and Boo spoke to me as though I was a fellow pilot. I remained silent but I thought that perhaps Joann might have let my secret slip.

Boo invited Joann and me to have dinner with him and his wife, Annie, in the restaurant bar of the White Hart in Godstone one evening. We were a little late and I was conscious of the fact that Joann had taken even longer than usual to get ready. She looked very attractive. She wore a trouser suit but, despite everyone's obvious approval, I preferred her in a dress, and she was well aware of that.

Annie, by contrast, looked anything but attractive. She was heavily pregnant, wearing an unflattering imitation fur coat, but worst of all she was smoking a cigarette, and I was dismayed when I saw that she exhaled the smoke through her nose. Boo stood and dutifully introduced Joann and me to Annie. When I kissed Annie on the cheek I smelt the strong, lingering odour of cigarette smoke, which I found distasteful. Despite that, I was sure that I would grow to like her. She was about my height with a pretty face, and there were two additional qualities that I quickly recognized; her sincerity and her kindness.

I was pleased to see that she and Boo were a loving couple and it was a delight to hear them going on about their lovely daughter, Sascha. We understood that their new baby was due in a few months' time and that they were hoping for another daughter. I made it clear to Boo that he was welcome to stay with Joann and me at 'Kent Hatch West',

Annie and Boo

our new home at Crockham Hill in Kent, while Annie was in hospital, and Annie was obviously delighted. She wanted to be sure that he was going to be well looked after ... and with the benefit of hindsight I know that he was!

My thirty fifth birthday belied the fact that Joann and I were less than happy although I should have read a lot into the birthday card which I received from her. It was full of hearts and kisses but it was sent to her hero... A 'superman' from his loving 'second class citizen' wife. She also gave me a book called *How to Live with a Neurotic Wife*, and inscribed in it, 'To my darling hubby ... After reading this book I hope you will agree that I could be worse'. I detected an inferiority complex but that was not fair ... that was my territory! I opened the book. The first page read:

Chapter 1

Understanding

a

Neurotic Wife

You must first of all, understand what makes your wife neurotic.

The answer is simple ...

It's you.

I did not need to read any more ... My eyes had been opened.

My family

Part Three

KEEP RIGHT ON...

Enter David Sullivan

Bernard Hardingham and David Sullivan, two young men with economics degrees from 'Queen Mary College', were making great progress in the industry. Still in their early twenties, they had built up a mail order company which was already more successful than ours. They had succeeded by advertising on a grand scale in a way that left the customer in no doubt about what they were buying.

Prior to their involvement, mail order companies, including ours, had pussyfooted around by being suggestive but gentle in their approach. Now these young entrepreneurs were 'telling it like it was' and the response was very positive. They were already making big money.

It was not long before David Sullivan and Bernard Hardingham had purchased every discountable magazine to sell through mail order and were on the lookout for additional supplies.

David Sullivan contacted Ron Coleman, who informed my brother and me of his requirements. We were not prepared to supply him because we were of the opinion that his aggressive style of advertising would provoke the establishment into taking even more action. Little did we realize that by refusing to supply him we were making a rod for our own backs ... A new publisher of girlie magazines was, of necessity, in the making. When his early titles, *Up the Mini* and *Blockbusters*, were released, we were not overly concerned. The magazines were over-priced, the quality was mediocre and his distributor was only average. The only thing that they had going for them was that they were prepared to be a little more raunchy than the competition. It paid off and before long new titles such as *Private* and *Climax* came on to the market.

Bernard Hardingham succumbed to external pressure and left the partnership. In monetary terms, Bernard must have kicked himself, as his former partner went on to make millions.

David Sullivan came in where others had left off but now the threat to us was greater. However, we decided not to increase the level of eroticism in our publications. The police had unsuccessfully attacked *New Direction* and *In Depth* twice, and we believed they could not possibly go for us again. But in spite of this, we took a board decision not to take advantage of the situation. We thought that we could create an understanding with the authorities that would allow us to trade without further harassment. With hindsight, that decision was wrong, as there was no let up and they were in no mood to come to any 'arrangement', despite the fact that it would have saved the tax payer a great deal of money.

Almost every household in the country now possessed a colour television and I was of the belief that it would not be long before the video would follow suit. I was one of the lucky ten per cent who owned one, but I was not sure that I had chosen the correct brand in buying a Philips 2000. It was certainly the most popular, but it was early days and both Betamax and VHS (totally different systems), were in close contention for the market leadership.

I saw the remote possibility of becoming the market leader with erotic videos, although, with the benefit of hindsight, I realized that it could not have been achieved without investing large sums of money. However, I was prepared to give it a try on a small budget.

My first task was to obtain the video rights to films which were mild enough to comply with legal requirements, yet erotic enough to have a demand in the market place. I had no knowledge of film production, and in any event this too would require significant outlay of capital, so I decided that the only way was to buy cheap, ready-made films. I realized that there was no prospect of obtaining British made films at low prices. Old films were so mild that there would be no market for them, so the only course to take was to buy from either America or from Germany. Their up to date, 'legal' productions would automatically be rejected by the British authorities, so I needed to purchase films which were at least ten years old. This suited me because it meant I could negotiate a good deal.

I felt like a jet-setter as I boarded my flight for New York. Jerry Levine was at the airport to meet me and, as was typical of him, he had prepared a three-day plan of action. He was not familiar with the film industry but he had managed to locate a few less salubrious producers, one in Greenwich Village and another in the Bronx.

I was a little nervous as our taxi drove through the city, but when it stopped and the driver said, 'It's right there,' I became very nervous indeed. Nevertheless, I had no intention of showing it, not to Jerry, not to anyone, and despite the unenthusiastic handshake from three rather ugly, aggressive-looking men, I acted as though we had been friends for ever and asked if they could get me a cup of English tea before we got down to business. They had none, but there was a 'deli' nearby, and when they said they would send out, I changed my request to coffee.

The meeting was a flop. Their films were far too 'strong', and although they were prepared to take out the really hot bits, I realized that there would be no story left. I told them that I would return in a few days to go over the films again and I would bring some money with me ... In a few days I intended to be on my way home, and telling them that I would bring money was one way of getting out in one piece.

The next visit, this time to the Bronx, was not dissimilar but this time the films were better. They were older and corny but at least the sexual content was about right and I was ready to buy. They wanted $5,000 a film for the world rights. I kept a straight face and told them that was quite reasonable ... for the world rights. But I was prepared to offer $500 per film for the UK rights only. The look on their faces was frightening and I immediately increased my offer to six hundred dollars. But I was not going to be further intimidated. The battle lasted for over an hour and Jerry was becoming fidgety. I had to settle and to settle quick. My final offer was to buy six films for $750 each, and just as they were about to throw me out, I said that I would pay them $1,000 in cash as a deposit, on trust. I am not a gambling man but I knew that the money was safe as there was another $3,500 for them to collect, and they could not hope to do anything further with those films.

Jerry was impressed, but he told me afterwards, 'Ralph, any more deals like that and you can count me out. I enjoy playing tennis with two legs.' I understood. I enjoy playing tennis that way, too.

David was becoming more qualified as a pilot. He had passed his night rating and, after many months of hard work, he was successful in obtaining his 'IMC' rating. This meant that he could enter cloud whilst flying under visual rules. Having this rating usually meant that longer trips, including continental flights, could be undertaken.

Both David and Boo progressed still further by achieving their twin rating and, with this under their belts, they decided to make a business trip to Menorca. Flying on instruments, the trip from Biggin Hill to Menorca and back should have presented no problem. The story of this flight was to be the first of many involving the Gold Brothers which David and I would recount over the years.

Boo had made enormous progress in the property business, and now sought to expand into house building. Whilst setting up a business, he was informed of a scheme in Menorca to build six villas on one plot of land and a luxury villa on another. He offered

David and me the opportunity to become involved in the deal which required an investment of £6,000. I was not happy about the idea because I have never felt that business and friendship go well together, but if David was satisfied then I would not object. Once David had handed over the money, Boo Marwood was quick to hire an Apache PA.28 from David Merritt at Biggin Hill Flying Club and was happy for my brother to take on the shared responsibility of flying it, taking one of Boo's partners, David Hale, as a passenger.

As far as flights go, their outbound journey was uneventful but the return was, for all concerned, a horror story. They took off rather late in the evening and the weather, as they approached the English coast, had deteriorated. Boo was in command for the final leg when the DI (direction indicator) appeared to be malfunctioning. PPL's (private pilots), especially the inexperienced ones, pick up phrases that cover a multitude of sins and 'instrument malfunction' is one of them. To a pilot, the word 'lost' is never used, and 'temporarily unsure of my position' or 'my flight instruments are malfunctioning', are tenuous yet more appropriate.

Boo, struggling to fly the plane and operate the radio at the same time in such bad conditions, asked David to contact Gatwick Control to obtain, via the wonders of radar, the plane's position. The aircraft was not equipped with a transponder and their height was known only to the pilots. As David made the call there was a terrible scream from Boo. Through the cloud, he saw looming up ahead and above the red light of the Wrotham Mast. He immediately handed over the controls to David. His fear and the violent turbulence caused David Hale, who was sitting behind my brother, to vomit, and every piece of his early dinner shot across the back of David's head.

They made it in one piece to Gatwick, and Boo was to be eternally grateful for David's skill and fortitude ... However, the £6,000 had been banked in Menorca and was never seen again by David or me.

*

David and his secretary, Penny McQuater, had become very close. She was often with him at the airfield in the evenings, even though she was terrified of flying. They had decided to live together, and David took a small, two bedroom flat in Croydon. They developed a close circle of friends at the airfield, but in particular they became close to Annie and Boo.

Penny was a great help to Annie during the last weeks of her pregnancy and she often stayed with her while their partners were flying together. I would like to have been up there with them but I realized the importance of getting on with my own flying. It was not going to be long before I would be allowed to fly solo and the thought of it scared me to death.

Boo was noticeably pleased to be in our company and when Joann invited him to bring Annie and Sascha to join us for Sunday lunch, he happily accepted. Our old friends, Don and Marie Wagstaff were also invited and they arrived an hour or so before the Marwoods.

We sat in the lounge with Bradley and Tina while Joann busied herself in the kitchen. Marie offered to help, but Joann seemed to have everything under control and insisted that she sit with us in the lounge. Boo's arrival was especially welcomed by Joann who by now was having trouble dealing with the dinner. He immediately offered to help her, which I thought was very considerate of him. I could tell that Joann thought the same and they went off into the kitchen whilst I took Annie and Sascha into the lounge and put on a Charlie Rich record.

Within an hour we were called into the dining room by Boo, who had brought in the steaming hot beef on our silver tray, and with a proprietary air proceeded to carve the joint. Joann looked flushed, but then she had worked really hard and the meal reflected it.

I was disappointed that Annie and Boo had to leave early. Annie was feeling very tired but she had done well. As she left she thanked us for a wonderful time and made us promise that we would look after her husband when she went in to have the baby. I was sure that the next time I saw her it would be born ... I was right. Two weeks later Jennen Paul Marwood was brought into the world. He was a big baby and the actual birth was very difficult, but Boo was there to help Annie through, and she knew that Joann and I were also there to take care of his needs during her confinement.

On the very day that Annie's baby was being born I was sitting alone in a Cessna 150 at one thousand feet above Biggin Hill airfield. 'Ralph,' I said to myself, loudly and clearly, 'what the hell are you doing here? You are 1,000 feet over Biggin Hill airfield, you are alone. In fact you have never been more alone! You must be crazy ... And to think that I am actually paying for this.' Then I thought, 'What if it all goes wrong? Do I have enough insurance? What about the business? What about Joann and the kids? ... Oh, Joann'll be alright. I'm sure she'll find someone in no time; perhaps the rugby player that lives next door to her friend, "Bee Bee", or the builder we met in Bromley, or even Mike from the garage ... The kids'll miss me, and so will David, Marie, Mum. Mick Roynane, he sent you up here ... He'll get the sack, and so he should, it's much too soon. There goes the runway disappearing to my left ... ! You must be mad! No there it is again. You're fine, do your landing checks ... Now just land this thing ... It musn't go wrong now ... I don't believe it, it's down! Brake hard. I've done it, I've done my first solo! Wait till I tell Joann, David, Boo ...'

I have discovered from other pilots that this kind of rambling is typical during their first solo flight, and the memory of it will stick in their minds forever.

At the office David shook me warmly by the hand before I phoned my friend, Boo. I first congratulated him on the birth of his son before telling him of my achievement. He was clearly delighted on both counts and he told me that he would join Joann and me, prior to Annie's homecoming, for a double celebration. He came but I was not at home. Boo, however, brought Annie and the baby over to see us a few days later, but once again I was at work and missed the opportunity to see them. I was not too disappointed, as all I knew about babies was that I did not want to know about babies, and leaving the happy moment for another time was alright with me.

The next morning I was driving to Biggin Hill for my next flying lesson when I happened to see 'Boo 11', a yellow Jensen, approaching from the other direction. I flashed him down, and my friend Boo got out to greet me. 'I've just been over to your house, Ralph. Annie left the baby's bottle and 'Joe Muggins' here, had to collect it.'

'Good for you,' I said. 'Must rush, I'm late for my lesson. See you soon.'

As I drove off, I thought, 'That has to be bad economics. A new bottle including the teats would cost him less than the petrol he'd used to collect them.'

Breakdown

On Thursday, 22nd of November 1973, I awoke to find that Joann was not beside me. She was sitting at the dressing table in a beautiful flowing plaid skirt with a pink mohair jumper and was applying the final touches to her makeup. We had enjoyed a pleasant evening the night before at the exquisite 'Marquis d' Montcalm' restaurant. Later we had made love, but it was noticeably passionless for which, in my mind, I was quick to accept the blame. I had begun to believe that my sexual prowess was lacking, but of late it was even worse, and on that morning I had a gut feeling that there might be an outside influence that was destroying any chance that we might have had to put it right.

'You're seeing him today?' I intimated, and I was not exactly surprised when there was no reply. What had made me ask the question I do not know, and I was already regretting it. But it was too late.

'Anyone I know?' ...Still no answer. 'OK Joan' (I used her old name, as though this was my first reprisal), 'I do happen to know,' I lied, 'but I agree that it's best that we say no more.' It was then that the bombshell really hit me.

'No you don't, Ralph, you couldn't possibly!' Her words confirmed it. My response was to look at her and say nothing.

Within a few moments, Joann began to cry. I walked over to her and put my arms around her. After a few moments I said, 'Stay here tonight by all means, but as soon as possible I want you to sort yourselves out so I can be left to get on with my own life.' As I write this, it all seems so clinical, but I have an in-built mechanism to deal with rejection. I like to think that it is a little more sophisticated than Godfrey's, 'Who fucking well needs ya?' but I suppose there must be some of his genes in me. The difference was that I did need her, I did love her and I did want her, but I knew that it was all too late.

Joann took the children to school without first bringing them up to kiss me good-bye. She did not return home and I lay in my bed feeling empty inside. I was very much unsure of what to do and needed time to come to terms with the situation, but what I really needed at that moment was someone to cuddle me and to tell me that everything would turn out fine.

I dressed and went to the office. In the car I could do nothing but think about Joann making love with another man – cuddling, caressing, talking about me, telling him how good he was in bed and how inadequate I was; how, if I had really loved her, I would have married someone else ... followed by a pause, a playful giggle, then back to making love.

What about the kids? All I had thought about so far was myself ('Typical!' I hear her say). 'I'll hire a nanny,' I told myself, 'and I'll carry on as normal.' I could have done a lot of things, but right then, all I wanted to do was get to work and discuss it. David would be there and he was the man that I needed at that moment.

David was there, but he could spare no more than three minutes. 'Ralph, it's all very sad, but let's talk it over later. Perhaps after work?' That was over eight hours away and if I did not talk to anyone in that time I would go mad.

Thank God for Ron Coleman. It was a juicy scandal with a tinge of mystery and Ron was more than happy to listen to every word. His advice, and subsequently everyone else's, was to remain calm and give it time. I knew that by the end of the day I would break down, and I did. Joann had posted a note through the door saying that she had taken the children to her mother's and she would contact me soon ... It was the beginning of a nightmare.

I was always proud of the fact that Marie was 'Akela' at her local cubs unit, and the next day I had promised to help out at an auction stall they were running to collect money for a local cancer hospital. She knew of my problem and had offered her sympathy, but what I wanted more was her support and that was clearly there in abundance. She suggested that I should cancel my contribution to the fête, but I declined. I insisted on going through with it, although it was the last thing in the world that I wanted to do.

I was more successful than I believed possible, and the money for the Royal Marsden hospital came pouring in. I momentarily forgot all of my troubles as my mind wandered back to the days of the markets; '... Now ladies and gentlemen, what am I bid for this beautiful dolls' house, once owned by a princess?' I lied as the offers came in to take Tina's once loved toy. 'And this rabbit's foot, guaranteed to bring you luck ... Well it has done for everyone with the exception of its original owner!' Everyone seemed to be happy. There was only one person who was not, and that was me.

As my stall gradually cleared I noticed my friend Boo standing on the outside of the now diminishing crowd. He was carrying his daughter Sascha on his shoulders. I was so pleased to see him. I was a friend in need ... A friend in need of a friend.

He had heard from David about my problem and was obviously, unlike David, concerned and prepared to sit and listen. He encouraged me to come with him to the airfield for a cup of tea at 'Dillow's' café. It was only a short drive and his gleaming yellow Jensen was ready and waiting in the car park. Sascha climbed into the back seat.

We sat for a time without a word being said. It felt strange. Then we both spoke at the same time. I could not understand why he was finding it so difficult to speak to me. I was the one that needed cheering up but he was making me feel worse. He let me speak. 'I still don't know who it is Boo, and to be honest with you, I don't think I'll know what to do when I find out. I've never been aggressive and I'm not sure that I know how to be.'

As I spoke, a peculiar thought crossed my mind. 'Suppose it's him? Suppose it's Boo?' I gripped the plastic cup from which Sascha had been drinking her milk. An impulsive urge to throw the remainder into Boo's face came over me. I did not go through with it. With the benefit of hindsight, I wish I had.

Joann came home with the children from her mother's on the Sunday evening. She appeared to be very relaxed and acted quite normally; she even gave me a kiss on the cheek. I wanted more, I wanted to hear that it had all been a big mistake, that she did not want to leave, and that we could sort it out. But she took her case to the spare bedroom, which said it all. After the children were put to bed we watched television and then following the second peck on the cheek, Joann said good night and retired to her own room. Joann informed me that she was taking the children from school and was going back to her mother's for a few days.

Despite my suspicions, I was prepared to let the mystery of the 'other man' continue for the time being. I was still living in the hope that we could go back to square one and we could forget that anything had ever happened. I was quite prepared for that, but the ball was firmly in Joann's court.

On the Monday morning I went to the office but I was unable to work. I did not care about the business or anything else. I was on the phone to my sister Marie for hours, then I would call my mother and as many friends as would listen to me.

I later phoned some of my business associates who were good listeners, and one of them happened to be Mel Walker. After dialling, an attractive female voice at the other end of the line said, 'Mel is on the other line, will you hold?'

'Yes,' I replied as long as you stay on the line and talk to me.'

She laughed, then said, 'He's free now, I'm putting you through.' Mel listened sympathetically while I told him the story, then I asked him if his receptionist was as nice as she sounded and whether or not she was small. When he answered in the affirmative, I asked him to put me back to the switchboard.

I asked Sarah if she would like to go out with me. It was the first time that I had asked for a date in more than ten years and when she agreed, I was more nervous than pleased.

I suppose that I was using her, because I made an excuse for her to phone me at home to confirm the time. I wanted Joann to know that I was not going to sit back and mope, but deep down I wanted her to be jealous.

Sarah phoned as arranged and Joann took the call. 'Is Ralph there?' she asked, with that beautiful telephone voice that I had fallen in love with.

'I'll get him,' Joann replied, indignantly.

Sarah lived in Streatham and was nineteen years old. A quick calculation told me that she was sixteen years younger than me.

'Ridiculous,' I thought, but just then I did not give a damn.

I planned to take her to the Sportsman Club in Tottenham Court Road where I had recently become a member, having been told that it provided the best restaurant in London. I was still very nervous but Sarah would never have believed it ... It was a great performance.

David was intolerant of my behaviour regarding Joann's affair. I had told him that I was convinced that her lover was none other than our mutual friend, Boo Marwood. David's response to this brilliant deduction was, 'Big deal.' The two words were drawn out to over-state the case. 'If it's true, Ralph, then I feel sorry for his wife Annie, but for you... you lucky bastard. Come on Ralph, you have not exactly been the happiest married man in the world. In a couple of weeks you'll be counting your blessings, and this one will be top of the list.'

The misery did not leave me within the suggested few weeks, despite my date with Sarah. She was young and very attractive, but it was all too soon. At the Sportsman we had what could only be described as a perfect evening. We lost twenty pounds between us in the casino and even that was fun.

I told her of my views regarding gambling, that 'the only way to win is to lose'. I had lost £20, but if I had won, then, in the fullness of time, the casino would have taken it back ten times over.

I took Sarah home and I knew that I had 'cracked it', when she asked me if she would see me again. I suggested that she join me on a trip to London again, this time with my friend Mike Behr and his crowd, who were planning to see the new film *Jaws* in the West End. Sarah accepted, and I was pleased that I would not be going unaccompanied after all.

She invited me in for coffee and to meet her mother, Joan, who was not much older than I. I stayed until about two in the morning telling them all my woes. Sarah listened but she occasionally yawned. Her mother didn't.

Coming to Terms

The fact that my private life was crashing around my feet made me more determined than ever to achieve things in the business world. Ann Summers had become the recognized market leader in sex shops, and Ron and I had made contacts throughout the world to improve the range of products, but much more needed to be done. I wanted to take on more shop units and to develop mail order so that our buying strength would be enhanced.

Also, at our pre-Christmas meetings David and I made plans to vastly improve the quality of our magazines. We considered the advantages of publishing more and importing less. Although we were selling many thousands of imported puzzle magazines our competitors were producing titles that outsold our imports on a scale of one to ten. There was plenty for me to do and I realized the importance of sorting out my domestic problem sooner rather than later.

Joann and I had come to a fair arrangement regarding the children though in the early stages of the break-up, it was agreed that they stayed with me at Kent Hatch, which they knew as home and we would keep things as normal as possible for them. Joann arrived early each morning and helped me get them off to school. She would bring them home in the evening and leave only after they were tucked up in bed.

Gradually it became generally known that she was with Boo,

and it was evident that Boo was in a total state of disarray. He had made no bones about his love for his wife, and two weeks after a difficult confinement was not a good time to say, 'I'm in love with a wonderful lady who just happens to be the wife of my best friend,' and he delayed the moment of truth for as long as he could.

Joann's parents were a port in a storm, and at weekends we took the children down to Basildon to be with them. I had hoped that they would have made a concerted effort to bring us back together but, on the contrary, Ethel (I delighted in referring to her by her real name) gave the impression that Joann must have been a saint to have stayed with me for as long as she did. Having found another man who could keep her in the style to which she had become accustomed was a bonus.

One afternoon I laid my head on their dining table and sobbed but, as they sat watching this pathetic character, I could feel them thinking, 'No more than he deserves.'

December 1973 had been the worst month of my life. Joann and I had a number of lunches which eventually took on a recognizable pattern. We would meet, kiss on the cheek, apparently the best of friends, but gradually the conversation would deteriorate until we were arguing. Joann would start crying before I called for the bill and we would agree to meet again soon, to discuss the children and the settlement and a million other things.

At these meetings, I was always hopeful that she would put forward a proposal of reconciliation, and I knew in my heart that I would jump at it. But it could only come from her, and it would only work if she was genuinely ready to 'dump' her lover.

Joann and I made Christmas Day as normal as possible for the children. Joann cooked a splendid meal for us. She arrived at 11 a.m. but by that time the children had already opened most of their presents from Father Christmas. As we exchanged our presents, Joann began to cry. She had bought me some flared 'Farah' trousers and 'Old Spice' talc. We visited friends over the next few days, but each of the occasions invariably ended in tears.

I wondered if every separation was as traumatic.

I was hoping that next year would be much better. I was certainly going to start it on a high note. Sarah came away with David, Penny and me to the 'Great Danes' hotel in Hollingbourne, Kent. I am not a heavy drinker but that night I let myself go – in more ways than one. Before the clock struck two a.m. on the first of January, I technically committed my first act of adultery.

David's relationship with Boo did not change much, but for me, of course, it changed dramatically. I often told the joke, 'My best friend has just run off with my wife and I miss him.' My other friends may have laughed but they knew that I was still hurting inside.

David and Penny had been close to Annie and Boo, and I was sure that under the circumstances they could not now remain friendly towards the new combination of Joann and Boo, but I was wrong. Boo acted as though it was perfectly normal, no different from changing partners on a dance floor and anybody who made a 'federal case' out of it must be crazy or, at very least, terribly old fashioned. I tried to be noncommittal but David knew that I was seething. Penny was also happy in both camps. She was young and modern and coped easily with the situation.

She was wonderful with Annie, who had now been told of her husband's infidelity. From the information that I had gathered, she was in an emotional state and Penny was helping her to cope. She enjoyed looking after the two children, especially the baby. I wanted to speak with Annie but I did not know her too well and the more I thought about it, the more I realized that I had nothing much to say. I was certainly the last person in the world who could offer her encouragement.

David and I continued to direct our energy towards breaking into the video market. I wrote to Klaus Uhse, of 'Beate Uhse', in Flensburg, suggesting that I visit Germany to buy some of his films. The samples I had seen were far too 'hot' for our market and I was keen to see his older titles which were tamer. I was aware that, unlike the American films, they would have to be dubbed. This also applied to the Russell Gaye silent films. I was trying to keep as many 'balls in the air' as possible. Unfortunately I had committed myself to the American deal and I was already regretting it.

Booking my flight to Hamburg and arranging to take the train to the north of Germany, I reflected on the change in my personal situation. I never liked leaving my family to go abroad and I was always concerned to see that such trips were worked around important calendar dates and Joann's arrangements. Now I was travelling without reference to anyone else, but it was a small consolation.

It was a lonely trip. I spoke no German, and sitting for two hours in a train compartment with Germans who spoke no English made it worse. A car waited for me at Flensburg Bahnhof to take me on the short journey to the 'Beate Uhse' head office. I had heard about their magnificent building but I was truly amazed when I actually saw it. It was new and it was huge, and needless to say I was very impressed. Before me I could see a vision of our future, and mentally I set my sights. I was also impressed to note that, with the usual German efficiency, everything was ready for me. After being introduced to the executive board, I was taken into a studio where a projector was ready to roll, and a cup of steaming coffee had been placed beside my chair.

I sat watching blue movies for the next three hours. There were films amongst them which I would like to have bought, but I knew that a great deal of 'blue pencil' work would have to be put into effect before they could be sold in Britain and the costs would have made it prohibitive.

I established a purchasing price with Klaus, but I told him of my dilemma and indicated that I would finalize matters within a few weeks. I took a taxi to the Hotel Flensburgerhof where I spent the evening alone. After watching those films I would have enjoyed some female company, but I did not have the nerve to do anything about it ... What a waste.

*

I received the first two films from Klaus Uhse and sent them to a specialist to have the parts that I considered would cause offence removed. I instructed them of my requirements.

I was very happy with the result and I arranged for Dennis Ewen, a former director of Ann Summers who was now a part of our organization, to arrange another specialist, this time one who had the facility to dub sound onto the 16mm master film. Within days Dennis had the whole set up organized and asked if I would like to go along to see that my two hundred pounds a day would be well spent.

The studio was in the editor's home. He had employed a female 'voice over' actress called Kate and a married couple who were supposedly very good. Unfortunately Dennis and I never found out, because soon after we arrived there was a phone call to say that their baby-sitter was ill and they were unable to replace her. The saviour of the day was Dennis who offered to take on the various male roles. I was relieved because I was not confident of my own ability, and Dennis did have a much sexier voice than me.

As it turned out Dennis was brilliant and he and Kate coped well with the newly censored film. They took their cues from Dennis's carefully prepared script, most of which comprised long moans with the occasional, 'I'm coming! I'm coming ... !' There was no doubt in my mind that the resulting video would be a success. At the end of the session I offered to take Kate to the nearby underground station. Kate was good fun, and although she was not exactly beautiful, as she read her script in time to the sexual movements on the screen, her desirability increased substantially. I was tempted to invite her out for dinner but instead I took her phone number which was the beginning of my 'little black book'... the book that for one reason or another was never to be used.

We produced a few hundred videos and I was hopeful of selling out within a short period. I didn't. I had clearly misjudged the market and the demand for videos was not yet there. Video machines were still a luxury for the rich, and my determination to be first was an error. In time, there were more sales and I was sure the tie-up with Russell Gaye, the publisher of *Fiesta*, would be the answer. His established video titles were already considered to be within the law, so censoring was not needed. They were silent but I now knew that dubbing was feasible, so I came to an agreement with Jan and Russell Gaye to pay, up front, fifty per cent of the costs to put sound on to their films. This provided them with sound as well as silent films to sell and I could also use their titles to put on video.

Over the next few months I took a number of trips to their main offices in Kilburn where Jan Gaye, her young assistant, Jennie, and I went through the films to decide which had the potential for dubbing. Once again, I found myself in a strange environment. The films had little effect on my colleagues whilst I felt just a little embarrassed. These movies were more suited for special occasions and it seemed strange to be dealing with them in this businesslike manner. After a time I too was able to treat the job with nonchalance. It was rather like making chocolates in a chocolate factory – after a while there is little desire to eat them. Mind you, I could have eaten Jennie, at the risk of over-indulgence.

I accidentally met Boo's wife, Annie, in a restaurant. She and her friend were just starting their lunch, and I asked if I could join them. Annie's friend, Jennifer, was a very attractive young lady but, like Annie, she also had two children and a marriage on the rocks, and was not to be pursued. I did not pursue either of them, but the food was good, and the female company was a bonus.

We talked for some time about the lead-up to our respective marital problems, and after the meal I was happy to take them both home. Annie wanted me to take her home first, because she saw the possibility of a relationship forming between Jennifer and me, which could well be the solution to all her friend's problems. I had no intention of fitting into those plans, but again I had recognized a quality in Annie that was rare.

David and I had by now taken over the Biggin Hill Flying Club, after hearing that it was in financial difficulties. It was not the best commercial move that we had ever made, although there were many compensating factors. One was that we would have a parking place for the old Piper Aztec David and I had bought, which we called 'Mike Oscar' because of the last two letters of its registration, G-AYMO.

As the joint chairman of the Flying Club I was expected to attend the annual dinner and dance which was planned to take place at the nearby Grasshopper restaurant. I needed a partner for the evening, and I thought that I would ask Annie. I wanted her to know that I would help in every possible way concerning her divorce if she needed it.

The evening was a great success. I had prepared a short speech which included a few jokes about flying, and the applause for it was long and loud. I felt happy that Annie seemed proud to be my companion. I took her home and we talked for a time, but it was very late. I pecked her on the cheek and said, 'I will call.'

When I was invited to another dinner dance I agreed to go, but I was unsure who to take with me. My closest girlfriend was the daughter of my neighbour at Kent Hatch, and I had started seeing more of her. We both loved classical music, Beethoven and Tchaikovsky in particular, and I had invited her into my home on many occasions to enjoy each other's company and the music. I was really pleased that at last I had found someone with whom I could share that particular interest. I was also very pleased that I was able to share other interests with her.

Some evenings when I had the children to stay, she would come over to spend time with me. As the evening progressed, I would bring down the duvet from my bedroom, and we would cuddle up in front of the roaring fire and make love. The lounge door was locked in case of interruptions, but my children did me proud. They did not disturb us once.

My relationship with her was wonderful, and we had fulfilled every fantasy imaginable, but, in view of the large age gap, I believed that there was no great future for us. I called Annie and invited her, and I knew immediately that she was delighted.

To say that the evening was a success would be an understatement. It was sensational. We joked and told stories, we laughed till we cried and then we danced until the band pleaded to go home.

After a rowdy farewell to our friends I set off to take Annie home. Stopping at a red traffic light Annie placed her hand on my inner thigh, kissed me on the cheek and said, 'Thank you for a wonderful evening.' On impulse I headed for Kent Hatch and replied, 'That Annie, is a little premature. The evening has only just begun.'

I took Annie to the bedroom and within moments our clothing was removed and we were making passionate love. As our bodies came together there was a feeling of unforgettable fulfilment. It took time but we each experienced an orgasm that seemed to go on and on. Annie had not made love for over a year whilst I had experienced, for the first time in my life, the excitement of making love to two different women within only a few days. This excess caused a change in me, and it improved my whole outlook on sex. It was less intense for me, and Annie was understandably in great need. What could have been better? Not only had I made love to both of my girlfriends, but they each clearly wanted me and were both prepared to give as well as to take, which was something I had not experienced in the past.

I could not cope with the deceitfulness of the situation for long, though, and I knew that I had to decide soon on the correct path to take. I fully realized that the move towards Annie was potentially a precarious route. She had, however, fulfilled me in a way that I had never known, and I wanted to progress my relationship with her.

Annie

Annie

David, Jerry and I went on our annual trip to 'Distripresse', the convention of book and magazine publishers which was being held in Hamburg. It was important for us to attend, although our business was growing and in future years we would probably be sending our sales manager to represent us.

On this occasion we had the opportunity to visit the nearby Reeperbahn, a wide avenue renowned as the red light district of Hamburg, in the hope of learning something more about the sex business. We passed a number of licensed red light zones where prostitutes were free to sell their wares. Brothels were also licensed and they were examined and approved by government officials regularly. It all seemed so cold and calculating, but nevertheless it was better than the ridiculous 'sweep it under the carpet' attitude of the British.

We also visited a number of sex shops, but I was not impressed with them. They were distinctly down market compared to the others that I had visited in Europe and I noted that they were not very well patronized. Most of their customers were the local prostitutes and their clients, and the items that they sold were, in general, for 'special' sex activity. I formed the impression that success in this business would be achieved primarily by selling to the man in the street via an outlet which caused no embarrassment.

What I saw in the Reeperbahn was a different thing altogether. I saw copulation 'in the flesh'. The performance took place in a first class theatre and I was surprised to see so many of my business associates and friends from the convention in the audience. Some of them were with their wives and I presumed that, like me, many were seeing a 'live' show for the very first time. It was fascinating, but far from stimulating or even erotic. The audience, however, had the time of their lives as they cheered on the leading male participant into achieving yet another erection in order to copulate for the sixth or seventh time ... It was very impressive.

I am sure that many people, like Lord Longford, would find this sort of thing repulsive, and the wonderful thing is that they are free to think what they like. Everyone present, including the performers, seemed to be enjoying themselves and, at the end of the day, there were certainly no victims.

Normally at the end of the 'Distripresse' convention David, Jerry and I would go back to London, but this time I had more business to take care of in Germany, so I said my goodbyes to my colleagues and took a local flight to Frankfurt. I arrived in the early afternoon and decided to settle down into the nearby Frankfurt Airport Hotel before visiting the 'Sex Fair' which was being held in the hotel's conference room annexe.

The taxi dropped me off at the elevator which was to take me up to the hotel reception. I was feeling uncomfortable as there was nobody to help me with my luggage. A young lady held the doors open whilst I put each of my cases into the lift. She spoke no English and I was happy to practise my German. I had recently purchased a Linguaphone language course, and was determined to put my few words and phrases to good use on this trip.

'Dankeschon,' I said fluently, 'Das war sehr freundlich von ihnen, wie ist ihr name?' With that she spoke at such a pace in German that I did not understand a word. I responded, as we arrived at the check-in desk, by saying, 'Kan ich mit ihnen abendessen haben?' She made a lengthy reply within which I recognized the words, 'Ja', and, 'Zimmer nummer'. She wrote down 410 and 8.30.

I was delighted. This was something that only happened in story books and black and white movies. I had a great deal of work to take care of at the 'Sex Fair', but I could not get out of my mind my pending date with the beautiful woman whom I had just met and whose name I could not remember. It was even harder as I watched the blue movies which were showing at many of the stands.

At 8.30 I knocked on the door of zimmer nummer 410 and my date was ready ... So was her mother, and she could not speak English either. An unforgettable evening ... Best forgotten.

When I look back, I find it hard to believe that I managed to find the time to do as much as I did at that time of my life. I was playing tennis, flying, engaging in a heavy social life and, at the same time, running a number of businesses with David.

Without Ron Coleman I know that it would have been impossible to continue with all of these activities. His contribution to the overall management of the business was considerable and I had no regrets about making him a director of 'Gold Star Publications' and 'Lydcare'. He had continued to keep in touch with most of the respectable dealers of sex products in the West End and he reported back at our meetings on the many developments. Sauna baths were opening up all over the place and Ron wanted us to get involved. David and I had reservations, and said that we would give it some thought. We half jokingly suggested that we would check one of them out ... For professional reasons, of course!

We went to a local parlour in Croydon which was reasonably up market, and we each had a luxurious massage carried out by a very attractive young lady wearing the shortest of mini skirts. We made no verbal suggestion of any kind to her and neither did she to us. But we commented afterwards that the experience was far more erotic than the massages we used to get on boxing or football gym tables.

On our way home we discussed the morality and the advantage of getting involved in that business. David had no doubts on the question of morality. He vehemently believed that this practice was a good thing. Even if it were true that 'extra' services were provided, then at least society would have done away with the need for street-walking prostitutes (along with the sickening routine of policing them).

Despite our support for the principle we decided not to pursue it although Ron was adamant that we were making a bad mistake and continued to press us to reconsider. He was an expansionist and wanted the business to grow at any cost, without too much consideration for nett profits, which was similar views to my father's. Ron and I, nevertheless, had mutual respect for one another. He was a good administrator and communicator, whilst I was the main negotiator for all of the companies, including the Flying Club.

Regardless of our involvement, the club was not profitable and it became common knowledge that we might be prepared to sell if an offer was made. However, we never let it be known that it was not making money – in fact, I often spoke of its great potential. The overall turnover was increasing and we were confident that it could become viable. But it was clearly in need of 'hands on' supervision, and David and I were always very busy.

After my date with Annie, I knew that I had to see her again. In view of our respective marital disputes I knew that there would be problems if our relationship progressed, but I had played it cool for long enough.

Annie and I had so much in common. She was only three years younger than me, and she too was experiencing an unexpected and unwanted break-up. She was still hopeful that Boo would return to her and I genuinely wanted her wish to be granted. She was, however, convinced that Joann, who, in her opinion, was far more attractive than she was, would hold on to him at all costs.

I knew that there had to be many reasons for Boo's affair with Joann, but one of them stuck out a mile ... Annie had been in hospital and Joann was available. I imagined Boo going back to Annie and Joann being 'dumped'. In my dreams I contemplated myself as 'the hero' who would be on hand to pick up the pieces. Joann and I continued to talk and the talks inevitably led to arguments. It had not been long before we got around to discussing money. My reputation for being mean was not altogether unfair. In business, I was known to be hard as I fought every inch of the way to achieve the best price. Paying one penny more than necessary left me feeling cheated, and any reduction from the initial asking price represented my achievement.

In my private life, I like to think that I was different. However, I had no intention of paying Joann more than I had to. As far as I was concerned, Joann had chosen to leave me for another man who just happened to be wealthy.

There were rumours that Boo's property business was in financial trouble, but I was still in no mood to be generous with Joann. On the contrary, I felt more inclined than ever to pay only what the law pronounced as her entitlement. I know that my first thought should have been for the children, and in a way it was. They had, from birth, lived in the lap of luxury and if, as a result of the break-up, their living standards came down a little, I felt it would do them no harm.

Although Joann had engaged a firm of solicitors to handle the divorce proceedings, Annie still refused to go to hers. She was convinced that Boo would treat her fairly, and she really believed that he was personally without funds, although I wasn't so sure.

'You don't know my Boo,' Annie remonstrated. I suggested that she forget the man she once knew and had loved. I knew that Annie would stand no chance of receiving financial support if he found out that she had slept with me. Although at that moment he had no reason to suspect that I had, I was well aware of the evils of scandalmongers. More people have been run down by gossip than by motor cars.

I needed Annie in more ways than one. Our lovemaking had been wonderful and she had made me feel as though I was the best lover of all time. I am well aware that thousands of men experience that feeling every day, but until then I had not been one of them – on the contrary, for years I had been filled with doubt. Just as condemnation and disapproval will cause a man to withdraw and become worse, praise and adoration will bring about improvement and so it was with me. Annie expressed herself before, during, and after, in such a way that I was left in no doubt that we had 'got it together'. To top it all, she loved my Charlie Rich records.

I knew that there was much more to a relationship than just making love, but I was concerned about making any sort of commitment. Annie was understanding. She fully realized and even told me that a man in my position would be a fool to get involved with a woman like her – with two young children, a husband who, despite his infidelity, she still loved and would take back at the drop of a hat. According to her, the enormous trauma that she had been through over the last nine months had left scars, some of which would never heal. As I write this, I feel a shiver run down my spine, Annie was right about so many things.

Boo had been good to Annie during the past months. He was clearly filled with remorse and regretted the fact that Annie was taking it all so badly. He wanted her to find a male partner and was delighted when she had accepted an invitation to go out with Brian, who was an unattached mutual friend. When Elsie, Annie's mother, was not available to baby-sit, Boo was very happy to take the responsibility.

When I came on the scene, Annie realized that it would be an error to let Boo know that she was going out with me. She made a point, however, of not lying to him. He often asked who she was seeing and Annie would not beat about the bush. 'Mind your own bloody business,' she would say. She might have still loved him but, under the circumstances, he was not one of her favourite people.

It seemed strange to be making love with Annie, knowing that her baby-sitter was the man who had run off with my wife. When I took her home, usually in the early hours, I would drop her off some distance along her road – my Daimler car was very distinctive.

One evening I asked her if she could get away from the children on the following Friday and Saturday night, and she told me that her parents would probably be happy to stay over. I took her to a local hotel for what I was sure would be a wonderful weekend. We made love after we were shown to our room, we made love before getting ready for dinner, and we made love before dropping off to sleep, exhausted but deliriously happy.

We had breakfast in bed and had no difficulty in finding what to do during the hours before going down for our lunch. As Annie descended the staircase, wearing a pretty summer dress, she saw somebody and turned to look at me in horror. It was Boo. Alongside him stood a fat, ugly man who moved towards me, as Boo walked towards the back of the reception area.

'Mr Gold?' the fat man asked. 'Ralph Gold?'

'Yes,' I replied, and looked at him as though demanding an explanation. He told me that he was a private detective employed by Clifford Marwood, and wanted to know if I had anything to say regarding the fact that I had spent the night with Mr Marwood's wife. I could not believe what I was hearing. I told the man that I had nothing to say and would he kindly get out of our way as we wished to go to lunch.

They went away leaving Annie and me to dwell on the new situation in which we had found ourselves.

'It makes no difference,' I told Annie. 'Although it proves I was right. How can you possibly still be in love with that man? After leaving you for another man's wife, he's stooped to having you followed. The only thing he could hope to achieve by finding out that you've slept with someone else is that the court may treat him a little better when assessing the settlement. The bonus for him is that it's Ralph Gold, and now I can assure you he will see that you get even less!'

I was determined to see that it would not affect our weekend altogether, but I was not entirely successful. There is no way of making a certain part of the body come to attention when the mind is on other things.

Not long afterwards, Annie and I went away for another weekend. We stayed in a magnificent hotel set in large grounds in

Cheshunt, and I went into our room and saw Annie sitting at the dressing table brushing her long dark brown hair. I remember the moment as if it were yesterday, I picked her up in my arms and carried her to the bed and I said, 'Do you know Annie, I think I'm in "like" with you.'

I know now that it was a lot more than that, but those horrible genes handed down by my father had made it very difficult for me to express my true feelings. It was unfortunate that tragic circumstances would eventually occur that would make it easier for me to do so.

Two weeks later, Annie stayed for the first time at Kent Hatch. She arrived in her old Ford Capri and we placed it discreetly in a lay-by, just along the road. We were snuggled up in bed when we were startled by banging at the front door.

I put my dressing gown on and walked tentatively down the stairs. There was nobody there. Only a note sticking through the letter box:

> Anna,
> Glad to see you having another great weekend lying through your teeth ...
> From now on tell the bloody truth.
>
> Love, Boo ... Your x to be.

Coming Together

Since the break-up there had been unbelievable trauma between Joann and me. The letters and affidavits were flying from one solicitor to the other. My auditor, Malcolm Harris, was requested to make a true statement of my affairs and he was not in a position to offer any cheer to Joann and Boo. I owned only one third of a number of companies in the sex business. Despite the high turnover, it was unlikely that a buyer could be found who would consider purchasing a minority holding in a business of this type.

Malcolm Harris also pointed out in his statement that the business was precarious, and there were police prosecutions and customs seizures to be taken into consideration. The nett profits had not been high and my salary reflected this, although I did have an expense account and various other 'perks'. However, I saw no reason why I should be any more generous to Joann than Boo was being to Annie.

Annie was gullible, and it had taken time for her to realize that 'her Boo' was not playing fair. She had been informed that their luxurious home was to be sold, and she had been instructed to look for a house more suited to his drastically reduced income. His income may have been reduced, but I was convinced that his capital was still intact. In view of this I planned to sell my Daimler and began to look for a new home more suited to my means.

From an advertisement in the *Evening Standard* I found a one bedroom flat in Tandridge that suited my newly found domestic situation perfectly. A block of apartments had been converted within a beautiful Edwardian mansion, surrounded by magnificent grounds that even included an orchard. The first floor flat was called 'Little Southlands', and for a month I lived in dread of the sale falling through.

Since I could not cope well on my own, I had taken on a lady to look after me. Mrs Clarke was in her late sixties. She was very small and slim and was just about the most lovable person in the world. Soon after employing her I went abroad leaving her in charge of Kent Hatch with only my mother to contact if there were any problems.

I made a big mistake in informing Joann of when and where I was going, and consequently I had only been away for one day when Mrs Clarke was confronted with a visit from her. Alongside Joann stood two burly removal men – their gigantic van parked in the drive. She stepped past Mrs Clarke and once inside ordered them to load the furniture that she believed was hers by right. Mrs Clarke was helpless, and had no alternative but to allow Joann the complete freedom to do as she wished. I returned to a half-empty house.

This was becoming a 'battle royal'.

Although the house was sparsely furnished, the children still seemed to enjoy coming to see me. Before they went home they would ask for, 'Mummy's money'. Joann always sent a list with them of items that she wanted to buy for them. I never complained, and I always paid up, although I instinctively pulled a sour face and fiddled in my pocket for the correct amount, as though that was all I had. Of course it was an act and the children soon grew wise, but it became a habit and to this day they jokingly mimic me.

This childish behaviour on my part was in response to similar behaviour by Boo with his children. Boo was paying twenty pounds a week for them, and even that was not paid on a regular basis. I had finally persuaded Annie to see her solicitors, and Boo's response to their letters was predictable. His solicitors claimed that their client was apparently so broke he did not know where the next penny was coming from, but they assured Annie that she would receive some money when things improved. In the meantime their advice was that she should get a job.

Boo had given up flying on the basis that he had run out of money but he had become involved in boating and, we were given to understand, he had the use of a large sea-going motor launch. He and Joann took all of the children away for a two-week trip to Jersey, which gave Annie and me the opportunity to take a ten-day holiday on a remote Greek island called Limnos.

What made us choose there, I do not know but it turned out to be paradise on earth for us both. We found such pleasure in each other's company and it knew no bounds. We took out a small motorboat and went off to little uninhabited islands where we made love on the rocks. On some of the evenings we swam in the bay and made love in the moonlight. They were wonderful times and when I look back on them, which I have done often, I realize that all the treasures on earth could not bring back even one of those precious moments.

I had moved into my retreat in Tandridge and from the first moment I knew that I would be happy there. I had come a long way since living in Green Street but posh homes with big rooms and luxury carpets were never important to me and I knew that my one-bedroom flat with a tiny kitchen and lounge would be perfectly adequate. In fact, I wanted for nothing more.

Annie went back to her equally unpretentious, newly acquired home in Coulsdon and we visited each other on a regular basis. On most Sundays, after I had played tennis at Limpsfield Tennis Club, Annie would either come to the flat and cook for me or invite me to her house. During the summer we would often have friends over to enjoy picnics on the splendid lawn which was conveniently situated just outside my front door. On summer evenings we would stroll for a few miles across the woodlands to have a drink at the Barley Mow pub. There we could sit in the garden with the children, drinking half pints of bitter, watching the world go by.

It was less picturesque at Annie's house because the garden adjoined the railway track between Chipstead and Woodman-sterne. The trains which came by on the hour seemed to shake the very foundations but after a time I was used to them and even enjoyed watching them go by. Annie cooked the best Sunday roast in the whole world and whether she did it at my flat or her home, I was equally content.

I soon became friendly with Annie's charming neighbours, Syd and Joan Potter, who had three children, Andrew, Neil and Lorraine. They had a small table tennis table set up in their garage and invited me to participate. Syd and both of his sons were too good for me but the games were always exciting and memories of Green Street were brought to mind as I stretched for shots that could not be reached without banging into the side wall or knocking over the garden rake.

Competition

'Gold Star' was well known for its 'girlie' publications, although they only represented a small proportion of the overall business of the whole group of companies. We were developing other areas of publishing that were of little interest to the media. We had established a niche in the puzzle magazine market. Although sales were high, we made very little profit, but it did wonders for our reputation. I was often asked ... 'What do you do for a living?' To which I would reply, 'Oh, I am in publishing.' The next question was automatic; 'Oh yes, and what do you publish?'

'Lots of different types of magazines,' I would say. 'But mainly puzzle magazines. Many of them are sold throughout the world.' This was all perfectly true and by now my listener would be completely convinced that I was more than just respectable ... I was practically a saint. I was honest in what I said. The 'dishonesty' was in what I had left out. In reality all of our other titles did not add up to one quarter of our sales of adult magazines, both in Britain and abroad.

Even so, David Sullivan's girlie magazines were now outselling ours. In less than two years he had become a well established publisher and now a force to be reckoned with. *Up the Mini* and *Climax* had been replaced with big selling titles such as *Lovebirds* and *Playbirds*, which were both selling more than 100,000 copies. A later addition to his range, *Whitehouse*, was such a contentious title that nobody thought that he could get away with it. Linking the pure and highly respectable Mary Whitehouse with a magazine which portrayed models in erotic poses and couples engaged in simulated copulation could easily be considered too offensive for the majority of shops to handle. But, on the contrary, it has great curiosity value, and the title is successful to this day.

David Sullivan was not only a formidable competitor in the magazine and mail order business but the growth of his 'Private' shop empire was also causing us concern. We had recently acquired several shops in the West End, bringing our total to nine, and we were still looking for more. Three of them were strictly Ann Summers sex shops and the others primarily sold books and magazines. Three of these accommodated 'Peephole' machines which were profitable. These were similar in principle to the old 'What the Butler Saw' machines. The viewer would put ten pence into the slot machine and, if he liked what he saw, he could pay another ten pence until he had seen as much of the film as he wanted. They were supplied to us by an independent company that provided the cubicle as well as the adult films which were changed every month. There were hardly any problems from the police, nor, in my opinion, should there have been. Nobody should have the right to stop an adult, sitting alone, watching a titillating film that he had chosen to view.

Although we were fierce competitors I used to keep in touch with David Sullivan, more especially at such times, to talk about our latest seizures as well as the titles which had been released by the courts.

On one occasion he was delighted to inform me that the appeal court had returned a large quantity of his reprinted American titles. He was as surprised by their decision as anyone. There were four titles all portraying pictures of John Holmes, the world famous 'porno movie' star, engaged in all kinds of activities including explicit intercourse. His twelve inch penis was unashamedly exhibited on one of the covers, only partially covered by the hands of two beautiful nude women who seemed to be treating it as a microphone for a singing duet.

'If they could be released then surely anything goes,' I thought, as I watched through the window to see the police loading four gigantic lorries with comparatively innocuous merchandise.

The unfairness of it all was illustrated yet again when Uncle David and my cousin Ian were taken to the Old Bailey and found not guilty by a jury. The 'offending' magazines, seized months earlier, were said to depict sadism and sexual torture. Our magazines depicted women in a state of undress and that was all. My brother was always philosophical and would say, 'The so-called experts seem to know more and more about less and less. This is, for them, one big game and all that we can do is to play along with them.'

David Gold and Son were one of the independent wholesalers supplying the newsagent trade, had been growing stronger, and as a result they had more power in deciding the titles which their retail outlets were to handle. Our titles were often dropped to make room for other publications because the publisher was prepared to give them a higher discount. Thankfully Uncle Dave had missed out on the David Sullivan distribution contract. Had he had control of that range he would have been in an even stronger position to dictate to us.

My cousin, Ian, was becoming more influential in Uncle Dave's business. They had begun publishing a few girlie magazines of their own and, although they were never highly competitive, we were unhappy that our main wholesaler was expanding in this way. They had produced a magazine called *Probe* which was not dissimilar to our own *New Direction*. It also promoted the improvement of sexual activity and, understandably, they went into the mail order business selling marital aids. 'David Gold and Son' was always there, snapping at our heels.

Although Uncle Dave and his brother Godfrey had never been really good friends, their relationship had improved since my father chose to go his own way. Godfrey looked to his brother for information about the trade and, I suspect, news about our progress. A very sad thing about the Gold family is that it has never been able to recognize the success and achievements of others. Or at least, if recognized, then there is an obvious inability to express it.

I certainly recognized my own son's ability and I was delighted to hear that he had done so well in his entrance exam for Sevenoaks school. There was now every likelihood that he would be accepted in the coming year.

One weekend he told me of a predicament in which he had recently found himself. He had been called into the headmaster's office to be told that a teacher at 'The Hill' school had discovered that a number of 'soft porn' magazines were being bandied around and in view of the fact that many of them were published by 'Gold Star Publications', there was an accusation being made by her that Bradley Gold was the culprit. Bradley told the headmaster that it was not true but he was unable to convince his accusers and their suspicions remained unchanged until a few weeks later, when the teacher informed the headmaster that her own son, who was also a student at the school, was the villain of the piece. She had found a large brown envelope addressed to him which contained mail order information from David Sullivan's company, 'Private'. Bradley was in the clear. But I could well understand his desire to become a solicitor.

I was now making regular trips to Germany, departing very early in the morning from Gatwick Airport, and arriving back by nine or ten in the evening. On one occasion I arrived home late, close to midnight, feeling weary and ready to collapse into bed. I opened the door to my flat and saw a note on the floor. It was from the caretaker. 'Dear Mr Gold ... In case you return tonight do not use your end sitting room as it is about to collapse. The builders will start work in the morning. Please contact me as soon as possible'. ... That was all I needed.

The next morning, I discovered that the foundations of the lounge beneath mine had collapsed and the whole building was about to fall. Under the circumstances I was asked to find alternative accommodation ... It was clearly time for me to move in with Annie.

On the Toss of A Coin ...

I was not surprised to learn that Uncle Gerald's company had failed. In the autumn of 1974 I was in Australia trying to recover some of the £155,000 that we were owed (I eventually managed to recover £17,500) when John Gibbins of Thorpe and Porter got in touch with Ron Coleman. The owners of Thorpe and Porter – which was now better known as 'General Book Distributors', or 'GBD' – wanted to put a proposition to me, and in my absence a meeting had been arranged between Ron, myself and the owners, Matthew Berdon and Ralph Fields. The arrangement was for us to visit their offices in Hill Street and later to dine at the White Elephant Club in Mayfair.

I was pleased that I was away when John called because it was then easier to make an excuse as to why I could not go on the day that they had suggested. I agreed to meet two weeks later which gave me time to prepare for the negotiations, and also helped to give the impression that I was not exactly over enthusiastic ... Of course the reverse was true.

There was an air of excitement as we drove into London. I needed to metaphorically pinch myself every now and again. I could not believe that there was now a realistic possibility that I would buy out the one company which had practically controlled the magazine and book distribution industry for the past twenty years. Thorpe and Porter had always been far too strong for us to make inroads into their market share and they also had the benefit of the £260,000 which, like highway robbers, they had taken from us when they went bankrupt and only days later set up again using an almost identical name and holding on to their substantial outlets and connections.

Our cash resources had taken a long time to rebuild, and now here I was approaching London to complete what I believed would be one of the hardest and most important deals of my life. I intended to call on all my skills as a hard negotiator and I had no intention of failing on this particular acquisition. I was determined to win back every last penny that Thorpe and Porter, had taken from us in the past.

I never liked the term 'hard'. It implies that I was an aggressive negotiator which was never the case – on the contrary my approach was invariably 'soft'. I had developed certain golden rules: one of them was not to start negotiations before lunchtime or after 4 pm ... Before lunch you are too eager and after four they will think you are desperate. My tactic was always to spend as much time on matters that had nothing whatsoever to do with the deal for as long as possible talking on subjects such as the weather, politics, sex or anything else on which I had practically no knowledge. The idea was to be sure that the other side brought up the subject of 'the deal' first and I would tend to purposely not hear or intentionally keep talking about other things. Once the asking price was put to me, I would automatically say, 'No ...' Then negotiations could commence.

By the time we finally got down to the real nitty gritty I had already given the impression that doing a deal was of little importance to me. Another ploy that I used after the deal had been introduced to the conversation was to talk, hypothetically, in terms of extremely low amounts. This had the effect of undermining the proposal and when more realistic figures were introduced, my counterpart would think he had achieved an element of success.

These negotiations were usually quite humorous and enjoyable. I always believed that the opposition should come out feeling that things could have been worse (not a lot, I would hope). I could live with myself in the knowledge that they were always free to say no! My intention was to establish the precise point at which a deal would fail and then to offer a fraction more.

Ron Coleman was not at all happy about my negotiating policy. He had reached a time in his life when his two sons, both staunch socialists, were influencing him away from his lifetime commitment towards capitalism and he would imply that there was a strong element of greed in my dealing. My response to that was to say that under capitalism it is dog eat dog ... Under socialism it is just the opposite.

Over lunch, Matthew Berdon began to raise matters concerning the business in hand. I had already worked out his reasons for wanting to sell and I knew that despite 'GBD's' profitability, Matty (we were already on first name terms) was aware that unless the company kept up with the trend and increased the sexual content of its magazines it was doomed to fail, and his partner, Ralph Field and he, were not prepared to go along that path. They had already made their fortune and the thought of police activity involving one of their companies was totally unacceptable.

During lunch I had spoken of nothing but the unfairness of it all, and how the police were hounding us, as well as even the publishers of 'softer' magazines such as Paul Raymond and Bob Guccione. I knew that this kind of talk was having its desired effect, and consequently made an offer for £225,000 which I knew was unrealistically low and considerably less than the nett value of the assets. Matty was clearly irritated and refused it point blank. Ron Coleman was like a fifth columnist when he said loud enough to be overheard, 'Surely Ralph, we could pay a little more, after all we have come this far and ...' He trailed off as he saw the resolve in my eyes as I continued to make my departure. I said my goodbyes, thanked them for their hospitality, opened the door and left. Ron soon followed and said to me, 'I think you're mad, I am sure that we have lost it.' I was not as confident as I sounded when I replied, 'They'll be back, you mark my words.'

The two week wait was unbearable but sure enough, John Gibbins called to say that Matty wanted to complete the deal and would compromise still further. I was only too pleased to make yet another trip to London, knowing that this time a deal would be finalized. This time I knew that if I stuck to my ground they would be accepting my offer.

Again, I was in no hurry to discuss the purpose for the visit. I left it to Matthew Berdon, and after a while he said, 'You win, I'm prepared to close the gap. We've analysed the company's solvency situation and it comes to £267,000, and I'm prepared to let it go for that figure and no less. Failing that, I intend to wind the company up. Which would be a tragedy for you but, I would lose nothing,' Matty said with apparent conviction.

'I came here prepared to increase my offer to £245,000.' I told him but that's my top figure, so we still have no deal.'

'Well that's up to you because I refuse to drop below the solvency figure,' he responded.

I told him that I would like to talk with Ron Coleman privately, although I knew Ron's view without him saying a word ... He was going to agree with Matty. 'For goodness sake, Ralph, accept,' he urged. 'I can't take any more.'

We went back to the table. '£250,000' I offered, 'and that really is final.'

'£256,000' he countered. 'And that's final.'

For the second time in two weeks I packed up all my papers and shook everyone's hand.

However, Matty had not finished. 'Are you a betting man, Ralph?'

'No,' I replied emphatically. Ignoring my reply he suggested that we toss for the £6,000. I could not believe my ears. I had never gambled more than twenty pounds at any one time in my whole life, and to put £6,000 on the toss of a coin was quite ridiculous.

'Sorry, Matty, but I don't gamble.'

With that my friend and colleague, Ron Coleman, whispered in my ear. 'Come on Ralph, you have just done the deal of a lifetime. Win or lose, what does it really matter?'

He was right, and after a moment's thought I agreed. I regretted it immediately. My principles on the matter were being disregarded. I had always said that the only way to win with gambling was to lose, and yet I could not bear the thought of losing this one. £6,000 on the toss of a silly coin ...

'Best of three,' I muttered as though the extension of the bet would make it less preposterous.

Ron was given the privilege of tossing the coin. 'Heads,' I called.

'Heads,' Ron clarified with visible glee. I was not as gleeful. If I had allowed the single call then I would have won by now.

'Call again,' offered Matty implying at the same time that he was happy for Ron to toss the coin.

'Tails,' I called nervously. Now I felt like a big time gambler, on a roll.

'Heads,' blurted Ron. The 'roll' had lasted for only one call.

'Here goes,' I thought. 'The big one.'

'Call again,' ordered Matty.

I did not want the responsibility but I felt obliged to do as I was told.

'Tails,' I called for the second time running as the coin was falling rapidly to the ground. When it landed I was afraid to look. £6,000 was resting on that single result. I could buy a house for that money. My mind rushed back to Green Street, to a time when £6,000 would have made us rich beyond our wildest dreams. 'Tails, it must be tails!' I was willing Ron as he went down on his haunches to look at the coin. He paused and I knew it was heads.

'Heads,' he called as his head dropped. I had lost £6,000 in less than six seconds.

I shook Matty's hand and congratulated him on winning the bet. I had just taken over a company for which I would have happily paid an additional hundred thousand pounds, and yet I was grieving over the loss of a mere £6,000.

Within two days Matty sent me a letter expressing his appreciation of my sportsmanship when losing the bet. He invited me to visit Ciro's, his own jewellery shop in Regent Street to choose a piece of jewellery valued at £1,000. I was most impressed and it made me think of how I would have reacted had the roles been reversed ... Not as well, I'm embarrassed to say.

Malta

The girlie magazine 'war' had not abated. David Sullivan continued to expand and the level of eroticism of his photographs and editorial had not declined. Ron and I decided to meet with him at his office in Upton Lane in Forest Gate to discuss working more closely together, as well as his contribution towards the formation of 'Bapal' (British Adult Publishers Association Limited), the industry's self-regulating body.

Upton Lane is close to Hampton Road where I was born, and only a short distance from my former home in Green Street, so I had no difficulty in finding it. I was not impressed with David Sullivan's office accommodation but I was impressed by him. He was clearly a sharp businessman and he was not prepared to automatically accept the demands of 'Bapal', nor was he going to easily fall in with our wishes to ease up on the erotic content in his magazines. It was a tough meeting which accomplished very little but we had made a start and I was confident that, in time, we would reach an understanding.

Ron Coleman, who had been elected to chair 'Bapal', was in his element. It involved a great deal of work for him but he enjoyed the challenge as he foresaw a successful outcome. David and I were less optimistic. We knew that through Ron Coleman, 'Gold Star' would be largely responsible for the work and for a disproportionate amount of the expenses. Nothing succeeds like reputation and we had a great reputation ... for footing the bill.

Eventually we came to terms and most of the adult publishers complied by paying a fee based on their turnover. Guidelines were established and a degree of sanity prevailed. An office was set up in Soho Square and John Trevelyan CBE, the former chief film censor, acted in a part time capacity as president.

The plan was that each adult publication was to be submitted to the board for approval to ensure that the guidelines had been adhered to. If they had not, a warning would be given and after three warnings all member distributors would refuse to handle that particular publication.

The council of 'Bapal' was set up at enormous expense but it failed to achieve its goal. It offered full co-operation to the Home Office, the Director of Public Prosecutions and the Metropolitan Police and at the same time requested that these bodies appoint representatives to serve on the council. In principle it was a solution to a problem that was costing the country a great deal of money. In practice it solved nothing. The police and the authorities in general refused to co-operate and they continued with their policy which was to seize, examine, present to the court, incinerate or return and then seize, examine and so on ... without considering the cost. 'Bapal' did its best, but in essence it was a 'paper tiger'.

The police were as active as ever in seizing girlie magazines. However, there were moves afoot which could ameliorate the situation. A committee had been set up by the government to review the laws concerning obscenity, indecency and violence in publications, displays and entertainment. It was chaired by the former husband of the politician, Shirley Williams.

Bernard Williams was a professor of philosophy at Cambridge and well respected in academic circles. Interested parties were invited to put their point of view to the committee and the formation of 'Bapal' was timely. At last it would appear that some common sense would prevail, although it was understood that it would take a few years for the committee to finalize its report.

*

I had given great thought to entering the Malta Air Rally. I was as determined as ever to improve my flying and follow in my brother's footsteps. David had performed exceptionally well, accomplishing a fifth place in the rally, but already he was hoping to do better. My own wildest dream was to actually reach Malta then to have a good holiday, and make it back to Biggin Hill. For me, that would be in itself a big accomplishment.

First, I had to learn to fly a twin-engine aircraft because I was not happy about flying over large expanses of sea in a single. Gordon King, who owned the club next door to ours, had a training twin aeroplane available and I hired him to teach me.

Soon after my training began, David suggested that we should buy a new plane and dispose of 'Mike Oscar'. It was as though he intended to 'put down' a lovable old pet dog. I would not agree to let it go as I was hopeful that I would soon be capable of flying it on a regular basis for both business and pleasure.

We agreed to purchase a new Cessna 337, which was a very unusual type of aircraft. It had two engines, one at the front and one at the rear which worked on a 'push, pull' principle. It is

claimed to be one of the safest type of aircraft available because it can fly more easily on a single engine than the more conventional twin, which experiences an amount of yaw within an instant of one of its engines failing.

After only seven flying hours of training with Gordon King I became a twin rated pilot and was in a position to take up passengers if I wished. However, I wanted first to be 'checked out' on 'Mike Oscar' and was eager to learn everything possible about that aeroplane before I would take full command with unqualified passengers.

Mike Wennig was an instructor who was highly skilled and after helping me to fly an 'Apache', he undertook to teach me to fly my own plane, 'Mike Oscar'. He started by joining me on all of my business flights, allowing me to be the pilot in control, but at the same time being there to see that I made no mistakes.

I was now making so many business trips abroad that my thoughts turned again to entering the Malta Air Rally. After all, I had flown to Belfast with Mike Wennig and practically the whole flight we were in cloud and I was in control (so much so that Mike went into the back of the aeroplane to have a snooze). The landings were good and Mike commented on the fact that I had done well.

All I needed was a co-pilot and, as most of the people that were going to Malta were already fixed-up, I was not hopeful of finding one – not until Donny Verne, one of the most experienced pilots on the airfield, offered to go with me. I discovered that he had an instrument rating (which is the highest achievable qualification for a private pilot) and it sounded as though I had fallen on my feet ... I was to learn however, that I had really fallen on something at the other end of my legs.

My preparation for the rally was, though I say it myself, proficient. The plane was thoroughly cleaned. Every panel, every nut and bolt and every tiny screw, in fact, every square inch was made to look as though it was to be used in an operating theatre. The object of this was to win the 'Concours d'Elegance'. David had been the runner up in this particular competition the year before and I had high hopes of doing well this time. A little help from David would have been useful but it was not forthcoming as he too was a participant; since I was a competitor it was understandable ... It was praise indeed that he saw me as a threat.

Donny Verne did not help. He was not interested in that sort of thing. He was a 'fun' person and that was that. As far as he was concerned, fun and work did not mix. I worked very hard on the flight plan, which was an integral part of the whole exercise. It not only assisted us to get there safely, it also had to be handed in to the judges, who marked it for information and clarity. These marks would contribute towards the final positioning in the rally. Donny was not interested in helping me with this either.

I was starting to have my doubts about him, but each time I expressed my concern, I was assured that he did have an instrument rating, albeit 'American', which meant that he was a competent pilot.

My friend Norman Sawtell mentioned that he would like to go to Malta and asked if I would take him and his girlfriend, Lynn. I was impressed because Norman was even more nervous than Annie about flying and he also knew that the plane was old and that I would be in the captain's seat. The only confidence booster for him was that Donny happened to be an experienced and, as far as he knew, competent pilot. I was delighted to have their company and Annie too was pleased that they were going, if only to keep an eye on me for the few days before she was able to join us. She was not really keen on flying in small aircraft, especially in cloud, over mountains and large expanses of sea, so she decided to travel there by a conventional commercial airline. She did, however, come to the airfield on a beautiful June morning to wave us off.

On the previous night we had loved each other to the point of exhaustion ... It was Annie's way of taking a little insurance.

She believed that a satisfied man was less likely to indulge in a holiday encounter. There might be something in that, and I just loved her for thinking that way – I loved her for thinking that I was highly desirable and that I would be some 'big catch'. At no time did I share those views, and she need not have worried because no woman could have taken me away from her.

Our destination on that day was Catania on the Italian island of Sicily, where we intended to meet my brother and his crew at a hotel near to the airport. There would also be many other Biggin Hill pilots who would be congregating for a few days before the final 'run in' to Malta via the Gozo beacon.

We intended to reach Catania in three legs via Clermont Ferrand, in France, and Bastia in Corsica. By the time we got away it was clear that we would not reach Catania until the following day. The flight to Clermont Ferrand was uneventful. Donny was as humorous as ever, making the occasional joke that instilled confidence in us, such as, 'The last time that I crash-landed nobody was hurt because the ground broke our fall.' We were all looking forward to our holiday. I knew that I would miss Annie but I was well aware that during the next few days my mind would be on nothing else but endeavouring to achieve as much success as was possible in my first competitive flying event.

Once we had crossed the Channel we were able to climb through the cloud to a height of 9,500 feet to enter French airspace, which was legal for a non-commercial pilot provided we were able to maintain visual conditions. We were given a transponder code number to transmit and it was comforting to know that from then on we would be under radar supervision. The weather was good and the journey was smooth. Donny Verne had absolutely nothing to do except make the mandatory radio calls and entertain the passengers.

Four hours and ten minutes later, we landed in Clermont Ferrand and the sun was shining. We were all very excited and everything was going according to plan, and after stopping for fuel and coffee, Donny and I went to the Met. Office to receive the latest weather report. It did not appear to be too important because all cloud had completely disappeared and the weather was perfect. When Donny showed me the 'read out', I was surprised that it was all so complicated. I knew that it was simple for an instrument rated pilot to interpret these reports, rather like a secretary when reading her shorthand notes, and I was pleased that Donny understood these things.

It surprised me, though, when he spoke to the weather man behind the desk. He spoke no English, so Donny's knowledge of the French language came in handy.

'Dis sez dat de weather south ist bon, oui?' The reply was positive because the Frenchman respected Don's knowledge of his language by speaking for five minutes about the conditions ... in fluent French.

Don had a perfect solution to the problem. He took the man outside and pointed a little to the right of the afternoon sun and said, 'South bon, oui?' The reply was even more positive and thankfully, this time short.

'Ah oui, très bon.'

Donny was satisfied. 'It helps to confirm these things,' he said to me out of the corner of his mouth. I believed that he was joking.

We took off into the clear blue sky. At 5,500 feet above the Mediterranean Sea with just over a hundred miles to run, we experienced serious turbulence. I was concerned for Norman and Lynn, who were cuddled up in the back and asked Donny to request a new flight level. This was given and we began our climb to 9,500 feet. A few moments later Nice control called us over the radio.

'Golf Alpha Yankee Mike Oscar, be advised that there are heavy intermittent thunderstorms in the Bastia area.'

'Roger, Nice,' came Donny's prompt reply, 'Message read and understood.' Then he repeated it to them.

I did not speak to Donny. I was concentrating on my climb and going through further in-flight checks as I awaited navigational instructions from my 'experienced' co-pilot. They were not forth-coming and it was not long before we were completely engulfed in cloud and the turbulence had returned with a vengeance.

'Did I see lightning?' came a gentle voice from the rear.

'No,' I lied, but one second later I saw a blinding flash and the plane lurched as I battled with the controls. My head literally hit the roof and I was forced to tighten my safety strap. This was it. We were in the centre of the storm. Donny was remarkably calm as he informed Nice control that he was going over to Bastia approach.

'Bastia control, this is Golf Alpha Yankee Mike Oscar, how do you read? Over.'

'Golf ... Ke ... Osc ... We ... Read ... Two's.'

'Bastia,' came Donny's reply, 'We read you two's also.' In telegraphy language, readings are marked out of five and a lowly two is a pilot's nightmare, especially when he is approaching an airfield in a mountainous area and being thrown about the sky like a rowing boat in a stormy sea.

He told them that we were approaching their airfield at a height of nine thousand five hundred feet in meteorological conditions, which meant we were still in cloud, and we requested landing instructions. There was no response, only a crackle and a few broken words that meant nothing to us. There were two landing aids at Bastia. One was out of commission and the other, an ADF (automatic direction finder), was unreliable under the inclement conditions that we were experiencing.

The fact that it was situated more than a mile to the south of the airport was an additional complication. Donny elected to position us at a point which, by referring to the albeit unpredictable ADF needle, he believed was directly above the airfield. From there we would operate in accordance with our let-down procedure. We were to fly outbound over the sea for five miles before commencing our descent, during which we would turn back into land, letting down to a height of five hundred feet. By this time, we hoped that we would be in visual conditions and would soon see the island of Corsica.

At 9,000ft Donny gave me instructions. 'Maintain your height and turn left fifteen degrees on to a heading of one three zero.' At his direction, I turned the aircraft immediately onto the new heading and repeated Donny's instructions back to him. I remained at nine thousand feet above sea level. Bastia had no distance measuring equipment in those days and our exact position was nothing more than a guess. On that basis, we could not possibly descend below the height of the highest mountain within at least ten miles, unless we were certain of being over the sea. Donny explained the situation to me on the outbound run and asked me if I agreed with what he was doing. I hated the question. After all he was the instrument-rated pilot and talking to me as if I was in that league sent a shiver down my spine.

'Donny,' I said, 'I am not qualified to make any judgement and our lives are entirely in your hands.' I knew, of course, that it was not strictly true – I was placed in the left hand seat and was, under those circumstances, the captain. I was doing very well and, had I been in a simulator, I would have been given full marks for maintaining a set height and heading. But as far as navigation was concerned, I had allowed myself to fly into conditions which would require skills beyond my capabilities. I was now beginning to doubt Donny's competence, and I was worried.

I spoke to Donny through the intercom and suggested that we should put on our life jackets. He made the point that it would unnecessarily alarm Lynn and, at this stage, I tended to agree with him. The turbulence was less severe as we slowly descended and I looked round at Norman and Lynn and did my best to give the impression that everything was under control. I knew that I had not convinced Norman ... But one out of two ...

We descended to five hundred feet above sea level, and to my dismay we were still in cloud. We continued the descent to three hundred feet. Norman said that he was sure that he could see the sea, although it took more than a minute before Donny and I could confirm that we could see it too. That was comforting and we all looked apprehensively ahead, hoping and praying for the island to appear. It did, and we began our search for the airfield, knowing that if it were unsighted within two minutes, we had to climb back into cloud to a safe height of nine thousand feet and carry out the same procedure. We failed to find the runway and I was instructed to climb. I respected Don for sticking to this procedure. Had he been totally incompetent, we would have stayed in intermittent visual conditions at a low level which would have enabled us to continue our search for the runway but, with mountainous terrain all around, it was too dangerous.

There were two other options; we could have flown to Ajaccio which was less than a hundred miles away, but by then we would only have had enough fuel for one approach and in any case, if the conditions did not improve, we would have been no better off. The second option was to make another two or possibly three 'procedural' let-downs at Bastia, although once we took that route, we were totally committed. We would have to find the airfield or ditch in the sea as close to the coast as possible.

Sweat was running down my face as I stuck rigidly to the correct climb rate. Mike Wennig had trained me well and I knew that I was handling the aircraft skilfully. I wondered for a moment just how I would cope in the event of a sea ditching. In training this was covered briefly ... but instructors are not too keen on giving practical tuition!

We made two attempts but each time failed to see the runway.

Donny called the airfield every two minutes and now he was using words like 'This is Golf Alpha Yankee Mike Oscar, transmitting blind, we require assistance, this is an emergency!' There was still no response as we approached the airfield for the third time. We reached the critical distance from the coast and I was anticipating further instructions from Donny. Instead, he let out a sound that will live in my memory forever. It was a sort of, 'Eeeeeeeeahh ... !' that ended with a little sobbing noise, a sound of total despair. The petrol tanks showed practically empty and the word, 'Climb!' would have been inappropriate as staying visual was now essential – although in doing so, we were being forced ever downward.

Suddenly there was a scream from the rear of the aeroplane. 'I've seen it! A runway... There!!' Norman was pointing dramatically out of the rear window. 'It was there, behind us, seven o'clock, turn left ... Oh God! It's gone, turn left! Turn left!'

We were at two hundred and fifty feet with rain pouring down, causing the forward visibility to be virtually zero. I applied full throttles and turned the plane practically on its side; it was a manoeuvre that I had done only a few times before and only then at a height which allowed for error. I was aware of the dangers but I was also aware that we could die if we failed to find the runway. More than once in my early training I had found it impossible to relocate a reference point such as a lake or a road or even an aerodrome and on those occasions, the conditions were perfect and I had the comfort of contact with a radio controller who was there to help me. This was different, and four lives hung in the balance.

When I finally saw the illuminating lights of runway 33/15 at Bastia, I cried with joy. I did not care to look for the wind sock or any other means of assessing the correct landing procedures, I just reduced my speed, put down the undercarriage, adjusted the flaps and put 'Mike Oscar' on the ground. It was not the best landing that I had ever done, but in a situation like that, any landing is a good one. And as far as my passengers were concerned, it was sensational.

Quality Of Life

As far as the Rally was concerned, it was not my year. I came 32nd out of 50, which was not bad considering. It was, however, David's year. He actually won the arrival competition and came second overall. The results were not announced until the fourth day, and by then Annie had arrived, courtesy of British Airways. The celebrations were wild, but Annie and I had our own celebrations during the day, and that evening we were almost too tired to stand up. Thankfully, the prize-giving took place in the hotel in which we were staying which meant that we could get back to bed without more travelling.

As we walked through the corridors of the Hotel Vedala we saw a number of photographs of well-known people who had stayed there. The most famous of them was that of Rock Hudson, who was a regular guest. I was told that he came each year accompanied by a number of young and handsome men. His picture was honourably hung in the hall of fame. Only a few years later my brother David's picture was added, in recognition of his brilliant flying achievements.

The six-day holiday went in a flash. All participants and their partners were invited to attend various functions which included beach barbecues, dinners and supper dances. A whole day was spent at 'Luzzu Beach Club' with the use of their water sport facilities, and another visiting the beautiful island of Comino.

We had a wonderful time, but for one small comment that Norman made to me. Annie had mentioned to Norman and his girlfriend, Lynn, that a small lump had appeared under her chin. She was a little concerned about it, but did not want me to be worried as I had a long flight to concentrate on. It was typical of her but I would have wanted to know, if only to offer her more reassurance, but I decided to broach the subject as soon as we returned home.

The lump was easily detectable and I raised the matter with Annie. She told me that she had seen her doctor who said that it was probably a cyst and he had given her a letter for the hospital. She apologized for not having told me about it earlier.

We visited Dr Knapton at Croydon General Hospital and he arranged for a specialist, Mr Courtney-Evans, to do a biopsy within a few weeks. Annie was not apparently worried by the developments and I acted as though I, too, had all the confidence in the world that there was no cause for concern.

Annie was admitted overnight and, when I collected her from the hospital, she informed me that we might have to wait up to a week for the results. Her follow-up appointment was only a few days ahead and I went with her. She did not seem to be worried and I did my best to hide my anxiety.

I decided at this point that I should stay with Annie each night until this thing was cleared up. I realized that my staying could have an adverse effect on her divorce settlement but that, now, had to take second place. I spent an anxious week in which I threw myself into my work.

Our receptionist rang through one morning to inform me that a young lady named Anna was on the line. I thought immediately of Annie but I was a little confused. Annie never called me at the office. She had always implied that she was nervous about doing so because she thought that my time there was so precious.

The call was put through to me and her nervousness was evident, more than that, she was in a state of obvious anxiety and I needed to calm her down. I joked about her using the name 'Anna', which was the name Boo always used. She apologized and then told me that her surgeon's secretary had called to tell her that Mr Courtney-Evans wanted to see her. She was told that it was quite urgent and an appointment had been made for the following week. I told her that there was no need to worry and that it could not be terribly serious or they would have asked to see her immediately. I suspected that I was wrong but at least my comments had eased her concern. I went to her directly but I could do no more than offer reassurance. I took her to dinner.

I was pleased to find that she was less worried than she had seemed to be earlier. She had clearly adopted a more positive attitude and we enjoyed our evening. Annie was incredibly loving, and clearly delighted that I was with her.

I promised to stay with her until the weekend, when we had arranged to go to Brighton for a few days. I had believed that there was no possibility of enjoying each other's company more, but I was wrong. Our lovemaking improved in both quality and intensity. I had found a partner who wanted me, needed me and most of all loved me. I knew this, not only because she told me (and she did on many occasions) ... I just knew. I did not love her any less, but I was still reluctant to make a bigger commitment and she both respected and accepted my wishes.

I went with her to the hospital and sat for hours waiting for her name to be called. We were eventually informed by a nurse to wait outside Doctor Elliot's office on the fourth floor. The young doctor (he could not have been more than twenty four years old) personally invited us in and, after checking Annie's neck and looking inside her mouth, sent her off to have a blood test. As he closed the door behind her he said to me, 'I am afraid that having removed the lump, we have discovered that your wife has lymphosarcoma.' The blood drained from my face. I did not tell him that Annie was not my wife but went on to ask him if that meant that she had cancer.

'Yes,' he said. 'Lymphoma is a malignant tumour which arises from the cells of the lymphatic system. It is a rare type of cancer that even today has no specific classification.' My mouth went so dry that I could hardly speak.

'And what's your prognosis?' I asked, close to tears.

'It's not good,' he replied. 'Six months.' But after observing my total despondency, he added, 'Perhaps more.'

'Please say nothing to Annie.' I begged. 'I'll take care of that.'

'Well, first she must see Dr Knapton and he will decide what is to be done next.'

'I want to speak to him first,' I spluttered.

'I'm afraid that he is seeing patients at the moment, but if you go down there ...' He motioned his arms, as if there were a fifty-fifty chance of seeing him.

I ran down the stairs two at a time and walked up to the nurse on reception. I told her that I needed to speak with Dr Knapton urgently, and she asked me to take a seat while she checked out the position. I kept looking at my watch as the minutes ticked away and I expected Annie to join me at any moment. After three or four minutes, I could stand it no longer and I knocked on his door.

'Come in!' He called. I stood there hardly knowing what to say. An elderly man lay on his examination table and they were both looking at me.

'Yes?' he asked at last.

'I'm sorry to barge in on you like this, but I'm in a dreadful panic and I need just a few moments of your time.'

'I am sorry', he replied, 'but I'm with a patient and you will have to wait ... Please wait outside.'

Ignoring his instruction, I pleaded with him. 'Dr Knapton, my partner – ' (I should have said wife) ' – is about to see you, she is about to be told that she has cancer and I must speak with you.'

'I am sorry but you will have to leave. What's said between my patients and me is not your concern,' he said, forcefully, as the nurse ushered me out of his consulting room. Once outside, I saw Annie coming towards me.

'Is everything alright?' she enquired.

'Everything's fine,' I lied. 'Doctor Elliot asked me to bring down your notes.' Annie seemed to be quite satisfied with the excuse as we sat down to wait for another hour before we went in to see Dr Knapton. I went in with Annie, but he did not acknowledge me, and made no reference to what had gone on before.

'The lump which we removed has been tested and I am afraid that there was evidence of malignancy. I propose sending you to the Royal Marsden Hospital, where they will decide upon the best form of treatment.' He spoke in a matter of fact way, as though he were sending her for a dental check up, and I hated him at that moment more than I have hated any other man in my life, even Boo. Now, as I reflect back, I realize the need for doctors to speak frankly with their patients, and any form of delay or indirectness can prove to be cruel in the long term.

Annie's appointment for the Royal Marsden was made for early the following week. Her reaction to the whole incident was beyond belief. In the car going home she spoke only of the fact that while I was with her, everything would turn out alright ... As she spoke, Doctor Elliot's words were pounding in my ears.

I carried on my life as normally as possible, but there was not an hour that went by when I did not think of Annie and how she was coping, and even of how long she might have to live.

Before she was due to go to the Royal Marsden, she had to undergo various tests. She was examined by a gynaecologist, followed by a bronchoscopy and a thorough examination of her throat and mouth. We were told that, as the primary tumour had not been found, they would give radiation treatment in the area from where the lump had been removed. This was to cover the possibility that it had in fact been the primary. A mask was to be made to protect the rest of her face, which would take some weeks. In the meantime, I asked for permission from her assigned doctor, Dr Ford, to take Annie on holiday. This was granted, and our friend Mike Behr asked us to join his girlfriend Mandy and him in Corfu.

Our holiday, under the circumstances, was superb, and soon after we returned home Annie began her treatment. I sat with her each day during her long wait. Occasionally the treatment apparatus would 'go down' and we would be forced to wait for many more hours. Each day Annie became more uncomfortable, as her mouth became dry and ulcerated. She was also became very tired and agitated, but each day I loved and admired her more.

The course of radium lasted six weeks and took us to within two months of Christmas. By then, Annie was very ill, but Dr Ford told me that she would be much better by Christmas and I should be able to take her on another holiday which he knew I was anxious to do. Annie's condition improved – she started to eat more and the scarring around her neck and face looked less angry. On the negative side, her hair had started to fall out in the region of the treatment and she was now forced to wear a scarf. I promised to take her to a hair clinic in London in the new year.

Initially, we went to Allders in Croydon to buy a wig. It really looked good but she was uncomfortable wearing it. Annie had been wonderfully brave in every respect through her illness and its treatment, but she was horrified at the thought that the bald spot would be there forever. Until then she had a head of beautiful dark brown hair of which she was naturally very proud and I was determined to find a way of, at least partially, restoring it.

The only solution was to take her to a 'weave' clinic, one of which I had seen advertised in the West End of London. They produced a weave that was tightened to her existing hair and beauty was partially restored although, within a short period of time, it became loose, which necessitated a periodic re-tightening programme. In addition to the visits to the Royal Marsden Hospital, we were to make regular trips to the Svenson hair clinic and I invariably chose to accompany her. It presented us with the chance to be together more, which pleased me enormously.

As the months went by I wanted Annie to see as much of life as was humanly possible, which involved visiting as many of our friends as we could. I took her to see Don and Marie Wagstaff who had been horrified by the events of the past few months but they were as determined as I was to see that Annie enjoyed life to the full. They had loved her from the first moment and were clearly happy that I had at last found a partner who was right for me.

Someone once said, 'It matters not how long you live, but how well.' They were great words, but with two young children it was understandable for Annie to say, 'Ralph, I only want for one thing in this life.'

'And what's that?' I asked.

'To be old one day.'

I could only reply by saying, 'You will be, Annie, you will ...' It was easier to convince her than it was to convince myself.

Business As Usual

Our overall group of companies had now expanded to the point where our turnover had well exceeded the magical five million pounds per annum and we were still growing. The prospects were good but David and I were very much aware that every penny was still hard to come by. Having said that, one day Pam, our receptionist, called to say that a Mr Miller was in the waiting room and wanted to see me. I never like to see people without an appointment but equally, in those days, I was reluctant to turn him or anyone else away.

'Send him up, Pam, but tell him I've another appointment in five minutes.' It was not true but I did not want to waste valuable time.

'Mr Gold,' he said after shaking my hand, 'you have a shop in Tottenham Court Road, number sixteen.'

'Yes,' I replied, indignantly, as though I was expecting a complaint or something worse.

'Well,' he went on, 'I have a five thousand pound cheque here for our rental and I would like to negotiate another three-year agreement.'

'What had you in mind?' I responded, as I took his cheque, not knowing what it was for, or indeed, what he was talking about.

'I think that you should give me your lowest price and then I can talk with "my people" and we will see if we can meet it.'

I was becoming frustrated but intrigued. It was not every day that someone put five thousand pounds into my hand without my knowing what it was for.

He went on to inform me. 'The advertisers will not pay more than we are asking for the site and that leaves very little scope to pay you more.'

The penny was beginning to drop.

'Advertising ... What advertising?' I thought. 'Well,' I said, 'I am looking for at least a fifty per cent increase,' presuming that whatever I was selling would now be too dear and I anticipated the word 'no'.

'No,' he replied. 'But I am sure that we could go to £6,400.'

With that I said, 'Please put your offer in writing and I will consider it.' I held the door open and he left. I kissed the cheque and went immediately into David's office. He could not believe it any more than I, as we tried to reason it out. When I mentioned advertising David suggested that it could be something to do with the hoardings on the wall above our shop in Tottenham Court Road. Although the advertising boards were attached to our neighbour's wall they were in our air space and a deal had obviously been struck with the previous owners. We had inherited the continuing arrangement ... Very nice, thank you. With this kind of luck, how could we fail?

With that, Pam called again. David picked up the phone and he looked at me in despair.

'I don't believe it!' he said. 'Six officers ...? Five lorries ...? Arrange tea and make them comfortable. Mr Coleman or Mr Tizzard will no doubt join them in a few moments.'

He put his hands out to his sides.

'The leveller,' he said. 'In one hand out the other.'

Chief Inspector Shepard was in command of the 'raid'. It was the biggest so far and the removal of stock took nearly two days. We were 'up in arms' about it and arranged for photographs to be taken of our police force at work, intending to alert the country to the real obscenity – the criminal waste of police time and public money.

Once again we helped by arranging for our employees to co-operate by supplying regular tea and biscuits and allowing the police use of staff and equipment. We reflected on this pattern of behaviour and wondered whether it was ultimately the right tack. The answer, with the benefit of hindsight, was 'no'. We were like lambs to slaughter and no amount of gentle baaing was going to save us.

We put pen to paper. It is said that the pen is mightier than the sword, but whoever said that got it wrong, particularly when it is related to the Obscene Publications department at Scotland Yard. At least the 'sword' had to be dealt with, whilst our letters were easily thrown in the bin.

We wrote immediately in protest to inform the Chief Inspector that we saw no rhyme or reason for his action. It had taken place at a time when final judgment was about to be made by the divisional appeal courts concerning similar publications, seized in an earlier raid. Most of the magazines were returns and were in the process of being exported. The best-selling titles had been proof read by counsel who certified that, in their opinion, they did not contravene the Obscene Publications Act. Finally, we pointed out that the Williams Committee was about to publish its findings which were clearly going to be relevant regarding the necessity for this sort of police action. However, our pleading clearly fell on deaf ears, even though we offered to give the revenue from the export sales to a charity of their choosing if they returned the stock. We were desperate to hold on to our export business, but after so much disruption it took many years before we re-established our markets.

'Bapal', under the chairmanship of Ron Coleman, had taken up our cause in a debate which was held on television. I was away at the time of its transmission, but I remember discussing it on my return with my good friend and solicitor, Michael Bauer. Having seen the programme, in which a number of 'Bapal' members were filmed in conference, he commented that they appeared to be 'seedy' and disreputable. I never responded, but it hit home how many people perceive us ... and not necessarily only the bigots.

*

Ron and I continued to visit Germany on business. Each year we attended the German 'Sex Fair', where we met up with a number of friends in the industry. Hans Binzer of 'Bimex', a pleasant man who spoke very good English, was one of my favourite suppliers. His wife and two beautiful daughters, who were probably in their late teens or early twenties, tended his stand, and I enjoyed talking to them – practising my German was a bonus.

It seemed strange at first that this ordinary and unquestionably decent family would work together in an environment of sexual explicitness. They offered for sale some of the most outrageous prosthetics and sex toys whilst around them were video company stands showing selections of their pornographic movies on large television sets.

As the years passed, I began to realize that sex is like any other pleasure product; in short measure, it is highly stimulating and its allure can tantalize and, under certain circumstances, it could have serious consequences. In the other extreme, like chocolate in a chocolate factory, over-indulgence can make you totally uninterested. I understand that some people may think that over-exposure to sexual material could possibly result in a complacency towards sex and, more seriously, towards loving, but I failed to see any detrimental signs in the Bimex family or, even more so, in my own.

In Britain, the judiciary had turned a blind eye to the 'Williams Report'. It had taken more than two years for Bernard Williams and his twelve committee members to finally submit their findings to the Secretary of State, Willie Whitelaw, on the considered effects of pornography. They had heard arguments about most aspects concerning the subject and its effects on crime, marriage, and general life in Britain and, in the final analysis, their statement read, 'There is often a real difficulty in identifying what the harmful effect of the material is supposed to be.'

These were not the words that the establishment wanted to hear. Nor had they wanted to hear that, after looking closely into the matter of readership, they had established that four million people read one or more girlie magazines each month, and after looking at all the available evidence regarding sexually explicit material and crime, they found it, 'Striking that one can study case after case of sex crimes and murder without finding any hint at all that pornography was present in the background.'

There were even suggestions made to them by psychiatrists and psychologists that 'cases more frequently occurred in which the effects of this material were beneficial rather than harmful'.

The report was extensive as well as being expensive to produce, and yet it became known as the 'forgotten report'. Government money was used to no avail. They sent thirteen highly competent people on a fool's errand, and having 'begged the question' they refused to listen to the answer.

Our distribution company, GBD, had no option but to handle David Sullivan's range of magazines because the customers demanded the 'more explicit' titles. David's distributor, 'Walton Press', in fairness purchased large quantities of the 'Gold Star' range, which made it more equitable.

Walton Press had made a lot of money with the Sullivan titles, which gave John Sheridan, the owner, a cocky confidence. It was even rumoured, jokingly, that business was so good he had to employ someone to insult new customers! Courtesy of the business he and his wife lived in a house valued at more than £200,000, which in those days was affordable only by the very rich, but their company was not going to provide for much longer.

'Gold Star' were buying out many of the small wholesalers, and we were also improving our magazines to compete favourably. Ron Coleman and I went again to see David Sullivan, at his request, to ascertain whether there was a possibility of formulating a deal which would end this seemingly hopeless battle for the marketplace. The competition between us caused both companies to increase the explicitness of their publications.

On this visit we went to his house in Chigwell, which was on the same road that Bobby Moore, the England football captain, lived. We had read so much about David Sullivan, who was said to be a flamboyant character with a home to match. Magazines and newspapers were filled with articles about this 'pornographer' who had made millions. He had allowed himself to become high profile, and was either reaping the rewards or paying the price. Ron and I were nervous of getting too closely involved with him and from the outset we were cautious. However, despite the bad press he was a likeable person, and we succeeded in outlining a deal whereby we would link up to become joint publishers. In essence it could work, but only with a great deal of trust and goodwill on both sides. We took the idea back to my brother, who was enthusiastic and excited at the prospect of controlling a large proportion of the 'girlie' market. Over the years the wholesaler had played David Sullivan and 'Gold Star Publications' against each other to our detriment but under this new association this would no longer be possible.

It took months of negotiation, but finally we were able to come to an arrangement in principle, and David Sullivan was left with the job of telling John Sheridan that he had no intention of renewing his yearly contract. An alliance was in the making.

Despite the 'partnership', we each continued to be responsible for the production of our own titles. The joint publishing paid for all of the outgoings and this money was set against receipts from the distributor. The nett profits were shared but both of the devotees, as a matter of pride, were determined to see that their own titles sold more. We continued to be the distributor which made good sense because in the 'girlie' field we were clearly the best. Only Uncle David could offer any effective competition.

Team Work

Early one morning I was discussing the latest shop sales figures with Ron Coleman when he received a telephone call. I could detect that the caller sounded young and, by the look on Ron's face, appealing.

'Why don't we have lunch?' Ron suggested. She obviously agreed because I could see the smile on his face. As he put the phone down, Ron grinned at me and said, 'That was very interesting. That lady works for a party plan company, and is keen to sell our products at her parties.'

'I agree, Ron, interesting,' I said. 'But hardly worth you devoting a whole lunchtime discussing it. If she were a man, you wouldn't even give him the benefit of a visit to your office.'

'That may be true,' he said with a smile. 'But I think that it's our duty to explore every avenue to sell marital aids, especially now that licensing controls are being applied to our shops.' I knew he was right. When Ron returned from his luncheon he informed me that the meeting had been very worthwhile, because in his view we could make the idea work.

Ann Galea was, according to Ron, a young and attractive housewife who lived in the South London borough of Thamesmead and was working in her spare time as a demonstrator for 'Pippa Dee'. To provide further income, she had been buying sex aids and novelty items which she found easy to sell at her parties. Not only did she make a small profit for herself, but she found that the ladies at her parties were having fun.

Fun was the operative word because this was the beginning of a new concept in party plan. 'Party plan' parties had invariably involved a dozen or so people gathered together for the express purpose of being shown merchandise that was not normally sold in conventional stores.

A party organizer would find a person who was prepared to 'host' an evening at their home. Provide food and drink (usually alcoholic) and in return for her hospitality usually received a gift and had the benefit of buying goods at a discounted price.

Ron promised to send Ann some of our 'Lydcare' mail order catalogues and agreed to supply the goods at a discount normally enjoyed by large sex shops. We talked for some time about the ramifications of selling marital aids through party plan. David and I were confident that it would work and I thought that we should look into the possibility of becoming more seriously involved.

Following her meeting with Ron, Ann Galea and her friend and colleague Chris Rogers introduced at least a dozen girls who worked exclusively in the Thamesmead area. They sold our product as a sideline using a small selection 'kit' of our products. The package needed to be manageable as the organizers had to take it with them to every engagement. There was only a limited amount of items for them to offer and we realized that the range had to be increased.

A meeting was held with Ann Galea and Chris Rogers present. In preparation we had spent a great deal of time debating our next move regarding party plan, having closely watched the orders as they came in from Ann. They did not reflect our expectations and we were immediately to realize that the needs of women had been wrongly interpreted.

With party plan we were providing an opportunity for ladies to buy sexual items out of the glare of the male counterpart who had, over the years, both dominated and arrogantly over-protected them. During the parties they were free to have a chat and a drink with the girls before the arrival of the organizer who would soon involve them in playing games that invariably caused them to laugh until they cried. They had the opportunity to try on garments and to show off their figures before getting down to the ordering which was always done without pressure, in fact orders could be placed into sealed envelopes and handed to the organizer for our attention.

We were somewhat enlightened by the information that the orders revealed and we were able to come to certain conclusions. Vibrators were being bought for personal use and we were going to need a bigger range. Novelties were bought primarily as gifts to give to partners and their inclusion was important because they were the 'fun' element of the parties.

David's elder daughter, Jacqueline, was now married and had worked in various departments within the company. She was very interested to learn what was happening with regard to party plan, and went along to a party anonymously with my assistant Jean Mills.

It was held in a semi-detached house in south London with about fifteen ladies in attendance. Although she and Jean were there on a mission, it was not long before they were involved in the overall enjoyment. The demonstrator had organized a game in which six 'Angel's Delights' (a peculiarly shaped vibrator) were literally raced across the carpeted floor, while each of the party-goers placed bets on which one reached the other side of the room first. They had a great time showing off and modelling the garments and everyone bought something, if only as a gesture of appreciation for the evening's entertainment.

On her return, Jackie suggested that we should offer an increased range of lingerie. She was confident that there would be an even bigger demand if the price and quality was improved and the range increased. Until then we had sold only very small quantities of lingerie through our shops and mail order. We had purchased a few lines such as see-through, 'Baby Doll' negligées and some sexy knickers which were crotch-less. These items were sold in our shops and later through mail order, mostly to men who would give them to their partners as presents. Few women, we believed, would have been happy to wear them, let alone actually buy them. 'Ann Summers' party plan' was to prove us wrong.

We discussed the possibility of running parties to sell our product exclusively and to do that we would need a catalogue which could be handed out at parties, but in view of the small number required at the time it was impractical and far too expensive. The current mail order catalogue was too explicit, and it was considered that it might offend partygoers. A solution had to be found, So David proposed that we arrange for photographs to be taken of a variety of items which we would place into photo albums.

The idea was brilliant. We elected to put it into effect and called the finished items 'Blads'. Once we had a response we could make a judgement regarding our next move.

More than six months had passed since Annie was told of her illness, and I was in a constant state of trepidation, although she was never aware of it. I had the ability to cope exceedingly well with the problem whilst I was with her, but when I was alone I would suffer terribly. I had every reason now to believe that the young doctor had made an error when he implied that Annie's illness was incurable. She had survived the six months and, apart from the lump which had been removed, was as well as ever. Her quality of life was high, and if I had anything to do with it, it would remain so.

Our visits to the Royal Marsden had been reduced from weekly to monthly, and recently to three monthly. Dr Ford had told us that the cancer was in remission, and long might it last. I made sure that I was available to take Annie to the hospital for her regular check-ups. We made early appointments, in the hope that we could be attended to before lunch, enabling me to go on to work. We would wait for a minimum of three hours and sometimes all day. I could never understand why. There had to be a way in which people would be seen at least within one hour of a set appointment but we never were. It was cruel, and I swore that one day I would go to my MP to protest or at least write to the hospital governors, but I didn't. Nor, to my knowledge, did anyone else, because over the years I saw no signs of improvement.

I made conversation with a number of cancer patients and I discovered the wonderful change in the way in which people had come to terms with what is a dreadful disease. When I was young, the very word was spoken in whispers or people would say, 'So and so had the big "C",' as if it were a dirty word. Now, remarkable advancements were being made and a cure was very much on the cards for many of the patients. But it still irked me that whilst sitting there for so long, the most precious of commodities was being wasted ... Time. Surely it is not beyond the intelligence of man to come up with a solution.

Annie's agreement to come to Malta in 'Mike Oscar' delighted me. I had convinced her that it was safe, especially now that my flying had reached such a high standard and my co-pilot, Graham Balls, was extremely competent. She loved to be with Graham and his girlfriend, Bobby, who would also be flying with us. I had been through enough flying trauma to last a lifetime and was convinced that it was now a thing of the past. I was as keen as ever to achieve a high placing, and my entire crew pledged that, at the very least, they would help me to win the 'Concours d'Elegance'.

David had planned to go with Penny and our friends Mark and Sue Cambell. There was no hope of my beating David in the rally, but when it came to the 'Concours' my aeroplane had the edge because handicap points were given to entrants with older models and I qualified for the maximum. David's brand new aeroplane, needless to say, was at the other end of the scale.

I came second out of sixty four international contestants in the 'Concours'. The judges awarded first place to my brother, who was more upset than I was at their verdict. He believed that they were wrong and he wanted me to have his winner's trophy. I couldn't accept his offer, but to this day, I treasure the runner's up prize which has pride of place in my trophy cabinet.

David had already won every other category of the competition. By winning the rally and coming second in the two previous years, it left nobody in any doubt that my brother was the best non-professional pilot in the world, and I could not have been more proud of him.

The trip home promised to be as comfortable as the journey out. The conditions were excellent when we took off from Malta, and the forecast was for near perfect weather for the entire flight to Cannes. Our fuel tanks were filled to the brim to ensure that we would arrive at our destination with plenty to spare.

David and his crew departed less than forty minutes after us and it was good to hear their voices over the radio. There were a few times en route during which we could talk freely to each other, albeit only for short spells, on our own independent frequency. Our tracks were identical, although David, with the luxury of pressurization, was able to maintain a height of more than twice my ten thousand foot limit.

Everything looked good and, as we overflew Cagliari, we changed our fuel supply from outboard to inboard tanks and set course to fly directly to Ajaccio in Corsica before taking up a heading to cross more than two hundred miles of the Mediterranean Sea to reach Cannes.

I had flown the aircraft to this point, but I relinquished control to Graham and called Ajaccio radar to advise them that we were now twenty miles to the north-west of their zone, and that I intended to stay with them until we were within range of Nice radar.

Five minutes later Graham mentioned to me over the intercom that he was a little concerned about the controls. For no apparent reason the plane was yawing to the left and he was being forced to apply pressure to the right-hand rudder pedal in order to keep the aircraft straight and level. I immediately took control and confirmed that there was indeed a problem.

Another five minutes out to sea and it became more apparent. We noticed that whilst the outboard tank gauges were each showing almost empty, the inboard gauges were not equally aligned. This, coupled with the yawing problem, made Graham and me anxious, and we discussed the prospect of returning to Ajaccio. Every second that we took in making the decision took us closer to the point of no return.

Graham called Ajaccio to inform them that we were increasing our height and would shortly be leaving their frequency to contact Nice radar. It was at this point that our minds were made up and we determined to go on. Our eyes barely left the fuel gauges. Minute by minute the left needle went down but the right one remained on full. Graham constantly tapped the glass in the hope that the needle was stuck.

'It's no use tapping it,' I said. 'One tank is feeding both engines and I think the fuel line from the port tank is blocked. We'd better make contact with Nice.' I picked up the microphone. 'Nice, this is Golf Alpha Yankee Mike Oscar, do you read? Over.' There was no reply. 'Fuck it! I don't believe it, Graham. Nice, this is Golf Alpha Mi... '

'Ralph, is everything alright?' came a voice from behind. It was Annie.

'Yes, darling, everything is fine. We'll be landing in about forty five minutes from now.'

I called Nice again, but there was still no reply. I continually adjusted the overhead rudder tab control which released the pressure on the rudder pedal, but by now the imbalance was such that my foot was practically down to the floor and beads of sweat began to appear on my brow ... (They still appear now as I think of it).

I put on the fuel pumps and advised Graham to turn the cross-feed lever to 'on'. This was something that normally would only have to be done in cases of single engine failure, but I hoped that it might unblock the defective part of the fuel system. It did not, and now the right-hand tank was showing less than a quarter full ... not enough to get us to Cannes.

There were two reasons for increasing altitude. Firstly, with greater height, we would be able to make contact with Nice control sooner. Secondly, there was comfort in knowing that when the fuel ran out, we would have more time to prepare, before the dreaded 'meeting with the waves'.

I transmitted blind in the hope that Nice radar were receiving me.

'Nice Radar, this is Golf Alpha Yankee Mike Oscar, do you read ...? come in please.' Still no response. Graham had already worked out that Cannes was approximately twelve miles closer to our present position than Nice so we continued with our track heading calling Nice blind yet again to inform them that we had insufficient fuel to reach our destination and requesting assistance.

With thirty minutes to run, our estimation was that we had little more than twenty five minutes of fuel remaining. Graham was reading the manual to ascertain the most economical fuel consumption speed when, over the radio, we heard a familiar voice. It was my brother David and the sound of it was music to my ears.

'Nice, this is Mike Alpha Golf Sierra, I have contact with Golf Alpha Yankee Mike Oscar, who have fuel problems and are trying to contact you. I request permission to transmit direct to Mike Oscar.' This was followed by a silence that seemed to last an eternity. Nice was responding to David but I was unable to hear the controller. However, he could, because of his greater altitude.

'Ralph,' David said after a few moments, 'check that your fuel pumps and crossfeed are on. Now make your heading three three zero. Nice have you on radar, squawk 4730. I have declared an emergency and air-sea rescue have been alerted. You have sixty two miles to run to Cannes airport.'

I then heard him inform Nice that he was at full speed, attempting to catch us up. In the event of our ditching, he would remain in 'a hold' above us, which would assist the rescue services in locating our position. I was still unable to hear their response.

David's knowledge of the Aztec was extensive. I told him of our attempts to clear the blockage and he advised me that in the event of the engine or engines spluttering, I was to immediately select the outboard tanks.

Then I heard Nice radar. 'Mike Oscar? Do you read? Over.'

I advised them that I had spoken with 'Golf Sierra' and that I was maintaining a height of 6000ft and a heading of three three zero.

'Roger, Mike Oscar, you have fifty six miles to run, approximately nineteen minutes to touchdown. Make your heading three four zero. Now change frequency to Cannes approach. Good luck, Mike Oscar.'

David came back on the frequency. He suggested that I should change the tanks to outboard in order to first drain them (on the basis that the crossfeed was not working). I understood what he was getting at and acted accordingly although all three tank gauges now showed empty.

The bay of Napoule was clearly visible, and we looked intently for our first glimpse of Cannes airport.

'There! There on the nose,' exclaimed Graham.

'Where? I can't see a thing.'

'One o'clock!' he yelled, as he pointed directly ahead.

'I've got it, I've got it!' I cried out, as I too could just make out the welcoming lights of the runway.

'Maintain your height for a little longer, Ralph,' came David's wavering voice, 'I'm just to the left of you.'

I turned to see Golf Sierra no more than fifty feet away.

'Maintain your height,' he repeated, 'If your engines fail, you will have more time.' Mark Cambell's voice came over the frequency, 'Hang in there Ralph, you are doing fine, we're all rooting for you. We're going to be down soon and dinner's on me. Just stick with it'. He sounded close to tears.

Neither Annie nor Bobby was aware of the danger, as the radio was transmitted only through our headphones. Annie tapped me on the shoulder and asked me if I had seen the beautiful yacht sailing towards the harbour. I made a cursory glance and nodded approval ... she was happy, although any minute now I might have to instruct them to put on their life jackets.

Suddenly both engines began to splutter as we hit turbulence. I calmly asked the girls to take their life jackets from under their seats and hold them on their laps. I knew that this would frighten them, but I had no alternative.

With only twelve miles to run, the engines began to splutter and then failed. Graham immediately changed back to the single inboard tank which we knew was practically empty, but we lived in hope that the dregs would help us to reach our destination. The engines burst back into life as the vital fuel reached them.

David had been in contact with Cannes approach obtaining clearance for us to make a direct downwind landing. I was advised by them that the circuit had been cleared and the runway would remain closed until we were safely on the ground. As I lined up the runway we could see the fire engines and ambulances and we realized that the airport was on full emergency alert.

'Be ready to stand on the brakes, Graham,' I warned.

At six hundred feet, and a mile to run I reduced my speed by pulling up the nose and lowering the undercarriage. The sight of the three green lights signifying that the landing gear was engaged was a relief, and the sight of the runway was even more comforting.

I could see holidaymakers on the beach and wondered about the many times that I had looked up at planes coming in to land, dreaming of one day being at the controls of one. Here I was at the controls of one, dreaming about being on a beach ...

It would have seemed unusual to them because aircraft normally land in the opposite direction in view of the prevailing wind and the mountainous terrain which impedes the overshoot.

I landed with a fifteen knot wind on my tail, with only one chance to get it right. Graham and I had to literally stand on the brakes as we came to a stop less than ten feet from fencing which was beside the road, crossing the end of the stopway.

'Well done, Ralph, Well done Graham!' came the excited voice of my brother, who had disregarded all compliance with radio protocol.

We taxied to stand thirty two and Graham leapt from the aircraft, knelt and kissed the ground. We were exhausted and so happy to be alive.

'What's going on?' exclaimed Annie, clearly distressed. I hugged and kissed her in sheer relief.

'Nothing darling, nothing at all. It was just a small problem.'

We called for the bowser to fill up the three tanks, and from the chit we did a calculation to discover that we had less than a pint of usable fuel remaining.

The Party Plan

The party plan organizers were increasing in number and the business was quickly taking shape. David, in his inimitable way, was working out the profitability as well as the practicability of expanding beyond the London area. We continued to keep the opposition aware of the problems, which was not too difficult ... there were plenty of them. Nevertheless, we knew that Ann Summers' party plan had great potential providing we could discourage all forms of competition.

There were two possibilities that could seriously affect our success. One was if a quality party plan organization with experience and vision moved into our type of business. The second was if one of our competitors set up in opposition and moved down market.

My brother David projected an increase of fifty girls a month and, if he were accurate, we could look forward to a guaranteed success. I made the usual comment about 'the leveller' and guaranteed David that, 'As sure as eggs are eggs and God made little green apples, it would come.' Regardless, I agreed to hire Charco's restaurant for a big celebration if we ever reached three hundred girls. 'And,' I commented, 'if we ever reached a thousand, then we could hire the Savoy.'

Jacqueline had strong views about improving our image and we were more than ready to go along with her. She recommended that we enforce a proper 'control of quality' as our product needed to be of the highest standard. This, I could understand but, as the buyer, I knew that it would take time.

We were experiencing some teething problems, such as non-payments, returns and non-starters and the only way to make things viable was to ensure that we produce a satisfactory mark up. Jean and I were said to be very capable, but we could not perform miracles, and it was inevitable that the quality in the early days would suffer. From the start we were worried about girls running mixed parties, and through the company minutes I put it on record that under no circumstances would we tolerate them.

To maintain our profitability we provided novelty items which had a high mark up and made the parties fun as well as guaranteeing enjoyment to the eventual recipient. Jean and I got in touch with as many companies selling novelty items as we could find. From their stock we selected the rudest items and if the price was right we would buy them. The price, however, was rarely right for us and we finished up with lots of samples knowing that we needed to either find the manufacturer or to imitate the idea and to produce them ourselves. It was rare that sexy novelties would have a copyright registration. 'Copying' was, and always will be, a necessary aspect of that business, but it worked both ways.

Ron Coleman and I continued to attend the sex fair each year. With the prospect of a successful party plan organization, it was important that we kept abreast of the industry. We added a number of products to our mail order catalogue, which were of great benefit in improving sex, whether it was with a partner or alone. I had been offered an item called 'Real Feel' which was an imitation vagina that lived up to its name. I only know because – for professional reasons, of course – I put two of my fingers into it. I was impressed and I bought a large quantity. They were very expensive, but they sold very well, I understood that it gave pleasure to a great number of men. In some cases it helped a lot of women too ... they were able to get some sleep. Blow-up dolls also fell into this category, and the response from grateful customers was proving to me that there was not only a demand for these things, but an actual need.

Another item for which there was a need, especially for the man with a small penis, was the 'penatone' penis training programme. Ron Coleman negotiated with the inventor, a Doctor Richards, for the sole marketing rights, but without success. We nevertheless continued to handle it on a wholesale basis and it sold very well. It gave me pleasure to know that many men who were concerned about being small in that area had an opportunity to do something about it.

Numerous types of marital and masturbation aids were being introduced daily and because of our prominence in the industry several of the new lines and prototypes were presented to us first. I felt a little like Caesar as I indicated 'thumbs up' for the moving finger vibrator and duo balls (ball bearings loosely encased in a plastic container which is inserted into the vagina to act as a stimulant), and then 'thumbs down' for the goat's eye and the tongue probe ... it was all in a day's work.

One line which outsold the rest was the 'Stud' delay spray. I found it interesting that there was such a demand for this product, but what ultimately was more surprising was the numbers of sprays sold to the women who attended parties, obviously for their men. The average person's sex life was dramatically revealed before our eyes as the orders began to flow in.

When I heard that within a month Ann Summers would definitely have more than three hundred 'active' party organizers, I was delighted.

The planned celebration took place at Charco's as agreed, and we needed to book the whole restaurant for the evening. As the champagne flowed, we were already contemplating the next milestone – to reach five hundred girls, which seemed like an impossible dream. Rather like, 'One day we will be millionaires' ... Inconceivable.

By now the use of the 'blads' was impracticable and the gamble

Jackie and Vanessa

of producing a catalogue exclusively for the 'party plan' was in prospect. Jacqueline, who was now controlling Ann Summers party plan', came up with an exciting idea. She proposed that we print a volume run and actually give the catalogues away. It sounded irrational ... after all, I had never given anything away in my life! But the more we thought about it, the more we began to realize that it could work. We agreed to make the first print run of 100,000 copies.

The first Ann Summers catalogue involved a great deal of time and effort to produce. Jacqueline took responsibility for organizing the photographic session, which was very successful. The catalogue was well designed and proved to be an excellent selling aid for the three hundred or so party organizers.

Lingerie comprised only a quarter of the overall sales in the early days, but it was clear that as we increased the quality and decreased the price we were on our way to becoming a substantial business. Crotchless and see-through knickers were the early best-sellers, and often the higher priced items consisting of less material were in bigger demand so both customer and supplier were happy.

'We are selling holes,' David would say to me on many occasions, as we discussed the price of the items that should be included in the catalogue. Apart from selling 'holes', we sold lotions and potions and oils which were inducements to enhance sexuality and sexual intercourse. 'Sex Sugar' which originally had been imported from Germany was one of our biggest sellers. Jean and I had succeeded in getting a small company in East Grinstead to make it for us. It was a 'wonder drug', and at £2.75 for a small jar, the customers would wonder if they could afford it. The more she or he paid, the more convinced she or he would be that it worked, and I can vouch for that.

Annie was always on at me to bring some of the Ann Summers items home and I used to joke with her about it by saying, 'Annie, you should attend a party and buy it yourself. Now that we are on computer I daren't take stock from the warehouse.' She laughed and said, 'Right I will.'

I thought no more about it until a month later when one afternoon, we were alone in the house. To Annie's dismay I happened to notice a jar of Ann Summers sex sugar in the food cupboard.

'You so and so!' she complained, as she saw me looking at it, 'You never go to that cupboard! I bought that at my friend's party and I wanted to use it on you, just to see what happened!'

I was so sorry that I had discovered it, and some quick thinking was required to stifle her disappointment.

'Annie,' I teased, 'I have taken two spoonfuls half an hour ago ... and now I'm crazy for you.' We did not wait to get upstairs and made love right there and then, over the kitchen sink ... Another satisfied customer.

Tragedy

On my second attempt, I had come close to achieving my great desire of becoming an instrument-rated pilot. I had passed the Civil Aviation Authority's flight test with the most proficient flight of my life, and now only needed to pass the written test to become fully qualified.

I had no success in finding a co-pilot for the next Malta Rally, and I finally decided to miss the event altogether. As the business was getting bigger I was not happy about David and me being away from the company at the same time.

David and Penny were again making preparations to go to the rally with Sue and Mark Cambell. David had by now put his name into the history books by winning the Malta Rally twice, and there was a good possibility of his winning for the third time. With Mark in support, they were the firm favourites.

Sue had made arrangements to leave her children with Mark's parents and was able to go, but much to David's disappointment, Penny, who had been a great contributor to his previous successes, became sick at the last moment and was unable to join them.

David and Mark did very well, slipping back only a few places on the arrival competition. Their other placings were good and there was still a strong possibility that they had won the competition overall. After the customary wait of several days the results were to be announced and everyone made a point of relaxing and enjoying themselves.

Mark's old team mate was Teddy White, with whom he had won the competition years earlier. Teddy had lost the determination to win again, although each year he competed and was the life and soul of the British contingent. This year, however, he was entering his Harvard T6, a Second World War American aeroplane, for the 'Concours d'Elegance'. Since buying it, he had allowed the American registration to remain along with the original American colours, and it was the talk of the show. Victory in the 'Concours' looked a certainty.

The day before the awards were to be announced, Teddy offered to take Mark up for a trip around the island. David, and Mark's wife Sue, decided to watch the flight from the balcony of the hotel while they were having lunch.

The runway at Luqa was so large that it could be seen from any high spot on the island. They took off in the early afternoon and within a minute the Harvard was clearly visible. Seconds later, they were giving Sue and David, and nearly every other guest at the hotel, a display of 'fly passes' and 'wing waving'. They were so close to the hotel that the roar of the powerful engine was deafening. As a finale to the show, they made a tight turn towards the airport.

David and Sue watched in horror as they realized that something was wrong. David recognized that they were in a stall configuration which, at a greater height, would have presented no problem. Under the circumstances, the pilots were in great danger. David said nothing to Sue but mentally pleaded with Teddy to pull the Harvard out, but as each second went by he realized that he would not succeed. The plane plunged into the grounds of a school and immediately burst into flames as everyone, including David and Sue, stood and watched. There was no doubt that Mark and Teddy had been killed on impact. Sue became hysterical and David could do no more than hold her in his arms to comfort her.

That night David accompanied Sue on a British Airways flight to Gatwick. Teddy's co-pilot, Gordon Mills, was also on board. It was academic in view of the tragedy, but Teddy White had won the 'Concours d'Elegance' whilst Mark and David were placed second in the overall competition. My personal view was that David and Mark had in fact won, but awarding the main prize to David (in his absence) and to Mark (posthumously) would understandably cause even greater upset to the already deflated organizers and competitors at the award ceremony.

I have no doubt that the highs and the lows of the rally had a profound effect on David and he would carry the memories forever.

The *News of the World* has never been able to live down its reputation for publishing as much 'down market' material as it could get its hands on. 'Good luck to them,' I say, but what I find so offensive is when they take a 'holier than thou' attitude towards their fellow 'pornographers'.

Someone told me that they had read in the 'Screws of the World' that my father had been jailed for importing and selling so-called 'pornographic' videos. I was not as concerned as I should have been because for so long we had gone our separate ways, despite David's and my own many attempts at reconciliation. Perhaps Godfrey had gone beyond the realms of acceptability with regard to his video importations; nevertheless, it could not have justified this cruel sentence. The newspaper referred to him as a man who had built a booming 'filth' trade and claimed he owned a 30,000 square feet warehouse that was stacked with 'porn'. This was a ridiculous exaggeration but, once the tabloids are aware of a conviction, they have the freedom to report as they please, and are free to cash in on 'pornography' to their hearts' content.

Godfrey was to serve his 'time' in Wandsworth Prison, and I was very interested to learn about his unusual behaviour from a fellow cellmate whom I met up with by chance, many years later. My father's reputation of being a 'character' had applied equally on the 'inside' as it had on the 'outside'.

He had bragged about the hundreds of girls whom he had seduced (not one of them over nineteen years of age), and about his wealth, which had been so vast that he hid £20,000 in the warehouse because he was going out one night and the last place that he would leave his 'petty cash' would be in his safe. After all, only a few years previously, the thieves had 'blown' it and had stolen several hundred pounds in small change, which he had taken from his bingo hall. Having hidden the £20,000 (I remembered it as £2000), he had forgotten where he put it.

Because of his age and perhaps his reputation, he was given some 'cushy' office jobs whilst in prison. However, after being sacked from the solicitor's office and the library, he finished up in the kitchen, where he did a considerable amount of business in tobacco (if I were to feel any shame at all, this would have concerned me most). He did not smoke, but hoarded his supplies, using them for trade. He became overloaded with stock after reaching the final of a knockout 'Kalooki' competition in which every contestant had invested a half ounce of tobacco. On reaching the final, he did a deal with the other finalist and they agreed to split the booty, which still further increased his stock-pile. I believed this particular story and remember well how he nearly crippled 'Gold Star Publications' through hoarding stock.

As 'Goddy' came out of jail, another member of my family, my cousin Ian, went in. It was the biggest miscarriage of justice since the Reiter brothers had been sent to prison for publishing the 'Hank Janson' books, more than twenty years earlier.

Two jurors at the Middlesex Crown Court found him 'innocent' (sic) of sending indecent books, magazines and mail order brochures through the post, but the remaining ten put the thumbs down and by a majority verdict he was found guilty. I would imagine that the ten jurors were disgusted with themselves when they heard the judge sentence him to twelve months imprisonment and fines exceeding £12,000.

During the trial, Ian described the difficulties that were faced by booksellers handling sexually explicit material. This con-stituted only a small proportion of his business (which applied to most booksellers). 'There are no official guidelines, but I have never handled anything which I consider to be indecent or obscene. The whole thing is like playing Russian roulette,' he told the court.

The purists would argue, 'If you play with fire you expect to be burned,' but I would hit back by saying, 'People are divided into two groups, the righteous and the unrighteous – and it's the righteous who do the dividing.'

In Wormwood Scrubs my cousin Ian met up with other associates of ours. David Sullivan and Mel Walker were also 'inside', both for so called living off the immoral earnings of women through their involvement (albeit indirect) with the 'sauna' businesses. Mel was the owner of 'Maw', a company which sold advertising space within our magazines. Although he no longer owned a sauna business himself, he had allowed other saunas to use his credit facility, and when they were raided he was drawn in with them and sentenced to twelve months imprisonment. David Sullivan had been imprisoned on a similar charge but, fortunately, his sentence was quashed after he had served just seventy one days.

I was told by Mel and other people in the trade that the sauna-bath houses were frequented by all and sundry; politicians, doctors, judges, famous actors, authors, as well as regular everyday men. But when they were raided the customers were allowed to leave without so much as their names being taken, or even given a warning. I believed then, and I do now, that sauna baths provide a perfect outlet for the sexually unfulfilled male. There is little doubt that some of the masseuses offer more than a relaxing rub down ... but so what? Providing they take care of someone's needs without hurting anyone else, who are we to condemn them?

As well as David Sullivan and Mel Walker, Ian also met an old friend of mine, Karl Slack. It seemed ironic to me that, at a time when violent crime was on the increase, and with insufficient space in prison to accommodate the perpetrators, individuals such as these were jailed. Surely, to satisfy the likes of Mary Whitehouse, they could have been heavily fined. To add to the irony, Ian's fine was reduced on appeal while he, a charity worker and happily married man with three lovely daughters, had to serve eight months of the twelve month sentence. It was a dreadfully long and unnecessary deprivation of his freedom, and was particularly cruel in view of the fact that his life was to be tragically shortened when he died from cancer at the age of forty five. I personally believe that these stressful proceedings had taken their toll.

When David Sullivan was released, he sold the interests in his chain of sex shops, as well as relinquishing his involvement in the top shelf more 'explicit' girlie titles, to a company in which he had no stake. He continued, however, to participate in the publishing of 'softer' magazines. He was determined to see that his deal with us remained equitable to himself, as well as to his former company. As time went by, we began to realize that a confidence and respect for each other was growing. Our long-term business adversary was becoming a friend.

He applied his energies in other directions than publishing and sex shops. He became a race horse owner but concentrated more on buying and selling property, which made him a great deal of money. However, with his highly active mind, that was not sufficient and he was destined for bigger things, which I am pleased to say involved the Gold Brothers.

It was evident that David Sullivan was preparing to go into direct competition with us in party plan and we had to make contingency plans.

We had reached the level of five hundred organizers, and there was every prospect of our achieving the magic thousand. One moment, David and I were regular businessmen, and the next, we were potentially millionaires. Just thinking about it was a little frightening for me, although for David it was very exciting and he was full of enthusiasm.

It was brought to our attention that a small wholesaler and mail order company based in North London by the name of 'Silver Rose' had started advertising for party organizers and it concerned me that this was the beginning of a number of 'copycat' enterprises.

Jackie sent anonymously to them for details and we discovered that they were worthy contenders. The catalogue, which was produced originally for the exclusive use of their mail order, was tasteful and of high quality.

My concern was such that I began to make extensive enquiries, and it was not long before I found out that Jeff Silver, the owner, had controlled at least three companies that failed. According to a close business friend who knew him very well, we had nothing to worry about.

'Jeff Silver,' he told me, 'couldn't run a bath. Ralph, Jeff Silver is no different from Sergeant Bilko, full of ideas that come to nothing.'

It would be more serious for us if David Sullivan were to go into party plan as we would be up against a competent businessman with large resources. It was rumoured that he was considering such a move and I decided to visit him at his house in Chigwell. Jean and I had flown in the past to Stapleford Tawney and taken a taxi to David's house, but since Mark's tragic accident, I was less enthusiastic about flying and went by car.

Our negotiations took no more than an hour. My reputation went before me and there was no way that I would easily get the better of David Sullivan. He knew that he could dramatically affect our progress, and if he was expected to stay out of party plan then he would require adequate compensation. It was a figure that was impossible to evaluate and how we managed to work out a solution in such a short time I will never know ... but we did.

We worked out a deal which was equitable and when we shook hands I knew that it was sealed. David had been tough but fair which, I was to learn, was his way. As part of the agreement David would never compete with us in party plan.

Different Attitudes

It was not long before the media realized that Ann Summers was big business, and many newspapers, magazines, and television programme presenters capitalized on the subject by sending someone to a party to report on what actually took place. With very few exceptions, everyone had a wonderful time. Politically, each reporter tackled the subject differently. Polly Toynbee pompously reported in the *Guardian* that the twenty or so women, who were from a 'poor' part of London, were forced by the 'hard sell' into buying something which, in 'the cool light of day', they would regret.

She had attended the party under the guise of being a friend of a friend and found that ... 'There was absolutely no way out ... which of that frightful display could I bear to buy?' She actually bought a pair of fishnet stockings only because the party organizer advised her that we did not sell tights.

'Passion killers!' she told Miss Toynbee.

Roslyn Grose, a reporter for the *Sun* newspaper also went to a party, but she had gone along to find out the 'secret of our success', and by the time she placed her order into a plain brown envelope she was left in no doubt. According to her, 'When the parcels arrive, a lot of husbands and boyfriends will be in for a frothy surprise when their favourite women peel off ready for bed.'

Roslyn Grose interviewed Jacqueline, and she was able to relay some facts about the amount of money that was being made by the party organizers. Roslyn went on to talk with them and discovered that there were many reasons for working for Ann Summers. It enabled them to get out and to meet people in the right kind of atmosphere. Knowing that they were helping to supplement the family income, their husbands were only too willing to look after the children.

A friend of mine, Cliff Taylor, who ran a taxi service, told Annie and me that he had been banished to the bedroom to watch the television while his wife, Stella, held a party. He did not object and thought that the idea and the rules were excellent. I told him that it was one thing to have rules and another to make them work. We intended to make them work!

We lost both Ann Galea and Chris Rogers, as well as many party organizers, to Silver Rose. They offered so much that even the most loyal Ann Summers organizer must have thought long and hard.

Gradually, the swing away from us slowed down, and we heard more and more that the girls who had left us were unhappy. I saw Jeff Silver on more than one occasion in the hope of doing a deal with him. However, we were clearly too far apart and it was now a 'fight to the death'. We continued to expand and soon reached 2,500 parties a month, while we estimated that Silver Rose had reached fewer than ten per cent of that figure.

They were not the only company in contention. There were a number of lingerie companies that offered their product to party plan organizers, causing many entrepreneurs to take us on. They all failed because they could not supply the most important ingredient of all ... which was service. We were seen by many as not only the best in the sex business but the best party plan operator of them all.

We were considering extending the business into Europe, although so far we had experienced unbelievable difficulties expanding into the islands away from the mainland. We managed to attract a few agents in Jersey and Guernsey but they struggled to survive. There was the same enthusiasm for our product but the authorities seemed determined to see that the 'decadence' of the mainland did not spread to their own 'comfortable' shores. In my view they would have done so much more in protecting society if they had concentrated their efforts on banning killer drugs like cigarettes and alcohol and allowed the women in their protectorates to decide for themselves about sex and contraception.

Our deliveries were often seized by Customs, and although most of the lingerie was released, the novelties and sex aids were strictly taboo. The biggest joke of all was when we were informed that our publication, *All That Men Understand about Women*, had been confiscated. The book was a joke in itself.

On the cover and the back page it relayed the technicalities of the subject; the competence of the author and a number of accolades from the editors of various publications: 'A slap in the face,' – *Swish Magazine*; 'This is the work of pure genius,' – *Parade* magazine; and 'Every detail exposed,' – *Rustler*.

The book was intentionally cellophane-sealed to protect the 'innocent'. Enough, I suppose, for the predominantly male Customs committee to discard it out of hand. What they had not realized was that, *All That Men Understand about Women* contained *nothing* ... only blank pages.

Celtic ...

David and I had bought a villa in Portugal. It was an ideal holiday location which presented the opportunity for us to be together in a relaxed atmosphere to discuss various business projects, as well as to holiday with our families.

On one occasion, Norman Sawtell convinced David and me to go with him on a 'men only' long weekend. Since Annie and I had lived together we had rarely slept apart, but, although I missed her, it turned out to be a great weekend.

The return trip, however, was anything but great. Although we were on a full flight on the outbound journey we saw no reason to anticipate a problem on our return. We had been at the back of the queue and as we reached the check-in desk at Faro, David motioned to an old couple, who had arrived late, to go ahead of us. As they happily walked off to the departure lounge, we presented our tickets to the assistant who informed us that the flight was full except for one remaining seat.

We chose to stay together so we decided to accept three seats on a flight leaving for Manchester within the hour. We were confident that the onward train journey to London would present only a small problem, but we were wrong.

There were no trains leaving for London from Manchester, with the exception of a milk train which was due to stop at practically every station on the way. We were able to board at Warrington

David and me on holiday

and a taxi driver had to drive like a maniac to get us there with only a few minutes to spare. I bought three first class tickets only moments before the train departed. We walked up and down looking for the first class compartments but there were none. Cheated out of thirty pounds, we got into one of the three second class carriages and were lucky to find seats together.

Before the train started off we heard a scuffle and two policemen dragged a passenger backwards off the train. This was only the beginning of a nightmare as we sat back hoping to get some sleep. Less than five minutes from our departure point we heard a sound as though someone was talking in their sleep.

'Celtic'. It came from the end of our carriage.

'Celtick... Celtickk!'. The one word was said more than a dozen times, gradually getting louder as more voices joined in,

'Celtickkkk!'

By the time we reached Stafford station, dozens of football hooligans were running rampant up and down the three carriages, carrying the emblem flag of their beloved football team.

A teenage couple got on and walked through our compartment. The girl was so beautiful I thought that she might have been a model. Her black boyfriend, who was very handsome, was clearly unsure of what to do as the calls became more and more obscene and abusive. David, Norman and I, too, were unsure of what we would do but, for the time being, we just kept our heads down.

At the third station we thought that things had quietened down but a gruesome-looking thug carrying a flag got up from his seat and put his head out of the window and called to a porter. 'Hey, hey yoo!' His strong Scottish accent made him practically unintelligible, as he swayed in his drunken state. 'Yoo, I'm fuckin' tarkin' to ya.' Then as the porter acknowledged him, he said, 'I fuckin' 'ate ya, I 'ate fuckin' blacks.' With that the train started to pull away and, at that moment, he dropped a full bottle of beer which smashed at the porter's feet. He turned around and sat beside David. Norman and I were sitting opposite them waiting for the storm to break. David looked particularly small and frail as the big, ugly, drunken Scotsman spoke.

'Yoo,' he said, as if he were continuing his conversation with the porter. 'Yoo, what team d'ye support?' I looked at Norman and I knew that he was thinking the same as me. Not so much thinking, more attempting to use telepathy.

'He must say Celtic ... Please David, say Celtic.' But no. 'West Ham United,' came David's meek reply.

'Oh no!' I thought.

'West Ham United, the bastards, I fuckin' 'ate em!' snarled the incensed Scot.

'Well, I don't exactly support them, I ... you know ... I look up the results.' He paused for a moment and then continued, 'I follow Birmingham City, too and Port Vale, and ... '

As David ran through a list of clubs the Scot lost interest, much to our relief. We survived the journey, and after leaving the train we stood patiently in the taxi queue at the station. We calmly waited until, as if from a horror film, we heard a noise like a herd of animals on the rampage, gradually getting louder. The same fifty odd Celtic 'fans', with their own flag bearer, joined the taxi queue ... At the front. We waited another thirty minutes for a taxi, but thankfully our ordeal was over.

As well as spending time at the villa with David and Penny, Annie loved being there alone with me. That became possible later in the year when we were able to go for a full week together. With only three days of the holiday left, I took Annie to a local restaurant to enjoy a romantic candlelit dinner and a bottle of wine.

Our conversations in the past would invariably be about the break-up with Joann and Boo. The question over the alimony payments was an on-going battle which would have lasted indefinitely unless Annie and I just let it drop, which we eventually did.

Now we were far more inclined to talk about ourselves and our future together. I had totally committed myself to being with Annie forever. We snuggled up in bed that night, too tired to do much more than cuddle and fondle each other. When we did that, however, it usually led to us making love but on that particular night we did not.

I caressed her face, her neck, her shoulders, but stopped there and dashed to the bathroom. I sobbed for a long time before Annie called, 'Are you alright, Ralph?' She was clearly worried.

'Yes dear, I'm afraid I've been sick and my stomach hurts,' I lied to the best of my ability. The truth was something that I could not reveal until we were home in England. I had discovered a small lump in Annie's neck, and in view of her medical history I was well aware that it was something sinister.

The last few days were quiet and Annie was worried that there was something wrong. Of course there really was, but I waited until the morning immediately after our return home. When I mentioned the swelling she told me that she had noticed it before the holiday but she was hoping that it would go away.

'I'm sure it will,' I prevaricated, 'but we should check it out all the same.'

That very day I made an appointment to see Doctor Ford at the

Royal Marsden within a week. Our worst fears materialized after the lump was removed and a secondary cancer was diagnosed. I will never forget Annie's reaction to Doctor Ford's alarming but gentle statement. She looked at me, held my hand and said,

'Ralph, don't worry, everything will be alright.'

She did not cry and neither did I. I do not know how I controlled myself. I could tell that she was more worried about me than herself and I was humbled.

'Annie, we have beaten it once and we will do it again,' was all that I could think of to say, and as I was saying it, I was thinking to myself, 'It's okay for you Ralph, you won't physically be going through what poor Annie has ahead of her.'

We went home. It was two in the afternoon and the house was empty. To my surprise, Annie wanted us to go to bed. We made love, but it was not as normal, although strangely enough it was more sensual than I had ever experienced. It was only afterwards that we both broke down and cried.

The next day I asked Annie to marry me. She was shocked and she was overjoyed and once again she cried. They were tears of real joy and I knew it.

'What a way to get a man,' she sobbed. 'But I don't care. I love you so much and I want you so much that if I died tomorrow, I will die happy.' They were wonderful words and I had to respond.

'You won't die tomorrow, you will beat this illness and we will be the star members of the Darby and Joan club in forty years' time. Now, stop being so silly, wipe your eyes and make me a cup of tea.' For once she did as she was told.

The wedding took place within a week at Croydon Register Office. We had agreed that we would invite no guests other than our close friends Syd Potter (best man) and his wife Joan. I wanted so much for my brother to be there but Annie had insisted on the minimum of fuss and I went along with her sentiments. The occasion was wonderful. We had a pre-wedding lunch with Syd and Joan and immediately after the photograph session, Annie and I went off to Brighton for four days to do nothing more than

we had always done there, only this time we had the added luxury of being in the bridal suite. It was wonderful.

I attended the Marsden with Annie every morning for the next four weeks, after which she was ordered to take a week's rest. Arrangements had been made for a smaller face mask to be designed for her as the radium treatment was to cover a larger area. Doctor Ford had prescribed the maximum permitted dosage of radium and he was calmly confident that it would, at the very least, buy time. Her mouth was filled with ulcers and she had lost all sense of smell and taste. Her suffering was acute and most of

Annie relaxing in the bridal suite

the time she was in absolute agony, but she did her best to hide it, at least from her children.

Annie's face was badly burned and permanently scarred and her hair was coming out in clumps, but she was determined to preserve her dignity, and our visits to the Svenson hair clinic needed to be more frequent in order to cope with the ever expanding size of her hairpiece. During the long wait I would shop at Selfridges or else sit in my car to catch up on paperwork.

Later we would go to the 'Ici Paris' restaurant which was close by. Eating there was not quite the same since Annie had lost all sense of taste, but we had become friendly with the owner and the atmosphere was wonderful.

On the journey home we regularly listened to our favourite Chopin piece of music, which completed for us a special day of togetherness. 'Now that I am a happily married man with big responsibilities,' I told Annie, 'I intend to give up flying altogether.'

I had flown much less over the past few months and I had always believed that flying was not a sport for part-timers. This was as good a time as any to hang up my goggles.

I reflected on my long ago decision to pack up boxing at a time when I realized that I could no longer give of my best. Both sports had a life-threatening aspect and I had come to appreciate just how precious every moment of life was.

At work, so much was happening. Ann Summers was now being run by Jacqueline, who was building a strong female management team around her. The company was growing at an enormous pace. We had reached a level of more than five thousand parties a month, each generating in excess of £100. We were giving away at least a million catalogues a year, which resulted in big mail order sales, and our expansion into Germany and Holland was well under way.

In addition to the Ann Summers side of our business, magazine sales were buoyant as we endeavoured to promote our softer titles through the leading retail groups. Our latest magazine, *Parade*, had been accepted by WH Smith, and we were hoping it would compete favourably with *Fiesta*, *Men Only* and *Penthouse*.

We were also expanding our retail shops and increasing our freehold property portfolio. We had bought the freehold of our head office and main warehouse at Whyteleafe as well as the adjoining warehouse and offices. It had been such a long time since the police had made any significant raids for our type of publications that we had every reason to believe they had at last seen sense. However, I arrived at the office one morning to find five huge trucks lined up outside the warehouse.

Ron Coleman and David Tizzard, our sales manager, were

chatting to a number of officers in reception. I went straight to my brother's office and, in his usual calm manner, he told me that the police were synchronizing raids at a number of our depots. It appeared that they were determined to put us out of business.

David Tizzard came into the office to inform us of his discussions with one of the police officers, who quite blatantly informed him that the 'raid' was vital to them (the police) because seizure figures of hard-core pornography had been very low for the year, and 'this lot' would certainly jack up the numbers.

That evening Ron Coleman brought in the *Evening Standard*. Under the headline: 'Yard Seize Tons of Porn' the article told of the carefully-planned raids which had started at dawn. Detectives had visited premises in London, Surrey, Birmingham, Ipswich, Manchester and Leicester. The whole operation was code-named 'Moose', which was the nickname of the man who masterminded the whole operation, Superintendent Ian Donaldson.

The police had already informed the newspapers that they had seized more than 250,000 magazines and some videos, which had a total value exceeding a million pounds. It was never reported that the police could have called on us at any time and we would have co-operated as we had done for the past twenty years, and that the need for a clandestine 'operation' involving scores of police officers was a joke. The stock that they had taken was, in the main, returns of magazines in the process of being sent to America, Canada, Australia and Europe, all having been cleared for sale by their respective Customs.

Despite the fact that they had 'raided' most of our depots and shops, they had found nothing that differed from what was readily available from any newsagent or bookshop in the country.

The 'raiders' were accompanied by reporters and television cameras and maximum publicity was assured. This gave prominence to the achievements of the 'porn squad'.

There was absolutely no publicity two years later, when all the stock, after thousands of hours of cataloguing, storing, sorting and filing, was returned to us at the order of the Croydon Magistrate.

The Spark

Godfrey, in the business sense, was finally out of our lives. After the *Evening Standard* article, David and I had recognized the need to sever all business connections with him. Although we held a 66 per cent majority shareholding in his companies and he held a minority 33 per cent in ours, we agreed to exchange and pay him a premium of £250,000.

The Gold Brothers group of companies had grown beyond recognition and we were soon experiencing the thrill of having a deposit account with a balance exceeding a million pounds. David and I were, at last, seeing the results of our hard work and commitment, and the years of struggling were well and truly behind us.

My daughter Tina was now working in advertising sales at Granada Television, and she had informed me that there was talk at Granada of David Sullivan's intention to spend two million pounds on television advertising to launch a new Sunday newspaper. I felt this was more than just a rumour, and his short call to me confirmed it.

He told me that he intended to go into the newspaper business and, though he was happy to go it alone, if my brother and I wanted some of the 'action', then now was the time to say so. I expressed an interest in going in with him, but only on the basis of a fifty per cent partnership. I asked how much capital would be required and he advised, 'In the short term, one million each.'

'What could we lose in the event of a worst possible scenario?' I asked.

'Anybody's guess, but I would say about double. Four million. Two each.'

I went straight to David's office and we briefly discussed the deal. We both agreed that David Sullivan was no gambler, and his record in publishing was first class. More than that, he was a hard working, 'hands on' man and we knew we could work with him. Ten minutes later I phoned back.

'David, we're in.'

The announcement that another Sunday newspaper, the *News on Sunday*, was about to be launched at about the same time as ours was not encouraging, especially when we learned that they were employing 200 staff compared to our estimated 15.

Eddie Shah's *Today* newspaper was effectively up for sale after only three months in business, and this too was not exactly heartening. Faced with a cash and circulation crisis, most of Eddie's backers wanted to pull out. His break-even sales figure for *Today* was in the region of 600,000 copies daily and he was barely selling half that number. He was ready to listen to offers from Richard Branson, Kerry Packer, the Al Fayed brothers, and Robert Maxwell.

Robert Maxwell's desire to expand his publishing empire knew no bounds. I had always felt that he did not really know where he was going, but he seemed to be in a big hurry to get there. He appeared to have money to burn when he challenged the London *Evening Standard*. His intention was to buy *Today* and to use their presses to print an evening newspaper which he was prepared to give away if necessary.

He was the type of man who took a bow every time he looked in the mirror. I did not like him, and I liked him even less when I discovered that he objected to 'Page Three' pin-ups, adult magazines and our Sunday newspaper. He had decided to show no more nipples in the *Daily Mirror*. Of course, he was perceived to be a 'pillar of our society' and his views were taken seriously.

*

My brother and I attended a meeting with David Sullivan at which he introduced us to Mike Gabbert. Mike, who had once been the deputy editor of the *News of the World*, had agreed to become the executive editor of our new Sunday newspaper. We deliberated over the suggested titles and settled for *Sunday Sport* which seemed to say it all.

From more than 200 applicants we had chosen Austin Mitchelson to be the first editor to work under Mike's direction and produce a newspaper that promised to be amusing, diverting, but most of all, fun. These were the words used in the *Oxford Dictionary* to describe the word 'sport', but with David Sullivan's input, it was also going to be sexy, titillating and rude.

We examined the break-even figures and the projections. Like most new ventures, the prospect of succeeding was in the balance. We needed to invest time and money, but more than that we needed a little luck ... some say it is better to be born lucky than rich.

Fortunately for us and our partner, we were less dependent on luck. There was a great deal of experience and skill going into this venture, but we were not risking more than we could afford. If we could not make it work, in my view nobody could.

Success depended largely on us getting the support of television advertising, not only because this would bring extra sales but it would also encourage the brand name advertisers to use our media, especially to target the 18 to 35 year old male market.

The proof copy, though I say it myself, was superb. It was clearly going to be an alternative paper to the *News of the World* which enjoyed sales in the region of five million copies. It included eleven topless girls, whereas the 'Screws' (a common nickname for the *News of the World*) had twelve. We had an excellent sports section edited by the great England captain, my football idol, Bobby Moore; other contributors included a sensational lady psychic racing tipster; comments on current affairs by Brian Moore, and an up-date on pop music from disc jockey Graham Dene.

In my opinion, the package was excellent, but it was not acceptable to the ITCA, the controlling body for independent television advertising and failure to get our message across to a large television audience, meant that our dreams of sales exceeding one million copies within eighteen months were dashed at a stroke.

In response to our strong protest, ITCA's general secretary, David Shaw, retaliated by saying, 'The decision reached was not, as you suggest, censorship, but merely reflects that the copy and product submitted would, if transmitted, have been incompatible with the ITV company's contractual obligation to the IBA' ... In other words ... censorship! They failed to convince, but managed to confuse us, and we gave up.

Everything possible had been done to win them over but their objection (in my view) had nothing to do with the pre-publication mock-up. It had more to do with David Sullivan himself and their jaundiced view about how he and his partners had earned their money. We were given leave to apply for a judicial review of the decision, which was made in private and the proceedings were confidential. Even that was eventually turned down and the authorities left us to do the near impossible. Selling newspapers without advertising is like winking in the dark ... you know what you are doing but nobody else does.

Our first lead headline, 'Fergie's Nude Photo Shock' was daring, but our readers were quickly informed that we were only objecting about some 'tampered' photographs which were printed in foreign papers. It would have been obvious to anyone that a lady, soon to be a princess, could not possibly be photographed without clothes. Knowing what I know now, the *Sport* could well have been first with the news.

Karren Brady, a highly competent and attractive young lady, was employed by the 'London Broadcasting Corporation' to sell radio advertising. David Sullivan placed our promotional advertising with LBC, and in so doing, he was in regular contact with her.

She worked hard to see that we were treated fairly, and, at the same time, achieved a high return for her company, which impressed David. He recognized that she was the ideal person for the *Sunday Sport* and we offered her a position as head of the advertising department. She accepted, and within a short period of time the sales of advertising space increased dramatically.

Karren produced a first class 'rate and data' document for potential up market advertisers. In it, we offered the opportunity to reach a specialized market which was essentially directed towards young adult males. Despite Karren's hard work, the response was disappointing. Advertising agencies were reluctant to recommend their clients to take space in the *Sunday Sport* for various reasons. The main one being the 'nipple count' which was some 20 per cent more than the *News of the World* and the *People*, and infinitely more than the *Sunday Mirror*, published by the highly 'respected' Robert Maxwell.

'Adult' telephone communication companies were on the increase and it was soon realized that the *Sunday Sport* was an ideal vehicle for them to reach their customers. Karren Brady was alive to this opportunity, and it was not long before she had maximized our advertising income from this source.

With our television advertising campaign rejected by the authorities, we were fighting an uphill struggle and were looking for different ways to promote our newspaper. Local radio stations took our adverts but unfortunately they were not cost-effective.

The 'sex' telephone line adverts in the *Sunday Sport* were financially rewarding, but they did not contribute to our prospects of becoming a 'family' newspaper. The other tabloids permitted their inclusion, but for them, the bigger percentage of more acceptable advertisements lessened the impact. However, the income we received from the 'sexy' telephone advertisers increased daily and the viability of the newspaper improved dramatically, whilst competitors such as the *News on Sunday* and *Sunday Today* were failing miserably.

The advertisers offering phone services were clearly making money, and it was not long before David Sullivan recognized the huge potential and set up in that business.

Nothing Had Changed

Lord Longford, Mary Whitehouse, and Winston Churchill MP had done their utmost to persuade the public that we needed to have obscenity laws similar to those 'enjoyed' by 'respectable' nations such as the Irish Republic, South Africa, China and other Communist countries. The fact that their objectives had not been realized might well be attributed to the likes of David Sullivan and the Gold Brothers who have stood against them and their supporters.

David Mellor, the Home Office Under Secretary, agreed to give Winston Churchill's bill to amend the Obscene Publications Act a second reading in Parliament. More time and more money was to be spent, and in return the benefits to our society were dubious (there were many who argued that such efforts had a contrary effect).

The bill was another move by the puritanical minority to abolish the choice of the tolerant majority. If it went through it would have prohibited newsagents from handling anything other than 'Page Three' material (and even that was in jeopardy) whilst more explicit material was only to be sold in licensed sex shops. It was being suggested that, as a result of a survey, the availability of adult material had increased rape, but figures produced to support this were spurious because rape victims had been granted anonymity and that resulted in an increase of rape offences being reported. Actual rapes may well have decreased during that time and it could be argued that the availability of erotica, marital aids and massage parlours, were responsible, a conclusion which had been reached by the Williams Committee. During that same period, offences of indecent assault upon females dropped by fifteen per cent, a fact which had been conveniently ignored.

David Webb was the Honorary Director of the 'National Campaign for the Reform of the Obscene Publications Act', and he and his committee were passionate in their desire to fight any move to restrict society's civil liberties. We naturally supported his cause and invited him to come to visit us at Whyteleafe. David and I were not only impressed with the work that he was doing but with the man himself. He was a very intelligent and likeable person and we were quite prepared to offer our support.

John Gibbins, the managing director of our distributing company and a director of 'Gold Star Publications', gave evidence in defending a quantity of magazines which had been seized from one of our depots. David Offenbach represented us and, by agreement with the police, the allegedly obscene magazines were classified into six distinct categories. Two magazines from each were chosen at random and this relieved the Court of the chore of examining each and every one.

Our co-operation did not help because in the final analysis the Stipendiary Magistrate, who was clearly out of touch with the real world, found all of the titles repugnant and a matter for regret, despite the fact that such material was readily available in newsagents and bookstalls. He took no account of the claim that, as a masturbation stimulus, the availability of these magazines was an alternative to penetrative sex and could even help in the fight against the proliferation of the deadly AIDS virus.

In making his decision he had referred to the findings of the Williams Committee but disregarded it on a matter of law. He also took into account the verdict that a jury might reach when counsel presented evidence of the David Gold acquittal (twice) for similar magazines. Again such evidence was not taken into account and the entire seizure was ordered to be destroyed.

*

I had strong views about the fortune that the Government had elected to spend with *The Times*, *Telegraph* and *Observer* on advertising. The advertisements expressed the important contribution that readers could make to help control the spread of AIDS by using condoms. They were prepared to advertise in all the newspapers with the exception of only one 'national' ... the *Sunday Sport*. It was clearly reaching the largest number of young virile males per thousand sales and would have been enormously cost-effective for the Government, who could only have achieved more if they advertised in girlie magazines. The government however had its own 'standards' to consider, which to them was far more important than AIDS control.

The death of Rock Hudson, Liberace and other famous people caused people to worry more about its spread. The government distributed millions of leaflets to households, hammering home the message: 'Use condoms, never share needles and stick to one partner'. They failed to take into account that there are millions of men who do not even have one partner to stick to, and for those men there is a choice between a prostitute and a wank. If a man were to choose the latter, which was socially more acceptable, he might have appreciated pictorial assistance. The magistrate was doing all that he could to see that such a man was deprived of it. Page Three pictures, in his opinion, should have been sufficient to keep the matter in hand... What a wanker!

Another Shadow

Before Annie's next check-up at the Royal Marsden, I decided to take her away for a week's holiday to the villa. Our flight was due to leave on the Sunday morning, and on the way to the airport I stopped off to buy a copy of the *Sunday Sport* from a small newsagent in Chipstead.

On the counter was the usual array of Sunday newspapers, most of them displaying explicit and outrageous headlines. Details of the resignation of Jeffrey Archer as Deputy Chairman of the Tory Party was the news story of the day. For no apparent reason, he had allegedly paid £2,000 to a prostitute (whom, he claimed, he had never met) to leave the country. Not for the first time, a so called 'pillar of society' was being compromised.

I was surprised that our newspaper was not on display and asked the young lady assistant for a copy. She looked at me strangely and then turned to the owner, a middle-aged man with a cigarette sticking out of the side of his mouth.

'This gentleman,' she muttered, pointing at me, 'wants a copy of the *Sunday Sport*.' They both turned to look at me. It was only for a few seconds but it seemed like an eternity before he went into the back of the shop and brought a copy through. As I gave him the money, I asked what it was doing in the back and why it was not on display.

'It's filth!' he said, with a face like Ebenezer Scrooge suffering from earache, 'and nothing short of pornography! This, sir, is a family store. They are going back to the wholesaler.'

I was flabbergasted and like a fool tried to make a 'federal case' of it by saying, 'How can you possibly judge what should or should not be sold? If you don't mind me saying, you made a bad judgement when you took 'that' product into your shop.' I pointed to his open cigarette display.

'How much death and misery do you think *that* is responsible for? You have your priorities wrong and the terrible thing is that you are not alone.'

'Get out! Get out of my shop,' he yelled. I was happy to oblige.

The holiday was superb, except for one thing. Annie had noticed a small spot which was an inch or so above her throat, and she asked me if she should mention it to Dr Ford when we visited the Marsden in a week's time.

Says it all, doesn't it?

'Mention anything that gives you even the slightest concern,' I told her casually, although I was well aware that it could be serious.

It was serious, deadly serious, and Dr Ford was quick to refer Annie to a skin specialist to decide on the next move. The spot grew each day and no time was to be lost. There was, however, a big complication because it could not be easily removed as it was situated in an area which had previously been treated with radium. Her skin would not heal there, and we were referred to Nicholas Breach, a renowned plastic surgeon, for his prognosis.

It was not good, although his optimism was comforting. He suggested making one attempt at removing the spot, which had been diagnosed as a squamous-cell carcinoma, in the hope that the skin would heal naturally. If it did not, then he intended to graft skin from Annie's thigh, which he was confident would work. The operation was quite simple, but when the skin failed to knit together, poor Annie was informed of the next step.

I was anxious for her to go to a private clinic where she could have her own privacy and some additional comforts, but it was a big mistake. She did not spend time in her 'posh' room because of a catastrophe that happened at three o'clock in the morning following the operation. I received a phone call from Nicholas Breach who told me that Annie's neck had started to bleed uncontrollably and he was making arrangements for her to be taken immediately to the Royal Marsden in Fulham Road, where they had the equipment to deal with this type of emergency. He no longer sounded confident.

I woke Sascha and asked her to take care of Jennen as I was going to the hospital. She did not realize the seriousness of the situation as she was hardly awake, and I had no intention of alarming her unnecessarily.

I found my way to the intensive care ward where Annie was lying, heavily sedated and bandaged. I sat with her as we waited to see Nicholas Breach. When he arrived, he immediately changed the mood from one of despair to one of hope. He told me that he would be operating on Annie again later that day and intended to join her throat to her breast.

'Don't be alarmed,' he said. 'In six weeks I will operate again to disconnect the link and by then, I promise you her neck will be healed.' It proved to be true, but during that time Annie went through a period of extreme suffering, both physically and mentally.

She soon came to realize that her outward beauty had been taken away from her. I first saw her in intensive care, only hours after her operation. She was not bandaged this time and at first sight I thought that the surgeon had removed her hand, and that her arm was linked to her neck but then, to my relief, I realized that the operation had gone according to plan and the roll of flesh was, in fact, coming from her chest.

I sat with her for a long time, dreading the moment when she would ask to see herself in the mirror. It took more than a day for her to ask and I was so proud when she made no fuss and even joked with Nicholas (we were already on first name terms with him) about her being a 'hoot' at the disco.

I had known from the moment we met Nicholas Breach that a special relationship would develop between the three of us, and it did. He informed me that Annie had needed more than six pints of blood during her operation and for a time he was very concerned that she might not make it. As he spoke, I reflected on the twenty years during which I had donated blood and, although I had been well aware of its importance, it was never more so than now.

Within a week, Annie was allowed to come home, but first she asked me if I would arrange for the hairdresser from the Svenson clinic to visit her in the ward, to adjust her hairpiece. Despite everything that had happened to her she wanted to look her best and I loved her for it.

The district nurse came each day to tend to her wound and I was happy to help. After a few weeks I was able do it by myself and the nurse called only to inspect my work.

I was even called upon to help Nicholas when he operated on Annie's lip a few months later at his London clinic. Annie had gone there for him to inspect her neck and chest which had healed well, but horrendous scars remained and Nicholas promised to take care of them in the near future. He was, at that moment, far more concerned about a small ulcer which had formed on her lip and decided that it should be removed immediately. Wearing a white overall and rubber gloves, I acted as his nurse and handed him instruments on request.

The small operation was a success, but to say that Annie and I were a little worried about what was happening to her was an understatement. I had given Annie a great deal of encouragement by telling her that her illness was under control and, although she would probably have the illness till the day she died, she would more than likely die of old age.

Annie was not convinced and asked me if I would take her to a spiritualist centre in Redhill. She had heard of the good work that they had done from her friends, Dennis and Joyce Drawbridge, whose daughter, Dawn, was enjoying many years of remission from cancer. I readily agreed to take her there although my faith in such things was non-existent. Under the circumstances, however, whatever Annie wanted I was prepared to go along with.

It was a strange coincidence that we met Dennis and Joyce in the waiting room. Dennis was suffering from tetanus at the time and he was sure that it was the spiritualist's healing power that was helping to cure him. His words gave Annie a wonderful boost and I was glad, even though I remained sceptical.

When Annie went in for her 'healing', I insisted on accompanying her and held her hand while a kind of ritual was performed. She was happy that, at least, something was being done to hopefully make her better, although I knew that it was nothing more than grasping at straws.

I was far more happy about our visits to the 'South East Cancer Self Help Group' in Purley, where we were given a great deal of help and encouragement from fellow cancer sufferers.

The small meeting rooms were used by courtesy of the South Eastern Water Board. Tom Perkins, the group leader, was busy negotiating a similar arrangement with Tesco, who were planning to build a giant store on the site. Tom had recently lost his beloved wife through cancer and he was determined to help alleviate the suffering of others. Help is too small a word ... he performed miracles.

Further complications ensued for Annie when a few months later she visited her dentist, Clive Gore, in Wimbledon. She was arranging to have cosmetic dental treatment but he was unhappy about doing it in view of an abnormality which he discovered on her cheek. He spoke only to me about it and I contacted Nicholas Breach who insisted that I bring her immediately to the Marsden.

Once again he operated within days to remove the affected tissue. He reassured her but my optimism was wearing thin. It was now evident that these carcinomas were secondary deposits and unlikely that the primary would ever be found.

Fun on Sunday

Without the help of advertising on television, the *Sunday Sport* was unable to make the progress required to seriously affect the competition. However, we managed to find a niche at the bottom end of the newspaper market and it was not long before there were signs that the paper could make substantial profits.

David's younger daughter, Vanessa, had joined Ann Summers at the time of its dramatic growth, and was working very well under Jacqueline's guidance. Jacqueline was naturally delighted that we were doing well with the *Sunday Sport*.

It seemed such a shame that we could not find a way to capitalize on the connection between our two companies. They were jointly selling to at least a million people each month, but there was pressure from both the management and customers of Ann Summers to distance themselves from the newspaper.

Sunday Sport, on the other hand, was keen to include articles on the success of Ann Summers. I had the job of diplomatically telling the editor, Mike Gabbert, that Ann Summers would not agree to this. However, my brother and I did agree to include an advertisement for the *Sunday Sport* in the catalogue, which went to more than a million homes each year.

I came up with a special slogan, 'I Get it Every Sunday' which, together with a small *Sunday Sport* logo, was printed onto car stickers and T-shirts. These T-shirts were sold through Ann

Summers, as well as by mail order. The T-shirt itself became a bestseller and it also helped to promote the *Sunday Sport*.

Every few months we met with David Sullivan in our private suite at the Tower Hotel. We would arrive in the late morning and take the lift to the top floor. After ordering lunch, we focused on business matters concerning our publishing ventures.

The view from the Nelson Suite, overlooking the River Thames, Tower Bridge and the Tower of London, was idyllic. The room was booked in the name of 'Apollo' which was the company that owned the newspaper. It was sufficiently unknown and attracted little attention, but with girlie magazines and *Sunday Sport* newspapers spread across the conference table at each meeting, it was not long before the waiters, and no doubt the rest of the staff, became aware that 'Apollo' and *Sunday Sport* were linked.

They also recognized David Sullivan, which concerned us about how we might maintain our low profile. Once a 'bug' had been planted in David's warehouse and he said that we should be alert to the possibility that there could possibly be an outside interest in our activities. It had been some time since the police had seized any of our publications but we were still concerned that the problem could rear its ugly head again at any moment.

We need not have been concerned because, at our next meeting, we found ourselves celebrating a victory after Magistrates at Newham Court had ruled that all of the magazines (more than 500,000 copies) and videos seized in 'Operation Sweetheart' earlier in the year were to be returned.

The *Daily Mirror* headline read 'Porn unlimited – £2 million of dirty books are given back to filth merchants.' Once again, the *Mirror* was cashing in on porn. Porn headlines sell papers and how wonderful it was for Robert Maxwell to spout off about the evils of pornography in his comment column. He lied and cheated by dramatizing the whole matter.

The magistrates had made a judgement that the magazines were not obscene, but Maxwell and his cronies supported Mary Whitehouse in saying that they were virtually 'hard porn', and that youngsters needed to be protected from it in the same way as from drugs, which in my opinion, was outrageous. Linking erotica with drugs, or even violence or smoking, is a disgrace, but as the *Mirror* probably sold an extra hundred thousand copies that day, it would have achieved its purpose.

We had not been able to persuade the television advertising authority to change its mind about the *Sunday Sport*'s acceptability even though our sales, in less than a year, had exceeded 500,000 copies per issue.

We were already discussing the possibility of bringing out a mid-week edition. Once again, to promote this we were limited to billboards, local press and radio advertising for which we would need to allocate a budget of at least £500,000.

Most of the daily newspapers had little to say about the Gold Brothers, but two publications that did give us coverage were *Private Eye* and *Digger*. Karl Slack made a very interesting observation when he jokingly talked about 'The *Eye*'. He said that they gave such unbelievably accurate accounts on the activities of Godfrey Gold, a sex shop owner called Tom Hayes, David Sullivan, the Gold brothers, and himself that if they ever said anything agreeable about any one of us, then it would reveal which one was the 'grass'.

The *Digger*'s reporter, Martin Tomkinson, was one of the first to discover the connection between David Sullivan and the Gold Brothers. His well researched articles were vicious in the extreme.The 'Slug' was the name he used to describe David Sullivan and he was quick to point out that the Slug's partners had made their money in the same way as David Sullivan had. He informed his readers that the Gold Brothers did not take a particularly active interest in the business as we spent most of our time in the more hospitable climate of southern Spain. David and I had spent no more than three weeks each year away from our desks and even now, my brother works no less than ten hours per day. The same was true of David Sullivan, and the 'Slug' analogy was offensive and disgraceful.

The article was ignominious and totally untrue, and I was

incensed. I telephoned John Gibbins to find out who the distributor of *Digger* was, and I was surprised to learn that *we were*! I managed to contact by telephone, a person whom I assumed was the editor and told him what I thought of his article. His response, 'Do your fucking worst,' did not warm me to him, and I immediately instructed John to see that every copy was withdrawn from sale. He informed me that this was not the done thing and that it could cost us in the region of fifty thousand pounds, to which I responded, 'John, you don't need road manners if you are a ten ton truck!' In response to his second point, I said that I would live with the cost. I was delighted to learn that within a few months *Digger* bit the dust. For the first time in my life I used my money, power and influence to get even.

Holding Back the Tears

The death of my cousin Ian through cancer was significantly one of the most distressing happenings in recent years. When Uncle David first disclosed the seriousness of Ian's illness I was put in a very difficult position. We had been negotiating to buy 'David Gold & Son' for some time, and I had already come to terms with the fact that his business was worth very little to us and, under normal circumstances, I wanted to put aside or even to drop the offer to purchase it. My bid of £500,000 had been made more than six months earlier and since then David Gold & Son had considerably lessened in value. Uncle Dave informed me that he was now prepared to let it go for the price that I had originally offered. I should have said that I did not want it, or that I expected to pay less. But, under the circumstances, that would have appeared to have been taking advantage of his unfortunate position. We went ahead with the deal.

Yet another death that I found hard to take was that of my football idol, Bobby Moore.

After his triumphant playing career as captain of West Ham and England, he did not succeed in football management. He was sacked as manager of non-league Oxford City and Third Division Southend United before seeking employment as a sports writer. Here, too, there were few offers of a worthwhile job and I had been pleased when he accepted a position as sports editor of our newspaper.

My brother David and I met with him on a number of occasions and found him to be a very likeable and sincere person. He was clearly delighted that we had offered him the opportunity to strengthen our sports section. He quickly established himself as an outstanding editor and was respected by staff and readers alike.

After his death I read many of his obituaries but none grieved me more than the article in *Today* newspaper, which concluded as follows:

> He hit rock bottom when he was forced to take a job as the sports editor of the *Sunday Sport* newspaper. For Bobby Moore, the perfect gentleman, this was the ultimate humiliation.
>
> It was hard to believe that 20 years after stopping Britain with that World Cup triumph he would be reduced to working hand to mouth on a tatty tit-and-bum newspaper ... (sic)

My brother David was furious when he read it.

'Where were you, Mr Editor, when Bobby was in need of a job?' he stormed. 'Did you offer him one? No you didn't, you sanctimonious bastard! You hypocrite!'

The article added nothing to the tribute and insulted the memory of a special man. As I write this I hope that Bobby is looking over my shoulder because *Today* newspaper is now out of business and *Sport* newspapers have gone from strength to strength.

Sunday Sport figures were usually on our desks by Tuesday morning, and David and I would attempt to work out why sales had increased or decreased. It did not take a genius to deduce that ... the bigger the tits, the bigger the increase. It did, however, require a genius to determine the limits of acceptability for advertisements, the strength of copy and the number of nipples that we could include. An error of judgement could cause us to be rejected by one or more of the major newsagent groups. Such a rejection could have a domino effect, whereby we would find ourselves on the top shelf and virtually out of the newspaper business.

The telephone service advertisers realized that the 'stronger' the ad content, the greater the response, and, as the advert copy was received, we had to take on the role of censors.There was a fine line between acceptability and vulnerability, but in the final analysis it was all about profitability, and we were inclined to give the service provider the benefit of the doubt. It turned out that we were right in so doing.

In view of the success of the *Sunday Sport* we decided to expand with a 'daily'. The decision was not taken lightly as we fully realized that there had not been a successful launch of a daily paper for more than a decade. Both the *Star* and the *Independent* were yet to make a profit.

David Sullivan was dynamic with regard to publicity. For the first birthday celebration of the *Sunday Sport* he held a party at 'Stringfellows' in Covent Garden. We were told that the evening was both exciting and outrageous, but my brother and I resisted the temptation to attend.

John Gibbins represented us, which enabled us to maintain our low profile policy. I had strong views about keeping to this and my brother David was happy to go along with them.There was much to celebrate and the party was an enormous success. For the men, the stars of the show were the new 'Glamour Girls Roadshow' and the female party-goers were treated to the 'Hunk of the Year' competition. The *Sunday Sport* was on its way to becoming the only successful newly launched newspaper in recent times.

Whilst in Portugal, on Monday mornings, David and I were able to purchase the *Sunday Sport* from the local kiosk – which was a thrill. I will never forget travelling with Annie and Penny on British Airways one Wednesday morning. We asked quite loudly for a copy of the *Sport*. Penny and Annie smiled knowingly at each other, as though they knew we would be unsuccessful, but to everyone's surprise, the stewardess brought us each a copy. This was only possible on a few more trips before the principals of BA decided that it was 'not for them' – cigarettes and booze, yes ... But a paper with at least twice as many naked nipples as the acceptable *Sun*? A definite No!

It was the same with the newspaper reviewers on television, in particular the 'Frost on Sunday' programme. For months we were at the top of their list as there was always something outrageous being reported, but after a time, pressure was clearly applied and our publications were left out.

For some reason the authorities did not bar us from radio advertising, and we speculated more than £500,000 to get our message across via this medium. It did help, although our biggest surge came as a result of a full front page picture of Tina Small. David Sullivan had been working on this idea behind the scenes. It came as quite a shock when Annie brought the *Sunday Sport* up to the bedroom with my morning cup of tea. There was Tina Small, showing all but the nipples of her 84 inch breasts. It was stunning, the scoop of the century!

I could not believe it ... Annie could not believe it ... Nobody could believe it, but that did not matter. It sold thousands of newspapers and made a lot of people smile. Annie spread her hands and asked me pleadingly, 'Surely Ralph, you don't believe it's genuine?'

I laughed and said, 'Of course I do! It's got to be true, it's in the *Sunday Sport*, isn't it?'

One of the most distressing moments of my life was when the telephone rang at five thirty one morning. It was my sister Marie. She was calling from Atkinson Morley Hospital in Wimbledon. Her voice was tired and strained, and she was hardly able to get the words out.

'Ken is in a coma,' she said at last. 'He's had an accident.'

She told me that it had happened at two in the morning when he was returning from his late shift. My brother-in-law loved motorcycling, and drove a powerful Honda. He had driven into the back of a van, parked in Godstone Road, not a hundred yards from our offices.

Within minutes I was dressed and after explaining briefly to

Annie, I kissed her and was on the road to Wimbledon. Marie had sat at his bedside through the night and was herself still in a state of shock.

Ken lay in the intensive care unit with wires coming from just about everywhere. Nurses frequently monitored him, all the time speaking to him as though he could hear every word. As each day went by, we were advised of further complications and it was becoming apparent that there was a strong likelihood of permanent brain damage even if he were to recover.

For six weeks Marie and I sat with him. I took some time off but Marie stayed by his side, taking only a few hours to sleep in a nearby bed which was provided by the hospital. She willed him to come round, but apart from the occasional gripping of her fingers, he never responded.

Ken and Marie's children, Steven, Julie and Christopher, shared with us that traumatic period of waiting and hoping. He was moved to Mayday Hospital where the vigil continued, and Marie, David, and I were at his bedside when, at three in the morning, he died.

Ken's funeral took place at the Beckenham Crematorium and was attended by hundreds of colleagues from both the ambulance and the fire services. As the procession of chief mourners approached the chapel a line of ambulances was parked each side of us, contributing to an atmosphere of intense emotion.

The chapel was packed and a tannoy had been set up for the benefit of those outside. I was privileged to be asked by Marie to read a message to the congregation. I remember, as I spoke, looking around and spotting Annie, who I knew would miss Ken terribly. She was in tears but I felt that I detected a hint of pride in her face as I made my short speech.

I also noticed my father and his son Mark who were near to the front. I wondered what was going through Godfrey's mind as he sat staring at me for all of three minutes. I suspected that it was not pride. Since our sporting days, he has never given any hint of recognizing any of David's or my capabilities, and it was not likely to change now.

An Ill Wind

I struggled to come to terms with the horrendous conclusion that Annie was going to lose her battle. I had not been told in as many words, but my studies on the subject of cancer had left me in no doubt that we had reached the stage when there was absolutely no prospect of winning through.

I will never forget the kindness, thoughtfulness and tenderness of Nicholas Breach who did so much to keep Annie's hopes alive. He never gave up hope himself, despite the fact that Annie and I came to him almost every month with further complications. Her mouth and face had required surgery which was either carried out at his clinic in Portland Place, or at the Royal Marsden hospital.

I made a point of always 'being there' for Annie. We were at the Marsden so much that we built friendships with a number of the nurses and patients. I even found myself dealing with menial nursing duties, such as helping to take patients to the bathroom and holding cups to the mouths of patients who were unable to tend to themselves.

Annie was in a ward of primarily ear, nose and throat cases, and many of the patients could only speak with the help of a device because their own voice boxes had been removed. I did my best to communicate with many of those patients and it was clearly appreciated.

Nicholas Breach once took me round to the neighbouring men's ward and I met a few patients there who were undergoing plastic surgery to improve the most horrible deformities imaginable. Although I had great sympathy for those people, I found it hard to accept that many of them continued to smoke. Memories of those sights caused me to find the habit even more distasteful.

Despite Annie's facial deformities, her appearance was everything to her, and I made special arrangements for her hairdresser to travel from the Svenson hair clinic to deal with the tightening of her hairpiece, and at the same time wash and style her own hair. Annie would remonstrate that I over-indulged her, and perhaps she was right, but it was the least that I could do ... I loved her dearly.

Annie's brother, John, was now happily married to Gaynor, who had two teenage children, Lianne and Paul. Annie and I visited them regularly, and I became friendly with Paul. He was only nineteen, and had been granted a place at Southampton University. I learned from his mother that he was undergoing tests at the hospital because he had been suffering from bad headaches.

Paul and I played chess, and although he beat me on every occasion, the games were close and I was determined to get the better of him. When I did, the victory was shallow. Paul's tests showed that he had a malignant brain tumour. He underwent radium treatment, but from then on his condition progressively deteriorated.

Annie and Paul were fighting a similar battle, and an affinity between them was established. We saw him more often as his health deteriorated.

There are days in one's life which are never forgotten; John Kennedy's assassination, Neil Armstrong's walk on the moon and England winning the World Cup to name but a few, but the day that sticks most in my mind is the day of the hurricane.

Annie and I were woken during the early hours by the wind howling through our garden and the adjoining woodland. We had always been interested in watching the natural beauty of a storm but this was different.

A new wooden verandah had been built just outside our bedroom and we were tempted to go out onto it. As we opened the door we realized that the wind was so powerful, to go outside was unthinkable. We eventually got off to sleep but the next morning the devastation was frightening.

Branches and trees had fallen in our garden and the adjoining woodlands looked as though an angry giant had walked through destroying everything in sight. I was forced to walk to work that day because a huge tree had fallen across our road, blocking all traffic.

As I left my house, I noticed that most of my neighbours were out clearing up the debris and I sheepishly returned home to instruct my gardener, Graham, to join them. By doing that, I felt I was at least contributing and could walk past my hard-working friends with a little dignity.

Our visits to the Royal Marsden in Sutton would be followed by a visually distressing journey from home. The magnificent wooded area on the edge of Purley Oaks golf course had been ravaged by the hurricane. There had been times when Annie and I had strolled through those woods arm in arm.

We often sat on one of the park benches which had been donated by the families of local residents and would read the plaque, placed in memory of a loved one who had passed on. We occasionally went there after our visit to the hospital when we were in a reflective mood. The sight of the fallen trees had taken away that luxury but we hoped that we would both see the day when everything was back to relative normality.

I heard from Annie that Paul had been admitted to St Thomas's Hospital after having collapsed during the day. We visited him at St Thomas's Hospital where he was staying in a small room with a view across the river to the Houses of Parliament. I remember the occasion well because Annie was suffering with a severe headache and a blockage in her nose that was troubling her, but she still had insisted on making the journey.

While we waited for Paul to finish his physiotherapy, his doctor arrived. We told him that Paul would not be long and to my surprise he sat down to talk to us. I presumed that he believed us to be Paul's parents and he explained that there was nothing more that could be done and he intended to send him to a hospice where they would take care of his needs.

We visited 'St Christopher's' hospice in Crawley on a number of occasions. One of the monks who helped nurse Paul was called Simon, and I enjoyed talking to him. He was a fine young man and I liked his outlook on life. He was celibate and intended to stay that way, but his views on sex were free and easy and he recognized the stupidity of society's desire to curb sexual expression ... An old head on young shoulders.

Paul died within a few weeks and Annie and I attended yet another funeral. The service was attended by a great number of Paul's young friends, many of whom we had seen only months earlier at John and Gaynor's wedding.

Only days after Paul's death, Annie and I were to hear of more bad news. The blockage in her nose was a tumour that needed urgent treatment. We visited a number of specialists who determined that an operation to remove it would be impractical because of the many secondary metastases. She would therefore need to go into hospital to undergo chemotherapy.

Poor Annie reacted with calmness and dignity, and I was very proud of her. I too managed to control myself but I needed to be somewhere away from her, to be alone, to allow myself time to cry. I knew, however, that she needed me at every moment and I wanted to be there with her. I had to suffer in silence – more than that, I needed to put on a brave face for her. It all seemed so cruel and unfair, but then I had come to understand that when it came to fairness, there was a world shortage.

My office was only fifteen minutes away from the Marsden and I made a point of calling in to see Annie in the mornings. During the six weeks of Annie's treatment, her friends Margaret Alderdise, Lynn Bauer and our neighbours, Pat and Margaret, were regular visitors and they would insist that I take a break. On those occasions, I went back to the office, not because I was a glutton for work, but more that I just wanted to be with people, and to keep my mind occupied. David would fill me in on most of the business details, and I still was able to take care of a few deals, which helped me to keep in contact with the business.

David's daughters Vanessa and Jackie would usually be there late at night as I returned from the hospital. Vanessa had taken on many of the buying responsibilities and, under the circumstances, it certainly made my life easier. Jackie, meanwhile, was receiving a great deal of media attention. I was never really happy about that because the media had given us nothing but 'grief' thus far, although David made the point that this time it was different. Jackie was not only a successful business woman, but she was extremely attractive, and the media would be likely to take a different approach. He has been proven right ... so far.

After three weeks of treatment, the doctors elected to give Annie a week off from the chemotherapy, which was fed to her intravenously. The side effects were devastating and although Annie was prepared to continue, her doctors insisted that for the time being, enough was enough. They told me that the quality of her life was now more important than the quantity. I agreed and I intended to make sure that her week was spent in doing exactly what she wanted to do, which was to spend the whole time at home with me and her children.

Although most of her symptoms had disappeared, she had paid a big price. She was tired and drawn and the rest of her hair was beginning to fall out. Nevertheless, we had our moments of great pleasure and we desperately regretted the fact that she had to go back for another three weeks to complete the treatment.

On the last day of her break, I arranged to take her and my mother to Greenwich Market which I now jointly owned along with my brother and David Tearle. This was a largely open market set on a huge car park owned by David and I, along with a business colleague and friend, David Tearle, with whom we were building a successful property company.

We picked Rose up from her shop in Green Street and within the hour we were walking through the market. I had a strong feeling of *déjà vu*, as though I were looking for the Inspector, but, of course, there wasn't one ... if there had been, I would have been employing him.

We looked at almost every stall before Annie and my mother went for a coffee. We agreed to meet thirty minutes later at the entrance to the bookstore, which was the prime building on the site. It comprised a number of book and magazine traders one of which was of particular interest to me as it had on offer a variety of old books and magazines wrapped in cellophane.

I saw one of the original 'Hank Janson' books, which made my skin creep. It was the very title which had caused the Reiter Brothers to be sent to prison more than thirty five years ago. Another 'Hank Janson' alongside had a red and yellow striped cover and I recognized it as one of the 'toned-down' titles that we had published.

I *had* to buy them, and I negotiated a deal with the stallholder – I can never resist the desire to deal (the asking price is invariably at least 20 per cent over the top). She asked for five pounds but agreed to accept three. I told her that my company was the original publisher of one of the books ... She was not impressed. Then I spotted a copy of *Golden Nugget*. 'I must buy that!' I told her. 'That was the very first girlie magazine that my company GSP ever published!'

After visiting other stands, I returned, to find that she had an American edition of *Tropic of Capricorn* by Henry Miller. Again I negotiated a price and bought it.

'I had to have it,' I told her, 'I attempted to import 5,000 copies of that title over thirty years ago, but the English publisher issued an injunction and they were ordered to be destroyed.'

She looked at me as if I were mad, and I walked away with

Annie on one arm and my mother on the other. I was wearing an old pair of jeans and an anorak and I had negotiated a reduction on each of my purchases. I could well understand the saleslady's total disbelief, and could almost hear her unspoken words, 'What a plonker!'

I told Annie what had been said and she responded by saying, 'No wonder she didn't believe you. Nobody would, especially after haggling over the price of a few books!' Then she asked, 'Did you tell her that you owned the market and you were her landlord?' I put my hand to my head in mock horror.

'No,' I told her honestly ... 'I forgot!'

Annie returned to her hospital bed for the completion of her therapy. During the last days of her treatment she became so weak that I could only take her out in a wheelchair. One sunny afternoon I took her to the Royal Marsden summer fête which was held in the hospital grounds. It may seem impossible to believe but we actually had a wonderful time. We were like young lovers as I wheeled her from stand to stand. We joked, laughed and cuddled. But later, when I was alone ... I cried.

Sex in Swindon

Peter Grimsditch, who had once assisted Derek Jameson as editor of the *Daily Star*, had been taken on to head the launch of the Wednesday edition of *Sport*. His experience with the *Sun*, *Mail*, and *Express* would no doubt be of great value as he clearly had the ability to build the *Sport* into a successful daily.

Peter set up the 'Wednesday' edition from a small, unpretentious office in Manchester with fewer than twenty staff. It was however not long before we were looking for bigger premises to facilitate the expansion into a second daily, which was planned to come out each Friday.

'Gold Star Textiles', the screen printing side of our organization, was called upon to redesign the *Sport* promotional logo. One moment the logo read, 'I get it twice a week,' and now the call was for, 'I get it three times a week'. It was getting harder to keep it up.

I agreed to Andrew Robertson's suggestion to write the occasional article for the *Sunday Sport*. I also enjoyed producing a sexy cartoon strip. Not very imaginatively, I called it 'Dave'. It was based on a sexy married man who experienced, at least once a week, some form of sexual enticement. Its popularity prompted Peter Grimsditch to request its inclusion in *Wednesday Sport*.

Another popular item in the *Wednesday Sport* was the 'Lonely Hearts' column. It was amazing that this should be successful when, proportionally, so few women read the paper, but successful it was. We received hundreds of letters, mostly from women, who told us that they had met the right man through our columns.

Fiona Wright, our agony aunt, wanted us to publish her diary which had been written during her affair with Ralph Halpern, the millionaire boss of Burtons. Hundreds of pages describing their daring and amazing exploits were sent to me but, after reading only a few, I decided against its publication. The revelations were too daring and too amazing ... even for the *Sunday Sport*!

Hardly a day went by without somebody telling me that they had read an article about Ann Summers or that they had seen a programme on television about us. 'It is like a "Tupperware" party with naughty bits', quoted the *Sun*. Other newspapers had made contact with our party organizers and carried articles such as: 'Sex Parties are My Business', and, 'I do it for Fun'.

More magazine printed an article with dozens of colour pictures of girls having fun at a party in Swindon, headed: 'Sex in Swindon'. Partygoers were more than happy to show off our products to the camera.

Articles about Ann Summers were invariably favourable and complimentary towards the company and the response from potential organizers and party hostesses was enormous. I felt that everyone involved in our organization had good reason to feel a sense of pride, even though the media tended to highlight the raunchier products.

We were climbing to the top but, on the way, we took nothing for granted and, while David and I reinvested profits back into the company, Jacqueline invested her time and personally dedicated herself to its success.

Her marriage had broken down, and one of the reasons for its failure might well have been her total devotion to the company. She worked very hard, not only to strengthen the business but to improve its image. In doing so, she was establishing herself as one of the best known business women in Britain, winning many awards, David and I were very proud of her.

At each conference, she was taking more responsibility and, although I continued to make the final promotional speech, David and I came to realize that we were little more than figureheads at these functions. Vanessa gradually took over responsibility for the buying, and as a consequence I had more time to spend dealing with other matters concerning the overall business and, more significantly, I was also able to spend more time with Annie.

Borrowed Time

For my fiftieth birthday, Annie bought me a magnificent gold watch. Chemotherapy had helped to clear the stuffiness in her nose, but as the months went by, it returned and her options seemed to have run out. Nicholas Breach was the only person to offer the slightest glimmer of hope, but to achieve a lasting result it would be necessary to perform major surgery. His plan, which he explained in detail, was to approach the tumour through an opening in her skull. Annie listened without emotion and readily accepted his proposal. I, too, had total faith and confidence in Nicholas. The operation was to be carried out two days after her admission to the Royal Marsden in Fulham Road.

Soon after reception Annie was required to undergo a number of x-rays and tests but first, with permission from the ward sister, I took Annie out for lunch. It was unusual for permission to be granted in such circumstances but Annie and I had, over the years, become friendly with the staff and the concession was made.

We went to a romantic Italian restaurant opposite the hospital. It turned out as special as any meal that we ever had together. There was a candle and a small display of flowers on the table, and I ordered a half bottle of Annie's favourite wine, 'Chateauneuf du Pape'. We stayed later than we should have done, and on our return the sister was in a flap because we had missed the anaesthetist, who could not get back to see Annie until the next day.

That afternoon we saw Nicholas Breach, accompanied by his colleagues who would be involved in the operation. He explained to Annie, for the second time, the plan of action and while she listened to the gory details I watched her expressionless face. She had placed her life in this man's hands but was fully aware that the operation could go wrong.

The following day I drove to the hospital to be there in good time for her appointment with the anaesthetist. I spent nearly an hour searching for a parking space and eventually left the car on a single yellow line. I expected to get a ticket but I had no more time to spare as I was anxious to be with Annie.

We saw the anaesthetist who was, we were told later, senior to Nicholas Breach, and talked with him about the proposed surgery. Ten minutes after he left, the sister came to explain that the operation would not now go ahead. We were stunned into a state of disbelief and anger. It was obvious that there had been a disagreement between the two specialists and Annie was to bear the consequences.

We were sent home that afternoon. Nicholas had uneasily explained that there was no more that could be done for Annie. She was prescribed steroids which would ease her suffering, but her life expectancy was now no more than a few months.

Annie's main concern, however, was how and when she would explain the situation to her children. I sat with her while she gathered her belongings from the ward. After a tearful goodbye to her favourite nurses we went to the reception area, close to the exit, and I asked Annie to wait while I collected the car which was parked less than fifty yards away. I was close to tears, but when I saw the clamp attached to the front wheel, they were even harder to control.

I took Annie back to the ward while I made the necessary arrangements to have the clamp removed. I telephoned the authorities who informed me that it could take up to two hours and that I should wait by the car. Fortunately, there was a small pub close by and Annie and I waited there.

It seemed unreal that just a few hours earlier, Annie had been told that her life was soon to end yet we were, laughing, joking and making friends with the barmaid. Outwardly, I was coping well but inside, I was suffering unbearably.

After the two hours had gone by I was becoming irritated with the clamp people and Annie clearly detected it. When they eventually arrived, Annie said to me, 'Everything comes to him who waits.'

'Yes,' I responded, 'except for the time spent waiting.' Although I did not say it, I thought to myself, 'Those hours were far from wasted, they were precious. Every moment with Annie was precious.'

The children had been with friends and in view of our late return, they were happy to stay over. Annie and I had a loving evening, and for the last time ever we physically made love.

A few days after Annie had been told of the hopelessness of her situation, on impulse I took her to 'Lane's of Croydon' where we bought a baby-grand piano. Annie had spoken to me a number of times about her desire to play and I thought that, in view of everything, it would be the best thing for her to do.

I paid £3,600 for the piano and insisted on the earliest possible delivery as Annie was keen to get started. It was delivered within a week, but in that short time, Annie's condition had worsened. The steroids had helped her to feel better in herself, although I was noticing that her memory was failing and she was forgetting some small but significant details. I have never been good when it comes to organizing things in the home, but when needs be, needs must, and I took on more and more of Annie's former responsibilities.

I managed to get her interested in the piano, although to start with it was the 'blind leading the blind' as I had no knowledge or, at that time, any interest in the practical side of music. I managed to help her to make a few tuneful sounds and I noticed her childlike response to them. I was saddened each time but, by then, I was coming to terms with the unhappy situation.

Our friends, Pat and Chris, recommended that we spoke to an acquaintance of theirs who was a piano teacher. He was Polish and they were unable to pronounce his name. Nevertheless, I did not wish to pursue this because I realized that the piano idea was no longer working. I had left it too late.

I was thankful for the help from Annie's many friends, but most of all from her parents, Elsie and Arthur. They were on call at any time and without them, I would not have coped for as long as I did. Annie was no longer able to think for herself and, like a child, she had to be supervised at all times. One evening, Annie's parents and I were watching television while Annie was getting dressed in the bedroom after taking a bath. Elsie called in to check that she was alright but came running down the stairs in a panic.

'She's not there!' she cried. I leapt up the stairs, three at a time, and peered into every room. It was true, Annie was nowhere to be found. I asked Elsie to stay by the phone while Arthur checked the garden.

I leapt into my car and searched the immediate neighbourhood. When I returned home, Elsie had the wonderful news that Annie had been found. Our next door neighbours had telephoned to say that she was in their house, having arrived on their doorstep only partially dressed.

Syd and Joan Potter had been wonderful friends to Annie and me, but I never needed them more than the afternoon they called in to see Annie. She was asleep and they joined me in the lounge for a cup of tea. That was the day I reached rock bottom and felt that I could go on no more. I broke down and sobbed.

Perhaps if they had not been there, I would have struggled on for a little longer. I had not wanted Annie to go into a home, but clearly the decision was taken out of my hands. It was Joan and Syd who begged me to ask for help and advice, and later that day I went to the Marie Curie home in Caterham.

I will never forget their kindness. They were so understanding

Annie

and helpful at a time when I needed it most. They took Annie in within a few days. I arranged for Ian Black, my doctor with whom I had been friends since my flying days, to visit on a regular basis, but there was nothing much that he, or anyone else, could do for her.

As I took Annie to her new bed she looked into my eyes and asked calmly, 'When are they going to operate?' She had become so used to the routine that her failing memory assumed that was the reason she was there. I saw no purpose in explaining the situation to her. It was sufficient for me to say to her that she was there, after all she had been through, for a rest.

In every hospital that Annie had been in we had made friends, and this was no exception. As Christmas approached, we were made to feel that we were part of a happy family, and on the day itself the matron, Miriam Jupp, and her husband Tony, set up a special trestle table with candles and decorations.

They suggested that I invite Annie's family to join us, and her parents, her children and John and Gaynor were happy to be part of what was clearly to be Annie's last Christmas. We enjoyed a meal that could not have been better cooked or served with more style at the Savoy Hotel.

The whole family came at different times to see Annie, knowing that each visit could be their last. David came one afternoon as I sat alone with her. He brought her favourite flowers but she was unable to recognise them. However, as he leant over to kiss her, her eyes lit up and she smiled. We sat there for several hours before I suggested that he left. I walked with him to the car but before he set off we cried in each other's arms.

Two days later on the morning of New Year's Day, Annie died. I held her hand as she took her last breath.

Sascha and I took care of the funeral arrangements. She was a pillar of strength to me and I believed that it also worked in reverse. Sascha wanted to see her mother once more and I took her to the chapel of rest for one last moment with Annie.

There were more people at her funeral than even I expected. I was surprised and gladdened by the fact that my father came. I saw this as probably the most significant statement from him; that our long feud was about to end. We shook hands warmly and I thanked him for coming, but beyond that there was not even the slightest move towards a reconciliation. For years Annie had expressed her sorrow at the rift, and she had offered on a few occasions to help to bring us together. Ironically, on this day, she had managed it. It was sadly to no avail.

I took up my neighbours', Margaret and Richard Lamb, recommendation to invite their priest from St Swithins to conduct the service. He knew Annie well and his prayers for her, coupled with the music of John Denver singing 'Annie's Song', reduced the congregation to tears. I, too, let my feelings go, and I well understood the need for that.

Out of Tune

There was a dreadful emptiness at home. Jennen had gone to stay with his Uncle John. Over the many weeks of Annie's stay at the Marie Curie, John and Gaynor had taken a special interest in him which I appreciated. Sascha, who was nearly eighteen years old, had a regular boyfriend, but during those early days, we helped to console each other. Most evenings however I sat alone in my lounge, not wanting company of any kind, just tinkering with Annie's piano.

I was occasionally invited to have dinner at the home of Pat and Chris who had once recommended Bob Maciejewski to teach Annie to play. They had told me that he had written a number of books on music and was a remarkable character. They suggested that I ask him to help me learn to play. I did not respond for many months, but eventually I made the move to follow up on their recommendation.

Margaret and Richard invited me on occasions to join them for dinner, either at their home or at a restaurant. I was already experiencing the loneliness of being the odd one out in mixed company and I welcomed the presence of their daughter, Sara, whose marriage had recently broken up. Although she was young enough to be my daughter, the company of an unattached woman was welcome.

I felt like the odd man out when I attended the annual meeting of the Residents' Association. Each year, Annie and I had participated and, invariably, after the proceedings we would finish up either at our house or at one of our neighbours' homes, for drinks and a chat.

This time, I was like a fish out of water as matters concerning road repair, parking and hedge maintenance were discussed. Under 'any other business', my friend Richard, the chairman of the committee, asked for the members' acceptance of one or two petty expenses.

I was astonished to hear of a complaint from a gentleman who lived nearby, concerning a cheque for ten pounds which had been paid, by the committee, for a wreath for Annie. It had been sent on behalf of her caring neighbours. Richard firmly and effectively dealt with the situation by telling the objector to sit down and shut up. He knew that I was both upset and incensed by the complaint. I recognize that here are some nasty people out there, and one of them was right there on my own doorstep.

Only in the last few months of Annie's life had I neglected my business responsibilities. David and I would invariably spend time on the telephone discussing company matters. The cash-flow, as far as I was concerned, was the most important consideration. If that was in good shape, I know there was little that could be wrong with the whole business. Thankfully, the cash-flow had been improving for such a long time that there was a tendency to take things for granted.

David and I were orchestrating a group of companies which was making millions of pounds each year. I knew of the saying, 'When contentment enters, progress ceases', but that could never be said of my brother. I had, due to my circumstances, delegated many of my day to day responsibilities, whilst David continued to be at his desk for a minimum of ten hours each day.

There were times when I would pass the office on my way to a restaurant or to see friends when I would see his car and I knew that he was still working. He often spent time in the warehouse, sometimes operating the fork lift truck. He claimed it was therapeutic after a long day in the office.

David and I had never thought too much about wealth. Our contemporaries, David Sullivan and Paul Raymond, were joining the band of the recognized super-rich alongside such famous people as Alan Sugar, Robert Maxwell, Richard Branson and the Queen. For David and me it was different. Knowing that publicity had never been good for us, we had endeavoured to maintain a low profile and live a conventional lifestyle, somehow avoiding this media attention.

Whilst most of the newspapers were delighting in the release of Nelson Mandela the financial papers were reporting details of the 1989 profits made from 'soft pornography' which were estimated as being £20 million.

I personally disliked the words 'soft pornography', being used to describe our product, but over recent years it had seemed to take on a new and less contentious meaning. Even publications such as *She* magazine and the Cadbury Flake advertisement could be interpreted as 'soft' pornography.

We were so incensed by some of the ridiculous statements being made by the press on the subject of 'porn and rape' that we invited a scholar at Reading University to produce a report on his own findings.

'Porn Linked to Rape', was a headline in the *Daily Mail*. The article went on to say that 'soft porn' magazines could be just the start ... Doctor Baxter, a specialist in animal behaviour, threw doubt on the Government's more recent tolerance towards certain forms of pornography. He stressed that this was based on the belief that there is no evidence that pornography corrupts. He thought differently and stressed that while studies disagree on the effect of 'soft porn', research (he neglected to say what research) now showed that massive exposure to soft porn led people on to read or watch 'hard porn'.

Our own specialist, William Thompson, made it clear in his report that, 'It is impossible to claim that clinical studies demonstrate a connection between pornography and rape, and that further control upon 'soft core' material is unlikely to reduce sex crime.' The Williams Committee had concluded more than ten years earlier that there was no evidence that pornography triggered abnormal sexual behaviour, so really that was nothing new.

The conclusion of the *Mail* article informed its readers that the Government was doing all it could: '... Home Office Minister, David Mellor, is waiting for the results of new research being carried out by two Government appointed scientists which are expected later in the year.' They were never published. After Dr Guy Cumberbatch and Dr Dennis Howett of Aston University claimed that there was no direct link between pornography and rape, the Government 'shelved' the report amid fears that it would cause a wave of protest.

More money had been spent to no avail, except that society had at last come to realize that its energy would be better directed at curbing the true obscenities, such as violence, drugs and crime.

Another team of 'experts', this time the Advertising Standards Authority, made the judgement that our *Sport* newspapers poster campaign; 'Start 1989 with a Bang!' did not conform to their stipulated requirements and ordered 2,000 posters to be removed from public display.

The contractors were reported to be 'red faced' in having to complete this task. Their red faces (in my view) should have been due to the fact that they had left, on public display, billboards promoting the sale of cigarettes bearing a large government notice practically guaranteeing the users death from either heart disease or lung cancer.

The Advertising Standards Authority were not the only official body we had problems with. There had been a number of complaints received by the Press Council which could have caused the paper to end up on the top shelf, and in that event our sales would have plummeted. The *Sport* editor, Andrew Robertson, did not help matters when he printed an editorial which read:

'BOLLOCKS TO THE PRESS COUNCIL'

...There comes a time when you've gotta deliver a sharp kick in the bollocks to the killjoys of life.

Cutting the bullshit, it's about time that the press council was press councilled ... But we will not take this heap of shit from trumped up newspaper bashers whose sole aim is to wet nurse the public and curtail our greatest asset ... Freedom.'

His sentiments were not wrong, but there had to be a better way of expressing them! There was no alternative but to reluctantly ask him to resign.

Birmingham

I kept in close touch with Annie's family. Since her death, her brother, John, had been concerned about Jennen and Sascha's welfare and he made arrangements for Jennen to spend some time with his father, Boo. I was rather pleased because I knew that if they could get along together then it would be better for Jennen in the long term. Sascha had gone to live with her boyfriend and appeared to be coping better. She had suffered terribly but time was already beginning to ease the pain. This applied equally to me, although I knew that there was still a long way to go. I pledged to keep in touch with Annie's parents. They had loved Annie as much as any parents could and their grief was clearly unbearable.

I experienced great difficulty in learning to play the piano. I am sure that it is difficult for most people, but, for me, it was even more so because I have hardly any sense of rhythm. Nevertheless, I persevered and it was not long before I was to take a grading examination. I had also begun to study the theory of music and I found the subject fascinating. My teacher, Bob Maciejewski, recommended that I should take the Board of Music examinations. He believed that I was good enough to by-pass the first four and to initially sit for Grade Five. It involved a long period of study but I enjoyed every moment, and was delighted when Bob gave me the go-ahead to attend the Fisher school in Carshalton to sit the exam.

I arrived in good time to find the hall, in which at least a hundred students, most of whom were in their early teens, were standing patiently waiting to be split into small groups in various classrooms. From the notice board I discovered that I was to be in a classroom with ten others. They all turned out to be girls and, not one was over the age of thirteen. Before the exam one of them chatted with me as though I were just another boy from her class. Stretching it, I could have been her grandfather ... I could have been everyone's grandfather except the teacher, and he could easily have been my son.

The girl beside me had an awful cold and sniffed throughout the exam. She finished well before I did and, as she left, gave me a knowing wink as though we were old friends. Despite the distractions I passed Grade Five and went on to pass Grade Six the following year.

To pass Grade One practical, I was expected to run through a few scales and play a few short pieces before an appointed examiner. There were a number of other students all between six and twelve years of age waiting nervously to go in for their tests, all of them no doubt taking a higher grade than me, but I believed that not one could have been more nervous.

The examiner must have found it strange to see a man in his early fifties taking the lowest possible music examination and showing such little confidence. I wondered what he would have thought had he known that I owned more than a dozen companies, with a staff of thousands.

Two months later I was informed that I had failed. Not by much, but I was enormously discouraged, and did not sit any more exams.

Norman Sawtell, David and I started playing pool on Tuesday evenings at David's house in Warlingham. It was good to get back into the old routine. We would play, have a meal at Charco's, and then return to David's house to complete the evening's pool matches.

As I walked into my empty home, late at night, I felt very lonely and missed Annie terribly. At these times the piano was a comfort and I would play into the early hours. On Monday nights I would invite my friend, Syd, to my house to play snooker, but first his wife, Joan, insisted on cooking dinner for me. They still lived next door to Annie's former home and as I enjoyed the luxury of home-cooked meals, little things would remind me of those early days, not least the noise of the trains that passed the end of the garden. Each time as Syd and I left for the game I realized how much Joan too was missing Annie.

I kept closely in touch with my former assistant, Jean, and her husband Ian. They invited me for dinner at least once a week. I had expressed my concern at being the odd one out at dinner parties and they introduced me to a few of their lady friends, one of whom was Susan, who had worked for our company some years ago. I was always happy to make up a four or a six at Jean's dinner parties. By way of reciprocation, I took Jean and Ian out to dinner and, on one occasion, I asked Susan to join us. I was delighted when she accepted.

I learned that she lived alone and worked at the Air Europe ticket desk at Gatwick airport. We had a delightful evening, and some time later, Sue invited Jean, Ian and me to her cottage on the south coast.

Our friendship developed, and in time I invited Sue to have dinner with me alone, at a romantic restaurant, close to her home. I was not yet ready to take the situation further, but, equally, there was no fun in spending too many evenings alone. As the better weather came, I suggested that we spend a weekend together at an exclusive hotel near Hastings, and she agreed to join me.

Although Sue was not a regular churchgoer, she had strong religious beliefs and I respected them. She was a member of her local church and attended meetings organized by the vicar and his wife. She had been to church a few times since we had become close friends and had told the vicar about our planned trip. His response, after she told him about my business activities, was one of horror and he clearly wanted her to think again before getting more deeply involved. Sue came to my defence and told him that she still intended to spend the weekend with me, in response to which he told her, 'God frequently visits us but we are often not at home.' I could just about work out what he was driving at.

When I called for Sue, her case was packed but she looked apprehensive and tired as she got into the car. I discovered that she had been up half the night with the vicar, who had called in an attempt to persuade her to change her mind.

'Ralph, he believes you are a force of evil and that I should resist the temptation,' she told me. I slowed the car, preparing to turn it around.

'No, please Ralph!' she insisted, 'I still want to go away with you.' In making that decision we experienced a weekend of bliss and, even in hindsight, the devil could have played no part in it.

I spoke to David Sullivan most days, and was growing to like him more on a personal basis. His love of football was similar to David's and mine and, although we talked about the game in general, we talked, in particular, about our boyhood teams. Mine was West Ham United, whilst his was Cardiff City. He told me how he used to pray each Friday before they played and how, if Cardiff had won, his prayers had been answered. If the other team won then he believed that their team's supporters had prayed harder.

We talked about Robert Maxwell and his apparent urge to buy up the whole of the Football League. David Sullivan saw him as a beggar on horseback who would one day come a cropper. We did not think highly of Maxwell and were aware that the feeling was mutual.

We were all interested in becoming involved in football. Being part of a soccer club would be an extension of what we were already doing, which was to regularly produce the best available entertainment for the largest possible number of people. We recognized, as did Maxwell, that we would have an edge over most of the other club owners because we were in a position to help promote our team through our own newspapers.

Birmingham City Football Club Presidents
David, David Sullivan and me

It so happened that only a few months after our chat we came close to buying a substantial, albeit minority, interest in a Premiership club. Having bought shares in the name of 'Sport Newspapers', we were literally cold shouldered by the club's board of directors and eventually we were obliged to sell our shares. We made a small profit but the club concerned (in my opinion) made a huge loss. The two Davids and I had been seeking no more than positions on the board and to contribute to the building of a successful team, whilst taking an interest in the club and attending matches on a regular basis. Their 'loss' was to be the gain of another club ... Birmingham City.

I was away on business when David Sullivan contacted my brother to say that he intended to invest £2 million to buy the club, which was in receivership. His conversation with David lasted no more than five minutes, during which time David Sullivan made it clear that he had done his homework, and was confident that Birmingham City was a sleeping giant which was ready to be woken. He said he would like to have the Gold Brothers on board, but if we declined he was quite prepared to go it alone. The conversation was not dissimilar to the birth of *Sunday Sport*, when David Sullivan spoke to me along similar lines.

'How much?' David asked.

David Sullivan answered that it would cost £1 million each to save the club from liquidation, and half a million each for new players. He made no mention of the millions required to build new stands.

My brother was given only two hours to make the decision, and was unable to contact me in time. However, I am happy to say he still went ahead. We have an unwritten agreement that we speak for the other, no matter how high the stakes, and this was no exception.

It turned out to be one of the most exciting things to happen to David and me in recent years, although we did not think so initially. I remember so well our first visit to St Andrews following the agreement to 'buy in'. On the journey we reminisced about the last time we were there, when we were young boys. The huge crowd, the 5–0 larruping of Manchester city, the 'Kop', the giant clock and so many other things. Our expectations grew as we approached St Andrews and saw the flow of supporters walking to the ground on a cold and foggy evening.

An official examined a list of names on a clipboard before letting us into the directors' car park and allotting us a bay situated on stony ground, fifty yards from the entrance.

They say that poverty is one thing that money can't buy, but we were far from convinced as we entered the directors' box from the board room. I looked at my brother and frowned as I stretched my arms out in a gesture of ...'what have we done?'. The small crowd reflected the fact that we had not won in the last seven games. David's response showed that he too was disappointed and must have felt, as I did, that his memory had let him down.

The only goal of the game against Oxford United was scored by our Canadian international, Paul Peschisolido, and we returned to the board room feeling a little less depressed. We were introduced to the chairman, Jack Wiseman, who chatted to us

David, Karren Brady and Paul Peschisolido

beneath a picture of his late father, the son of one of the club's
founders. The Wisemans had experienced some wonderful years
at the club, but recently it had fallen on hard times and when its
owners, the Kumars, went into liquidation in 1992, it looked as
though the once famous Birmingham City Football Club, would
disappear forever. David Sullivan had saved the club, but only a
few were aware that the Gold Brothers were his partners in the
whole venture.

David Sullivan's appointment of Karren Brady, the former
senior executive of 'Sport Newspapers', as managing director, was
approved wholeheartedly by David and me. The fact that Karren
was the first and only woman director of a substantial football
club led people to think that we were unwise, but, like my
brother's daughter, Jacqueline, Karren had learned to cope with
the bigots in our society and set out to demonstrate that she was
as capable as any man.

Still only twenty five years of age, she had already proven
herself at 'Sport Newspapers', and we had every confidence that
she would be equally successful in her new role.

The team manager, Terry Cooper, was a genuine and likeable
person who tried hard under difficult circumstances to instil
confidence in a disillusioned squad of players. We had a terrible

season, hanging on to our place in the First Division by the narrowest of margins by beating Charlton Athletic 1–0 in our last game. After a series of bad results during the following season, Terry resigned.

We subsequently engaged one of the most exciting and dynamic managers in the football league, Barry Fry. David Sullivan advised my brother and me that Barry was, in his opinion, the right man for the job and we agreed with him. Within hours of our discussion it was reported in the media that David Sullivan had made a direct, illegal approach to Barry for him to come to Birmingham for talks. The whole incident blew up out of all proportion and it was to cost the club £175,000 in fines and compensation.

Once again David Sullivan and Birmingham City were in the headlines. David Sullivan already had a high profile long before his involvement with the Blues, but it was to leap even higher as he became one of the most talked about individuals in the Midlands. It came as no surprise when he was presented with Birmingham's 'Man of the Year' award. Karren Brady too was idolized by the Birmingham fans, and her profile was increased enormously when she later married Paul Peschisolido, our high scoring striker.

Despite our input Birmingham City languished at the bottom of the division, and even after a magnificent run of unbeaten games, it was left till the last game of the season to determine whether we would survive in the First Division. We had to beat Tranmere away from home, while at the same time our Midland rivals, West Bromwich Albion, needed to lose or draw at Portsmouth.

We won, and during the closing stages of the match we listened anxiously to the radio commentary of the Albion game ... They scored in the closing minutes, condemning us to the Second Division.

We had little to say to each other on the way home. We were understandably depressed but early the following morning, I was woken by the telephone.

'Who's calling at this unearthly hour?' I wondered. It was my brother David.

'Ralph, we must buy Mark Ward. We'll make two million available for new players, win the championship ...' He said all this without drawing breath.

'David', I interrupted, 'do you realize that it's six o'clock in the morning? We've just been relegated to the Second Division. What are you so excited about?

'I'm convinced that going down is a blessing in disguise, and could be a brand new beginning. We'll complete the new stadium, win the Auto Windscreen Shield at Wembley, and become league champions. It'll light up the imagination of every Blues fan and act as a springboard for the future. I'm sorry for calling so early but I wanted to share my thoughts with you. Unless you can see a down side to what I've said, I'll call David Sullivan and get back to you later'. With that the phone went dead.

I lay for a moment reflecting on how dejected I had been over the results, and how David's telephone call had changed my way

Good As Gold: Gold Brothers with Blues captain Steve Bruce,
Kevin Francis and goalkeeper Ian Bennett

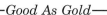

of thinking. His positive attitude has been an inspiration to me on many occasions and I fully appreciate my good fortune in having him as a partner who is as good as gold.

Paper Wars

With *Sport* newspapers we had achieved the dream of becoming a 'daily', but we were now reliant on the continuation of the advertising revenue from the 'adult' telephone lines. The watchdogs, ICSTIS, were constantly threatening to either pull the plug on service providers who failed to comply with their regulations or, worse still, to exercise power to see that *Sport* newspapers were only allowed to be displayed, by law, on the top shelves of the newsagents.

The attack on the adult message line companies was no different from the battle to suppress girlie magazines or the sauna bath services. There was clearly a need for lonely and frustrated men to practise safe sex in the comfort of their own homes or in the relaxed atmosphere of a massage parlour, but there were always people who saw fit to complain.

A so-called 'expert' on rapists, who ran a therapy centre for convicted offenders in Birmingham, suggested, in his book on the subject, that if a sex line caller was not completely satisfied, then he would be likely to go on to make an obscene telephone call. He further claimed that, 'The line between an obscene caller and a rapist is frighteningly thin.' In my opinion, it was his argument that was frighteningly thin. I cannot be considered an expert in these matters, but common sense tells me that, faced with the horns of this dilemma, surely censorship and its enforcement must cause even more frustration for the oppressed.

My own strong convictions on 'freedom' lose a little credibility when I expound the view that smoking in public places should be banned. But then I believe that I have a much stronger argument, especially when the latest studies were proving beyond doubt that even passive smokers were at risk of lung cancer, and children of parents who smoked faced more than double the risk of dying from cancer. That to me is frightening. Notwithstanding this, large companies dealing in that awful trade have received the highest national honours and recognition for their 'achievements'.

In the paperback book business, a number of respected publishers now include in their ranges a selection of blatantly pornographic titles which are distributed through conventional retail outlets. They make *Lady Chatterley's Lover* and *Fanny Hill* seem like nursery books, but neither the authorities nor the public have seen reason to complain about them. They are right but, on the same basis, they were undeniably wrong in condemning similar material and its publishers (me included) in years gone by.

Jacqueline had continued to put into effect her policy to improve the image of the company. She herself was becoming a household name and David was clearly proud of her. She had strong views about the future direction of the company and set about her plan to 'soften' its image. A range of swimwear was introduced to tumultuous applause at the annual conference, and Jackie pledged to the delegates that within a year we would be offering a range of lingerie for the larger lady. This too, practically brought the house down.

John Lawless of the *Evening Standard Magazine* praised both Jackie and Ann Summers when, under the headline of, 'The Unstoppable Sex Machine', he said we were the 'Marks and Spencer' of sex, which was fair comment. However, it was rare for any newspaper or magazine article to stay complimentary towards us for long, and this one was no exception.

I am fully aware that editors encourage their reporters to bring in 'sex' stories which will shock their readers. An article about an efficient, well run family business in the Surrey suburbs which was doing rather well internationally, selling goods that were 95 per cent British made, would hardly be newsworthy. The fact that it sold marital aids and was run by an attractive young woman, who was prepared to give her first press interview, did interest them, and the article was made raunchy and more interesting. This was to be, for Jackie, the beginning of a huge media hype that would make her nationally famous.

In 1992 the tenth annual Ann Summers conference was held in Jersey. It was without a doubt the most spectacular so far. Being on an island, every delegate was to be brought there by chartered aeroplanes. The stage equipment was transported by boat and to get it to the Hotel de France it had to be transported across Jersey in a container. It was so large that a police escort was needed to lead it through the narrow lanes at six in the morning. One poor man was dragged out of his bed to move his illegally parked car before the container eventually reached its destination.

By the time we arrived, the exhibition room was alive with the most exotic stage presentation that I had ever seen, and within hours we were participating in rehearsals.

In the opening routine, Jodie, one of the lead dancers from the Ann Summers Roadshow, set the scene by singing 'The Only Way Is Up', which was the theme for the conference. One of its highlights was the introduction of our 'Twice as Sexy' range of lingerie. Lingerie manufacturers had perpetually ignored the larger lady's need to express her sexuality, but now Ann Summers was offering underwear to fit all sizes, and a much larger percentage of the female population would be able to feel and look sexy. I could not help but think of the many ways in which our companies were changing sexual attitudes – in my opinion for the better.

When Jacqueline appeared on stage with a large red album in her hands, I guessed that she was about to present another version of 'This Is Your Life'. She had been present at a 'Gold Star' dinner several years before when I had called David on stage, and I wondered who was due for the big shock this time. It turned out to be none other than the company, Ann Summers itself.

Jackie had done her homework and the presentation was exceptional. There was a five-minute film of her being chauffeur-driven through London to the Ann Summers shop in Edgware Road where it all began, then on to Whyteleafe where an additional block of executive offices was being built, reflecting our progress.

Chairs were set out on the stage and while the film was being shown, executives were invited up. David and I were called first and, as Jackie spoke of our achievements, we saw on a huge screen an old picture of me from my boxing days, followed by an action photograph of David scoring the winning goal at Crystal Palace in front of a large crowd. She continued by bringing on a host of people, all of whom praised the company. David and I were filled with pride.

The hush in the hall during my speech indicated that it was well received, although it was probably the last one that I was to make for Ann Summers. The consensus of opinion was that we should reduce the male influence on the company, and I was not unhappy about that.

At the end of the conference a cake was brought on stage and, as I helped to blow out the candles, I thought of the ten wonderful business years that we had experienced. From the start, the only way had been up, and we had made it higher than our wildest dreams.

David had suggested to me that each year we invited some of our close friends to be there as special guests. The year before, Karin and David Tearle had been invited, and this time it was the turn of Michael and Sandra Vaughan. My friendship with Mike had started through the tennis club where he had become the chairman.

I had discovered that he was the sales manager for Eagle Brothers, a trading company which I had dealt with many years

Michael Vaughan, me and David

earlier. More recently they had been able to supply us with many party gifts at affordable prices. As a supplier and a buyer, Mike and I were to gain mutual respect and we had a great deal of fun in our negotiations.

On one occasion he sent along his best salesman, Mike Potterton, hopefully to finalize a deal with me on a large quantity of baskets containing toiletry items and a clearance parcel of suspender belts. Unfortunately he did not succeed, and after protracted bargaining, I received the following correspondence from Michael Vaughan:

[In Memoriam]

It is with deep regret that I have to advise you of the sudden death of Michael Potterton, after long and serious negotiation with Mr Ralph Gold of Ann Summers.

Mr Potterton was found early this morning clutching the Ann Summers order confirmation in one hand and a 34 page booklet on the technical specifications and manufacturing details of a suspender belt in the other.

When found, Mr Potterton's shirt was missing, clearly lost

in the fray, and four gold rings were missing from his right hand – obviously snatched by Mr Ralph on the concluding handshake. The autopsy showed that Mr Potterton's testicles had been twisted off and it is rumoured that these have been made into a paperweight as a trophy for Ralph's desk.

Mrs Potterton, saddened though relieved, she says, said that it was terrible towards the end. She said the look of horror on Mike's face when the phone rang, followed by the horrific spectacle of Michael cowering on the floor screaming, 'no more, Ralph, no more reductions ...' was terrifying and heartbreaking to watch.

Two of Mr Potterton's colleagues – Geoffrey Eagle and Michael Vaughan – have been certified insane since the deal was struck and four executives of the third party involved in the deal have been admitted to rest homes indefinitely.

It has been announced that 16 salesmen from allied trades committed suicide by collectively jumping from a high building on hearing the news that Mr Ralph Gold was looking to do another deal like this one.

Mr Ross McWhirter of *The Guinness Book of Records* has said that the number of reasons given by Ralph Gold as to why the price should be reduced and why more items should be included in the package for less money (the subject of the negotiations), has been confirmed as a new world record and will appear in the next edition.

David Gold said that it was tragic that he was away for the last week of the negotiations as he might have been able to help in the decision to clinch the deal and save Mr Potterton's life. Mr Ralph's business associate, David Sullivan, said he felt that Mr Potterton had done well to last four weeks. He added that he came close to suicide last week himself – and that was after only ten minutes on the phone to Ralph.

Ralph Gold said that he is very upset at the news and has offered to help Mrs Potterton to negotiate a good deal with the undertaker, starting with a bit less wood in the coffin ...

In a few hundred words Mike had summarized the whole of my business life. I include it to fulfil my promise ... 'Warts and all'.

Full Circle

I had come to terms with living alone. My housekeeper, Carol and her assistant, Carmel kept my house spotless and I wanted for nothing. I saw Susan at least twice a week and, even though we lived more than forty miles apart our relationship was very good. She came to Puerto Rico with David, Penny and me on a holiday over the Christmas period. Jackie, Vanessa and their partners also came and we had a great time. Jackie and David spent many hours each day with their briefcases open at their sides working on projects. I had always known of David's twenty four hour a day commitment to the company, but now I was seeing, at first hand, his daughter's equal dedication.

Because of their devotion to the business I began to relax much more, and I gradually found myself less and less involved. It concerned me that the 'spark' might be fading but I knew that I must come to terms with it. There was a time when I wanted to be what I am today ... but now I want to be what I was then! Ambitious and keen.

Bradley and Liane's wedding was only ten days away, when I saw that 'World In Action' was presenting an 'expose' on David Sullivan entitled, 'Sultan of Sleaze'. I wanted nothing to spoil their big day, and I was worried that the Gold Brothers would be mentioned unfavourably. David was totally unconcerned, but then again he always was about the media. His consistent response was, 'It is what it is, and all the worry in the world won't change a thing.' He was right, of course.

The programme itself was appalling. It attempted to decimate David Sullivan's character with the help of a few of his ex-employees and an intoxicated old man, Harrison Marks, who had been involved in producing some full-length movies with David. I was not surprised when the Gold Brothers were mentioned. A ridiculous photograph was shown which had clearly been unearthed from old archives. Incredibly young, we were dressed in 'bell-bottom' trousers and outlandish ties.

At the beginning of the programme it was suggested that David Sullivan lived in a mansion worth £6 million and was personally worth £100 million. So it made no sense when, later, it stated that he needed the Gold Brothers because we were the 'money men' behind his latest 'disreputable' projects. It did not reveal that he needed us for other reasons; our involvement with him diluted his risk and, that David Sullivan has learned from experience, that the Gold Brothers were as hard working and as determined as he was to succeed.

Predictably, not everyone saw it that way. David Sullivan, my brother and I are well aware that we have nothing to gain in challenging the media. It is sufficient for me to write this book in the hope that readers have the opportunity to see things (for once) from our side.

There are, sadly, a few people who want nothing to do with individuals who deal in adult publications, and I have no objection to their thinking the way they do – after all, it is a free country. My objection is only to people who choose to persuade others, more especially when they cheat and lie in order to influence their cause.

I watched a television programme recently about call girls advertising in phone boxes. What was so interesting was the various interviews which took place in the area to obtain the views of the local people. Most of the women interviewed had no objection to either the ads or the resulting activities so long as they took place in private, whilst quite a few men objected aggressively. It certainly made me realize how times had changed.

In the 19th century, editors of the *Oxford English Dictionary* considered the word 'condom' to be, 'Too utterly obscene to be included'. A hundred years later we have a national condom weekend, a Royal Princess has been tested for AIDS and, a young lady, Jacqui Power, has opened a condom shop in Dublin. One woman, however, wrote to the *Irish Times* to protest about it and, in her published letter she declared, 'I would rather my son died of AIDS than he wear a condom.'

It is my opinion that with the possible exception of China, Ireland will no doubt be one of the last of the bigoted nations to relax censorship and permit sexual expression. Thanks largely to satellite television, censorship will soon be a thing of the past and people throughout the world will be free to choose what they want to see and to discard what they do not. The problem regarding children and violence on television has to be addressed, although the recent findings of the mental health charity 'Young Minds' claims that there is no link between television violence and aggressive children. These people may be 'experts' but we have the right to disagree with them and to exercise our own censorship ... in our own homes. Which is where, in my opinion, it should remain.

The dispute between Godfrey, and David and me had become a fact of life which no one in the family, except the three of us, took seriously any more. The family had tired of trying to bring about a reconciliation of a twenty-five year long feud. When we raised the matter with any member of the family, the small amount of Jewishness would become apparent as they spread their hands in a gesture of, 'What can you do with this man?'

At a recent family wedding, David and I had our now traditional meeting with Godfrey. As we approached him to shake his hand, his comment was, 'Don't you look old,' to which I replied, 'Don't we all.' But it wasn't true. For his age he looked

A rare picture of me with my father

remarkably young, and only the bitterness on his face aged him. He wore a huge gold medallion and, behind his back, he was referred to as the 'Lord Mayor'. At Liane and Bradley's wedding I hoped I might be able to put an end to a few lingering hostilities that still existed in my life. In particular I wanted so much for the differences between my father and me to be resolved, but I did not hold out much hope.

On the evening of the wedding, I stayed at the same hotel as Joann and Boo. Bradley and Tina had arranged for them to meet Sue and me for a drink in the bar after dinner. It was all very strange as I shook Boo by the hand and kissed Joann on both cheeks. Twenty years had gone in a flash and a lot of water had passed under the bridge, but this was not a time to dwell on the past. Our son was getting married and this was a time for celebration and reconciliation.

As I sat down for breakfast on the morning of the wedding, I spotted an old couple at the next table and it did not take long for me to realize that they were Joann's parents. I approached them apprehensively, but confident that they too would want to forget the past and be prepared, for the sake of the occasion, to make amends. I was only half right. Fred at least shook hands with me, whilst Ethel made a point of totally ignoring my presence.

There was one more hostile person to be tackled ... my father. He had been invited but did not turn up to the morning gathering which turned out to be a great success. However, I was pleased to see Godfrey at the ceremony which took place at All Saints church in Lindfield. I made the usual move to shake his hand and in return I received the usual response ... 'One out of three,' I thought, I was not doing very well.

The wedding itself was a joyous occasion, and after the photographs Bradley and Liane were taken off in a magnificent horse drawn carriage. At the reception, the bride and groom and their parents stood in line to welcome each of the guests. I stood alongside Joann and experienced a strange feeling of *déjà vu*. The guests filed through. Each of them offered a few kind words and I enjoyed special long hugs with many of the ladies, including my mother Rose, my sister Marie, my daughter Tina and my step-daughter Sascha.

Godfrey and Ethel were conspicuous by their absence, but subsequently I caught sight of each of them out of the corner of my eye. They were possibly thinking that they should do the 'right' thing if only for the sake of the bride and groom, but they did not. Clearly they have chosen to take their bitterness to their graves.

Boo shook me warmly by the hand and said, 'I would like to speak to you in private when we can find a moment.' We found the moment during the evening and sat down while most people were dancing to warm sounds of a Country and Western group.

'I find this hard to say, Ralph, but I want to thank you sincerely for all that you have done to help bring up my children, but more especially for what you did to make Annie so happy. I think that you have been as good as gold and now is the time to forget the past and even for us to be friends again.' For the second time that day, I shook his hand, but this time there was added warmth.

While the lead singer sang 'Behind Closed Doors', which was one of the songs from the Charlie Rich Album that Annie and I had enjoyed and cherished during our happy times together, I sat alone in deep thought. 'I am fifty four years of age and I am as young now as I will ever be. My life is well past half way and whilst time might be a good healer, I only have to look into the mirror to see that it is a lousy beautician.'

From here the lamp posts left to count are, like the future, getting closer and closer. I have had a great deal of success and pleasure from life because I managed to get what I want.

Now, I look to the future and hope to find true happiness, which is not only getting what I want, but wanting what I get.

Boo's words were ringing in my ears ... Good as Gold?

What's it all about Ralphie? You know where you have been but now as you approach the autumn of your life ... where are you going?

Epilogue

The Algarve, Portugal. February 1996

By the time you realize how to get the most out of life, most of it has gone. As I sit here in Portugal in blazing sunshine, (it is 70 degrees in the shade), totally relaxed and very happy, I am able to reflect back on my life and add a little more about what has happened to the Gold Brothers since the wedding.

Business calls and faxed messages still come through to me, although my work involvement has lessened since beginning to write this autobiography more than three years ago. In that time Sue has found and married someone who offered more of a commitment and I have subsequently met Diane, a lovely lady who I affectionately refer to as 'Lady Di'.

She lives in the Algarve, having moved here some years ago, but as fate would have it, I met her in London. Since making my regular visits to Portugal, the completion of 'the book' has taken precedence over everything with the exception of our love-making. She knows how much I appreciate her and how grateful I am ... just for being here with me.

It was also coincidental that Diane originally lived in Birmingham and through her family I was to learn of the newly found 'fame' that the Gold Brothers are experiencing in the Midlands although it had taken a long time.

At the start of the new season the Gold Brothers were chastised when, one evening well before the start of a match at St Andrews, we went onto the pitch. A cameraman became annoyed because we were in the way of his filming. He asked, or 'ordered', us to move out of the way, as he was trying to film the wonderful new stand that had cost millions of pounds to build. We smiled and did as we were told.

The low profile saga continued when we were being driven home in our limousine, listening, which we regularly do, to Tom Ross the popular Midland radio broadcaster. His phone in programme invited football fans to ring in with their comments and observations. One fan, with a very strong Brummie accent, rang in to express his gratitude to the new owners:

'I'd like to thank David Sullivan – oh, yeah and those other two geezers – for all that they've done for Birmingham City Football Club.' It said it all. Along with David Sullivan, the Gold Brothers had already invested close on ten million pounds, and yet we were practically unknown to the Birmingham City fans.

In an effort to put things straight Tom Ross insisted on interviewing my brother for 'It's a Funny ol' Game', a radio programme, similar to 'Desert Island Discs'. I sat in on it and listened to a mini version of our life story, with the added pleasure of hearing records that brought back fond memories.

At the end of the show, Tom joked, 'Well David, the Gold Brothers are now so well known that they are a legend in their own lunchtime' ... At least that was better than being known as the other two geezers.

The year after Birmingham's relegation, there was another cliff-hanging close to the season, but this time at the other end of the league. It was critical that we immediately climbed our way back to the First Division, and once again the outcome was left until the very last seconds of the last game. We visited Huddersfield, where victory was our only certain way of finishing as champions. The tension was unbelievable, and when the final whistle blew with the score line at 2–1 in our favour, every Blues fan in the ground was ecstatic.

It was an unforgettable end to a wonderful season. Only a month earlier, we had seen David's other prediction come true when we went to Wembley to see Birmingham City face Carlisle United in the 'Auto Windscreen' final.

We met up with the army of 57,000 Blues fans on the approach to the stadium, where the traffic was at a total standstill. We realized then that this occasion would be more than just 'unforgettable'. Words could not express what was happening to the Gold Brothers. We were accompanied by Penny, Diane, and my sister Marie, as we travelled in our chauffeur driven mini-coach to Wembley. Diane was the only 'Brummie' amongst us. She was born and bred in Birmingham and for her this was a very special occasion.

Later we met up with Bradley and Liane, Tina, Vanessa and my nephew, Steven. They arrived with many of our staff from Whyteleafe in a coach party organized by the company's new chief executive, Michael Vaughan, who came with his family. My eighty year old mother would not have dreamed of missing out on this wonderful occasion and her presence in the Royal Box with her family around her was a delight for us all. Also in the Royal box, sitting alongside Rose was her new friend, David Sullivan's mother, Thelma.

Before the match we visited the players in their dressing room and returned directly to our seats through the famous Wembley tunnel onto the side of the playing area. As David and I walked side by side the crowd stood and applauded. I looked over towards the pitch and saw nothing ... slowly realising that the applause was for us. The feeling was euphoric.

Many people had said that winning this game was not important, that 'being there' was what counted. However, the Gold Brothers were of a different view. Winning was paramount, and when there was no score at the end of ninety minutes, we were on the edge of our seats waiting for extra time. For the first time at Wembley, it was to be a 'sudden death' play-off, where the first goal scored would literally end the game.

When Paul Tait headed the ball into the back of the net for Birmingham City I was overjoyed. It was without doubt one of the happiest moments of my life. The Birmingham fans were dancing and singing for hours. David and I heard them chant, 'There's only one Gold brothers,' which sent a tingle down my spine.

The team made their lap of honour while David and I stood in awe. We watched and listened as more than 50,000 loyal fans began to sing the famous club anthem, 'Keep Right on to the End of the Road ...'

Birmingham City football Club continues to provide enjoyment to my family. Bradley – now the father of three – is on the board of directors and comes to nearly every game in the now famous 'bluesmobile'. My sister Marie and my nephew, Steven, come to most games and enjoy the wonderful facilities in the exclusive Presidents suite. My mother along with David Sullivan's mother, Thelma are developing the Birmingham City Senior Citizens Club which has been instrumental in establishing us as a recognized family football club.

Our ambition to reach the Premiership remains undaunted but it can only be realized if we devote much of our time energy and money to it. Since our promotion and wonderful Wembley victory we have taken on a new manager, Trevor Francis, and millions of pounds have been invested but we don't intend to stop there. The club has successfully floated shares to the public which has enabled the fans to be financially involved in our success.

Most clubs have found that their ambitions are nipped in the budget but not ours, thanks to our ever growing business empire the future for the Blues looks bright.

'Gold Group International' was selected as the new name for our holding company. Previously, under its old name 'A & P Roberts (Holdings)', it had reached 234th in the Jordan's Financial Directory of Britain's top privately owned companies and all this was prior to successful restructuring and the formation of a number of additional businesses. One of them

My mother at the Gold Suite

Bluesmobile takes David and me for take-off

'Gold Air international', is an air charter company operating from Biggin Hill. It gives me great pleasure when I am flown to a match or business meeting in one of my own aircraft.

As our businesses continue to expand, David and I have reflected on how it has all been achieved ... Hard work, determination, skill, luck, call it what you will. All I can say, is that the harder we worked the luckier we seemed to get.

I was delighted to hear that Nelson Mandela had become the new President of South Africa. It was coincidental that on the same day I heard from my Group Chief Executive that he had been in direct contact with a high ranking police officer from Scotland Yard. He had been informed of new developments regarding police policy and that no further action would be taken by the authorities to repress 'top shelf' publications.

The establishment, at last, had come to realize that the sale of such material clearly contributed to safe sex. They also had come to accept that there was virtual total compliance with the self regulation regarding 'top shelf' product and, under the circumstances, no further action would be taken by them. After thirty years of police raids, court cases and time wasting we had won the battle for common sense to prevail.

To research this book, I found myself in the loft of my house where I discovered a case of old 8mm films. I knew that there would be some fond memories on them so I arranged for my friend Clive, an expert in this field, to put them all onto video.

It resulted in Tina, Clive and me burning the midnight oil to produce a three hour saga which was 'premièred' before the whole family. David, Marie and I saw moving pictures of ourselves dating back more than thirty years.

Marie's children were in tears when, to their complete surprise, they saw 'in living colour' their father who had died more than eight years earlier. It was emotional and rewarding for me, and endorses the fact that you invariably 'get out' from what is 'put in'. They say that all the treasures on earth cannot bring back one precious moment ... although my surprise film-show came close.

My book could have a similar effect. At the same time as being a catharsis for me, it has given me the opportunity to put into words my feelings about the many people who have helped to bring me happiness.

Some people think that they are rich because they have lots of money ... I promise you that I am not one of them. I *am* rich, rich in family and friends which is something that mere money cannot buy. My riches are not in the extent of my possessions ... more in the fewness of my wants.

As I reach the end of my book I take time to reflect on what life holds for me now. I fully realize that you can't cheat old Father Time but I do want to drive a hard bargain with him. I am still too busy to grow old but the years of real hard work are clearly behind me.

The high profitability of *Sport Newspapers* had been contributory towards our inclusion in the 'Wealth League'. Our personal fortune, according to the *Sunday Times* listing of 'Britain's

With my brother by the pool (Ron McMillan)

Richest 500', was amassing, and the Gold Brothers were climbing the ladder of the country's richest people. We were said to be worth £120 million and had been placed 130th alongside John Paul Getty II and Mick Jagger.

'For two boys from Burke Secondary Mod. with only one GCE between us, we haven't done too bad, have we?' David reflected. The answer to the question was obvious.

For anyone who might be interested in knowing the secret of how I made my fortune, I can put it down to two vital ingredients, the first was having a positive attitude. I see my goals and I mentally apply blinkers which prevent anyone, or anything, from stopping me from reaching them. I know that it is easier said than done but Henry Ford was of similar mind when he said, 'Whether you think you will succeed or not, you are right'.

The second is having a business partner who is as 'Good as Gold' whom I unashamedly love like a brother ... which is not difficult because that is exactly what he is.

THE END

Writing the words 'THE END' was a wonderful moment for me, but a year or so later I was made even happier. I was informed by my publisher that, after two reprints, we had again sold out of the hardback edition and Jeremy Robson asked if I would agree to having *Good as Gold* published in paperback. His only requirement of me was to bring the book up to date. Something that I knew I would enjoy doing as my life has improved with each passing day – long may it last.

My relationship with Diane has blossomed and I fully realise that, along with good health, this is of utmost importance if I am to achieve my ultimate aim in life – contentment. Something, incidentally, which has one big thing over wealth – nobody tries to borrow it.

One big thing I have achieved since completing the hardback book was making contact with my father. 'Matchmaker *extra ordinaire*' Mel Walker, who was instrumental in getting me together with Diane, had been seeing my father periodically. Mel phoned me to say he 'felt the vibes' and believed that Godfrey wanted to see me. I made it clear that I would be perfectly happy to go along with any suggestions he ma— He cut me short and said, 'Well, your dad's here with me. I'll put him on.' I could not believe it, I had not spoken to my father in years and here I was speaking to him as though we had never had a bad moment. It was as easy as that.

I wish it had been as easy for Birmingham City to get into the Premiership. During the 1997/8 season my brother David was asked by the board to take over as club chairman. Jack Wiseman, at eighty years of age, was ready to step down to become vice chairman, knowing that his vast experience was still to be of service to the football club he loved so much. An additional bonus for him was to know that his son Michael received a directorship and that ensured the continuance of the Wiseman family's involvement well into the next century.

David had not occupied the hot seat for long before he was in the middle of a controversy at the club. Trevor Francis, already a legend among Birmingham fans, had quit over an incident which he determined had been brought about by a lack of forethought and consideration for his own family as well as for his players and their families. Birmingham City was becoming an exciting and prestigious club in the Midlands and it was of vital importance to everyone concerned with the Blues that this misunderstanding was resolved without a moment's delay.

David and Trevor, after hours of speaking on the telephone, agreed to meet at a 'half way house' (which happened to be in a lay-by near to Oxford) at 10 o'clock at night. It was not until the early hours of the following morning that they came to an agreement, whereby Trevor would stay on as our manager. Several leading national papers had blown it up out of all proportion but, thankfully, David had managed to bring about a better understanding between club and management, and Birmingham City Football Club moves ever forward.

David was rapidly becoming one of the most talked about chairmen in the country. It was amazing that his skill in the day-to-day involvement of the club went without comment whilst this storm in a tea cup brought about unbelievable exposure.

During this exciting season we had our ups and downs but one great moment was missed by 'Mr Chairman'. David finally agreed to take a Caribbean holiday and accepted the fact that he must miss one game. We were playing away against Stoke City and I promised to phone immediately after the match with a ball-by-ball report. When I reached the fifth goal scored by Birmingham City he interjected, 'OK Ralph, enough messing around, let me have the true score.' It was three days before David received his newspaper and he phoned me to apologise. The newspapers confirmed what I had told him: Stoke 0 Birmingham City 7.

David and I have hardly missed a game over the years and Birmingham City were again engaged in a nail-biting end to the 1997/98 season. I wonder sometimes if this is fun ... it's agony, but just like the 100,000 or so other 'Brummie' fans, we love every moment. Playing at St Andrews in the last game of the season we heard over the radio that our immediate competitors for the final play-off position, Sheffield United, had lost their last game and all we had to do was win ours. With only 30 seconds to go that seemed unlikely until we were awarded a penalty. Our £6000 per week superstar, Peter Ndlovu, was elected to take it. I buried my head in my hands only to look up and see the ball safely in the hands of the Port Vale goalkeeper. It was difficult to keep my composure. Grown men don't cry ... shame.

After a wonderful start to the following season we are in no doubt that our team will be in the Premiership before very long. The Gold Brothers will have played no small part in this success. I must take the accolades along with my brother knowing that, apart from my investment and commitment, I personally devote only a small amount of my time to the club.

Having said that, my negotiation skills were called upon at the beginning of the 1998/9 season when our captain, Steve Bruce, was tempted away from us by Sheffield United Football Club who wanted to employ him as their player-manager. Steve had just signed a contract with us, although we had agreed not to stand in his way if an opportunity for him to go into management came along. When it did, I was subsequently confronted with a difficult dilemma. Taking Steve as a manager was one thing, but as a player-manager their gain was Birmingham's loss, and we were entitled to compensation of at least £250,000. I would not accept their 'final' offer of £135,000 (£60,000 of which would only be paid if they were promoted to the Premiership) and after hours of negotiation, their next 'final' offer, made late in the evening over the telephone, was £210,000. I would go no lower than £240,000. We had reached a stalemate. There was a knock on my office door and I motioned for my nephew, Steven, to come in, and sit down. I scribbled Steve Bruce's name on a piece of paper and Steven sat in silence listening to every word. Mike McDonald, on behalf of Sheffield United, was ready to pull out of the deal before I made another 'final offer', by reducing the figure to £215,000.

I was fed up with the whole business when Ian refused to accept this obvious compromise.

'OK,' I said, 'it's crazy that two men in our position should be arguing over £5000. I'll toss you for it.' I couldn't believe that I had said that, especially after my experience nearly 30 years earlier. Although the stake then was much higher and, of course, far more significant I still am of the opinion that gambling is a mug's game. Ian accepted this compromise, but, only hours later, he declined to go ahead with the wager and we settled on £212,500.

'You look exhausted,' said Steven.

I was. But I was happy to have been involved, albeit in a small way, in working towards a brighter future for a club that has given my family and me so much pleasure.

My mother continues to develop her profile at Birmingham City. At 84, with the help of Thelma, David Sullivan's 80 year-old mother, she ensures the progress of the Senior Citizen's Club. I have attended many of its functions and I have experienced, at first hand, the adoration and gratitude shown by the ever growing number of members, many of whom love my mother almost as much as I do. Even my sister, Marie, enjoys a high profile in Birmingham. The women's pages in the local press richly named her as 'The Golden Girl'. She is now set up in business with her son Steven selling a product that I feel could make them even richer than the Gold Brothers. The 'Chelsea Clip' which, placed in many restaurants throughout the country, is protecting ladies from the horror of having their handbags stolen whilst they are out on the town.

David's daughter Jaqueline remains at the 'top of the tree'. Now in her mid-thirties, she is not only beautiful and articulate, but continues to lead Ann Summers towards becoming one of Britain's foremost companies. It is already recognised as Britain's leading party plan organisation and now, with the success of our high street shops and the potential of a worldwide franchise scheme, Jackie with calm authority has taken the business to unbelievable heights.

Following the success of the book there have been a number of interviews which have at last put David and me in a fairer light and naturally I am pleased about this. Times have changed so much for the better and the media are latterly seeing us for what we are and not for what we were perceived to be ... it's refreshing.

Erotica is no longer a thing only to be viewed behind closed doors and sexual fun is no longer a pleasure to be enjoyed by men only. Women are now experiencing 'The Full Monty' and why shouldn't they? It's a free country and at last we have achieved an equality of the sexes.

One woman, who had preconceived views about the Gold Brothers, did read the book and was kind enough to write to me. I am taking the liberty of publishing her words verbatim:

Dear Mr Gold,

As the wife of a life long Blues fan, I am used to finding all sorts of football literature around the house, therefore to find your book was no surprise to me. What did surprise me was that I casually picked it up one day and was unable to put it down.

Having reached the age of 48, I can now see that I had a very prejudiced view of the industry you are involved in. Your book enlightened, and completely changed my views. I hope it has the same effect on others that read it.

I am ashamed to say I was very derisive about the source of the finance injected into the Blues, and I can only thank you and your book for bringing me to my senses.

Once again thank you for a great read and all my best wishes for the season to come.

Yours sincerely,
J. M. B., Surrey

Having read my book, readers are now aware that I too deplore hard-core pornography and would support any initiative to control it. It is, however, a matter of interpretation and I am sickened that in the United Kingdom, at the moment, some of the same bigoted establishment views of the sixties still exist.

I read with great interest the numerous articles written as a consequence of a statement made by James Ferman, the director of the British Board of Film Classification. After 23 years in office he claimed that the restriction on explicit publications showing consenting adults had encouraged a black market in far more obscene publications involving children, animals and violence.

He went on to say that it was time to recognise the legal difference between pornography and obscenity. Legalising 'conventional' sex publications and making them readily available in licensed sex shops would make it easier for the police to concentrate on 'under the counter' publications dealing in child porn and violence. Hallelujah! At last it seemed that intelligence was to prevail. But no!

Commentary from most of the establishment newspapers was unbelievably naive. Whilst writing about a particular world leader (a man of substance, a religious man, a man who would agree with their every word), a man who had just confessed to having had a blow job from an intern; they wrote of: 'Tortured logic', 'Curbs which will lead to looser morals' and 'A final outrage!': opinions that prove my earlier belief that, in the main, the media 'got it wrong' and sadly still have it wrong. Voltaire undoubtably 'got it right' when he said, 'The history of human opinion is scarcely more than the history of human error.'

This was to be proved only weeks later when the sanctimony of the media was totally exposed as they relayed the unbelievably explicit sexual behaviour of the President of the United States in graphic detail. Along with over half the world's population, I was able to read on the Internet and later in every single newspaper: 'The President unbuttoned her blouse and touched her breasts without removing her bra. "He went to put his hands down my pants and then I unzipped them because it was easier. I didn't have any panties on and so he manually stimulated me." According to Ms Lewinsky, "I wanted him to touch my genitals with his genitals and he did so. Lightly and without penetration." Then Ms. Lewinsky performed oral sex on him until he ejaculated...'

After reading this in *The Times*, I reflected on the quotation:

'We are all prostitutes, it is just a matter of price.' During my lifetime many of my associates and friends were punished and imprisoned for publishing far less erotica than this.

I was told that 'all fame is dangerous: good brings envy: bad, shame,' but I was happy when TeleVideo Productions asked to include the story of the Gold Brothers in the 'Blues' special end of season video. They did a wonderful tape with plenty of football, but also plenty about us, and I was so happy that, at last, David and I were portrayed as we really are. This was followed up by Carlton television production which was edited by Mitch Price. Mitch and his crew came to Portugal and filmed the Gold Brothers in relaxed surroundings at our villa as well as walking along the beach in sunglasses. The programme, appropriately called *The Blues Brothers*, was a great success.

The Sunday Times informed me that the Gold Brothers were now richer than the Queen and that there were only 76 people in Britain who were wealthier. One of them was Sir Paul McCartney. He is purported to be worth £500 million. Sadly, on the day of this announcement, Paul was sitting by his wife's bedside whilst she was dying. For me it brought the whole thing into perspective. Money isn't everything…far from it.

Although I had broken the ice with my father, I was sceptical about our newfound relationship, after all I had written a book that did not exactly put him in a good light. My music teacher, Bob Maciejewski, had advised me not to publish my work while he remained *compos mentis* – a sentiment I could well understand although I had not, in the final analysis, heeded his advice. The book was out there and selling very well. So well in fact, I was sure that he would, by now, have heard about it even if he had not yet read it.

I took Diane with me to the reunion and to my surprise he greeted me like a long-lost son. We hugged, which is something we had never done. We talked – mainly about him – I hasten to add, but at least we were talking. To my horror, he had read the book.

'Rags!' he demanded, 'when was you boys ever in rags?' I was pleased about his response to reading my book. It was not what I expected, after all, I had written much (all true I might add) that I thought would enrage him, but 'rags'?

'Dad, while you were away for much of the time, we were cold, hungry and yes, we dressed in clothes bought from the ragman.'

'Well I never knew, and I don't believe it. Your muvver was never kept short and...'

'Dad,' I interrupted, 'what difference! All I know is what I know, and I know that I had no soles on my shoes, there were times when there was no food on the table and I went to the ragman in Southern Road and bought rags. And another thing I know is this is not the time and place to be discussing it.'

Diane had noted his antagonism and calmed things down by changing the subject. I was happy that he only had one complaint about the book. However he was not satisfied with leaving it there and it was not long before he brought up 'old sores'. I was not enjoying this reunion although I had sensed he did not want us to go. It was strange but I did not really want to go either. It just seemed sensible to try again another time.

Four weeks later, at our villa in Portugal, I learned that my father had had a stroke. He was not desperately ill but, as before, he wanted to see me. Since then he has had a heart attack but continues to hold his own. I have visited him regularly and feel much better in myself, knowing that we are friends again.

More than a year has flown by and during that time my daughter Tina has married, my grandson is walking and talking, I have been to Thailand, learned to play golf, Birmingham City had all but reached the play-offs, I have watched at least 60 football matches, and, in addition to all of this, I have finally learned to play 'Moonlight Sonata' and 'Keep Right on to the End of the Road' on the piano. Now as I complete this final chapter of my story, I intend to see that I enjoy the rest of my life.

THE END ... I promise

Simple advice to would-be millionaires

Since completing my autobiography I have received many letters from people who have enjoyed *Good As Gold* but felt a few things were left unanswered. In particular, they had hoped that they would learn much about how my fortune was made and whether they too could achieve similar success. In other words, can anyone become a millionaire? And if so, what do they have to do?

The answer to the first part of the question is obviously, yes. The answer to the second part is, lots and lots. When I discuss this with my friends I am tempted to tell the joke about Abie, a Jewish man who went to Shul every Saturday and prayed to God for a fortune so that he could pay off his bills. In his prayers, he told God about his friend Solly who had recently won a million on the lottery. 'Why can't I win money like that?' he asked. After a clap of thunder, God's words came from the sky, 'Give me a chance, Abie, at least you could fill in your ticket!'

Ten rules which could help you achieve success in business:

1 You can't score a goal if you are not on the pitch. A fortune will not 'drop in your lap', you must always be available to wheel, deal and scheme at the drop of a hat.
2 Be positive and set your sights high. He who aims only for the stars is short on imagination.
3 Persistance is vital. Don't capitulate, whatever the challenge.
4 Don't gamble...it's a mug's game. To succeed in business only one policy should prevail: Heads, I win! Tails, I don't lose! Nevertheless, you must always be prepared to make a decision. Remember a bad decision has less than a 50 per cent chance of

being right...no decision has none.

5 Think small. Thinking big will put you under too much pressure. Start small but invest as much as you can, using the principal set in number four.

6 There is no substitute for hard work. Neither skill, education, enthusiasm nor ability will pull you through unless you are prepared to initially work hard and for long hours.

7 Delegate but never designate. Stay hands-on, at least until you reach your second million and even then you cannot afford to hand over control entirely.

8 Partnerships are like relationships...precarious but highly beneficial. Like relationships, however, they don't work well unless you have total commitment and absolute trust in each other.

9 Find your niche. In whatever you choose you need to provide something that is special and original.

10 Greed is one of the most despicable of characteristics but to maximise a deal there is, unfortunately, no substitute. Most entrepreneurs will agree with this but few will admit it. My only reservation is: don't do business with friends. If you do, you will compromise yourself to hold onto the relationship. In business you must put yourself first and work at all times for the long-term benefit of your company.

Ten useful tips but, 'I need more than that,' I hear you say. Well, clearly it is not possible for me to give you any hard and fast approach. Otherwise, I would be out there taking it from under your feet! Above I have outlined some dictates to work to, but first you must get 'off the ground'.

If I were starting again from rock bottom I would plan to buy a parcel of goods. Nothing would be simpler than that. The word you probably did not notice was 'plan'. A friend once told me to plan your work and work your plan. They were wise words but it must be said that he was not a successful man so planning is only one of the many vital ingredients. It is important that, sooner rather than later, you back your own judgement and make a definite move to hopefully realise your goal. I use the word 'hopefully' although I know that provided you have observed rule number four you will not have gambled and the parcel could, of necessity, be disposed of for no less than the amount you had paid.

Buying and selling, in my view, is the way forward for the would-be millionaire. As with all things in life the first step is the hardest and invariably the most important so put your heart and soul into it and prepare well, but be sure to seize the opportunity.

Get involved in a product with which you are familiar. Seek overage, soiled or damaged lines. It is often the case that large companies look to dispose of such items at a give-away price. Seize on these opportunities and if you achieve a good buy, don't automatically settle for a quick sell and a small profit. Consider selling direct, retailing, wholesaling or any other way of disposing of the parcel which will create profitable turnover. Make it happen!

This may be OK for starters but once you are buying and selling and profit is coming your way, there is still a long way to go to reach your goal.

Don't employ staff until you are sure that you can no longer handle the total day-to-day running of your company. Don't take on property until you have utilised every inch of the available space in your home, your garage or even the garden shed.

I cannot emphasise too much the need for being thrifty – watch every penny, do not be in a hurry to spend without thinking whether you really need it and when you know that you should buy something, take into consideration the strong possibility that it can be bought for considerabley less than the asking price. Don't buy without first knowing that your supplier would refuse to sell for less. There is an art in 'knowing', although you can be sure that he would not sell it for less if you were on your way out of his door and he fails to call you back. At this point you are obliged to pay more but you have, at least, satisfied yourself that you have not paid more than you need have.

Once you have made money invest only in your up and coming business. You cannot afford to indulge in luxuries until you have a cash surplus and even then there must be no room in your life for drugs, booze or addictive habits. Do all in your power to see that you remain healthy. You will have no time to be sick.

At the end of the day you must be able to look back and say: 'I did my very best. Then from somewhere I was able to find that little extra which put me above the rest.'

Good luck.

Money isn't everything.
I've had money and I've had everything and believe me they are not the same.

Index